ALICE MUNRO AND THE ART OF TIME

ALICE MUNRO
AND THE
LAURA K. DAVIS
ART OF TIME

UNIVERSITY *of* **ALBERTA** PRESS

Published by

University of Alberta Press
1-16 Rutherford Library South
11204 89 Avenue NW
Edmonton, Alberta, Canada T6G 2J4
amiskwacîwâskahikan | Treaty 6 | Métis Territory
ualbertapress.ca | uapress@ualberta.ca

Copyright © 2025 Laura K. Davis

Library and Archives Canada
Cataloguing in Publication

Title: Alice Munro and the art of time / Laura K. Davis.
Names: Davis, Laura K., author
Description: Includes bibliographical references and index.
Identifiers: Canadiana (print) 2024047984X | Canadiana (ebook) 20240479858 | ISBN 9781772128017 (softcover) | ISBN 9781772128208 (EPUB) | ISBN 9781772128215 (PDF)
Subjects: LCSH: Munro, Alice, 1931-2024—Criticism and interpretation. | LCSH: Time in literature. | LCGFT: Literary criticism.
Classification: LCC PS8576.U57 Z656 2025 | DDC C813/.54—dc23

First edition, first printing, 2025.
First printed and bound in Canada by Houghton Boston Printers, Saskatoon, Saskatchewan.
Copyediting and proofreading by Clorinde Peters.
Indexing by Adrian Mather.

All rights reserved. No part of this publication may be reproduced, stored in a retrieval system, or transmitted in any form or by any means (electronic, mechanical, photocopying, recording, generative artificial intelligence [AI] training, or otherwise) without prior written consent. Contact University of Alberta Press for further details.

University of Alberta Press supports copyright. Copyright fuels creativity, encourages diverse voices, promotes free speech, and creates a vibrant culture. Thank you for buying an authorized edition of this book and for complying with the copyright laws by not reproducing, scanning, or distributing any part of it in any form without permission. You are supporting writers and allowing University of Alberta Press to continue to publish books for every reader.

University of Alberta Press is committed to protecting our natural environment. As part of our efforts, this book is printed on Enviro Paper: it contains 100% post-consumer recycled fibres and is acid- and chlorine-free.

GPSR: Easy Access System Europe | Mustamäe tee 50, 10621 Tallinn, Estonia | gpsr.requests@easproject.com

This book has been published with the help of a grant from the Federation for the Humanities and Social Sciences, through the Awards to Scholarly Publications Program, using funds provided by the Social Sciences and Humanities Research Council of Canada.

University of Alberta Press gratefully acknowledges the support received for its publishing program from the Government of Canada, the Canada Council for the Arts, and the Government of Alberta through the Alberta Media Fund.

Contents

Acknowledgements VII

Introduction IX

1 | Genre, Narrative, and Time in *Lives of Girls and Women* 1

2 | The Past and the Present in *Who Do You Think You Are?* 33

3 | Time and Corporeality 69
   "Lichen" and "White Dump" in *The Progress of Love*

4 | Time and Narrative Framing 97
   "Friend of My Youth" and "Meneseteung" in *Friend of My Youth*

5 | Memory and Retrospect 127
   "Fiction" and "Child's Play" in *Too Much Happiness*

6 | Time and Life Writing 155
   "Corrie," "The Eye," and "Dear Life" in *Dear Life*

Conclusion 191

Notes 201

Works Cited 209

Index 223

Acknowledgements

I WOULD LIKE TO OFFER THANKS to the editors and staff at the University of Alberta Press who supported me in this work and were instrumental in seeing it come to fruition: Douglas Hildebrand, Cathie Crooks, Duncan Turner, Alan Brownoff, and Mat Buntin. Special thanks to Michelle Lobkowicz, acquisitions editor at the University of Alberta Press, who believed in my work. She encouraged and guided me through the process. I would also like to thank my editors, Joanne Muzak and Clorinde Peters, for their insightful work on my manuscript. Their suggestions were invaluable and improved its clarity, depth of thinking, and readability. Thank you to the anonymous peer reviewers, whose advice was detailed, astute, and important. Their reading of my work helped to better both my scholarship and my writing in this book.

Thank you to Red Deer Polytechnic for their support for this book. The Polytechnic granted me a sabbatical year to begin work on this project. I would like to thank the Professional Development Committee for granting me the funds necessary to hire an editor for the manuscript and for granting me a course release to complete the revisions. A special thanks to my colleagues at Red Deer Polytechnic for their support and encouragement, especially Peter Slade, who has been a mentor to me.

The students of my English 389 class on Alice Munro were great supporters of this project. We read many of Munro's stories and the students truly came to love and appreciate the author's work, bringing freshness and excitement to it each day. The studies we did in that class contributed to my own understanding of Munro and to this book. Thank you to those students: Marae Doble, Elizabeth Fleming, Leah Johns, and Asher Williams. I would also like to thank the professors who have taught me, mentored me, and have influenced the ways in which

I read and understand literature, especially Nora Foster Stovel, Smaro Kamboureli, and Luke B. Carson. Thank you to the scholars of Alice Munro's work and of Canadian literature who have greatly influenced my thinking on both and who have helped me in my interpretation of Munro's stories.

On a personal note, I am especially grateful to my family who supports me and each and every day: Roger Davis, Rachael Davis, Kai Davis, Clara Davis, Ken Strong, Wendy Strong, Greg Strong, and my best friend Nicole Prior. This work could not have been done without you.

Introduction

CANADIAN WRITER ALICE MUNRO, a master of words, constructs narratives that engage time in unique and complex ways. As we examine her prose, we are invited to contemplate the concept of time, each story a delicate balance of past, present, and future. Munro is well known as one of Canada's most preeminent literary figures, and she is regarded as one of the best contemporary short story writers in the world. She has won numerous prestigious literary awards over her long career, including the Governor General's Award (1968, 1978, 1986), the Man Booker International Prize for lifetime achievement (2009), and, most notably, the Nobel Prize in Literature (2013).

During the years when Munro was rising to notoriety, the concept of time was gaining traction in Canadian literary criticism and in Western society at large. As our world experienced rapid technological advancements and societal shifts, the exploration of time's nuances became an avenue through which writers and thinkers navigated the ever-changing contours of human experience. Cynthia Sugars and Eleanor Ty's edited book, *Canadian Literature and Cultural Memory* (2014), for instance, suggests that Canadian literature has exemplified a shift "marked by a concern with the ways the past continues to infuse the present—sometimes through intangible or unconscious means, but also in self-consciously manufactured and consumable forms" (1). Paul Huebener's *Timing Canada* (2015) examines time in various works of Canadian literature and argues that "the politics and power relations that saturate Canada's existence are *profoundly* tied to the broad understandings of time that have been advanced, assumed, and rejected throughout the country's history" (7, emphasis in original). This study builds upon these works to consider Munro's contribution to Canadian literature and how paying heed to time in her work can alter how we understand individual and collective identities.

This emphasis on time in Canadian literature assumes paramount significance in Munro studies. It is a cornerstone of her oeuvre, from her well-known early stories such as "Boys and Girls" in her collection *Dance of the Happy Shades* (1968), to her coming-of-age stories in *Lives of Girls and Women* (1971) and *Who Do You Think You Are?* (1978), to her final collection of stories, *Dear Life* (2012). Building on scholarship that identifies Munro's use and complication of narrative time, this study analyzes time in selected stories to show that Munro's narrative techniques disrupt linearity, progress, and chronological flow. To analyze the concept of time in the author's writing is to foreground the gaps and fissures of history—the unsettled truths that erupt into the present and derange it. Turning to the concept of time in Munro's writing enables us to consider contemporary literature's reassessment of the past; how perceptions of the past inform the present; and how the *then* and *now* cannot be separated, since our troubled histories, both personal and national, have often not yet been put to rest.

Alice Munro and the Art of Time examines how Munro challenges patriarchal time and embraces a more woman-centred concept of time by considering ephemerality and renewal in both the body and nature; Munro contests traditional narrative time by resisting a straightforward or easy progression from beginning to end. In this study, I explain how Munro mobilizes conceptions of time in an endeavour to work toward liberation rather than domination, empowerment rather than restriction. For Munro, it is primarily girls and women who have been restricted and who can be empowered by a conception of time that resists linearity and progression. Literary theorist, feminist philosopher, and linguist Julia Kristeva distinguishes between the symbolic order, the social world of language and communication, and the semiotic, that which is associated with the prelinguistic and includes the musical, the poetic, prosody, and tone. In relation to time, drawing on Friedrich Nietzsche's work, she explains that there are "two temporal dimensions: the time of linear history, or *cursive time* (as Nietzsche called it), and the time of another history, thus another time, *monumental time* (again, according to Nietzsche)" (189, emphasis in original). For Kristeva, cursive time is associated with identity and history, whereas monumental time is associated with loss of identity and anthropology. Monumental time is productive because it has the potential to upset and challenge the linear, historical time that opposes it. Kristeva's contemplation of language is relevant to Munro's writing, which is as attentive to form as it is to content. Specifically, Munro engages in self-reflexivity, intertextuality, narrative framing, and *mise en abyme*.[1] Through attentiveness to form, Munro meditates on the meaning of art and literature and seems to value the revolutionary potential of monumental time—the power of anthropology and semiotics to disrupt the status quo.

Scholars have lauded the ways in which Munro handles narrative time. In "'Clear Jelly': Alice Munro's Narrative Dialectics," for instance, Robert Thacker argues that Munro's narrative dialectics involve a retrospective form of narration in which the older, first-person narrator looks back on herself from the point of maturity, so that the narrative exists in multiple points of time. Her narrative technique, he explains, "is the means by which past and present comingle" (37). In that essay, Thacker discusses Munro's early short stories, including those first published in the University of Western Ontario's undergraduate literary magazine *Folio*, when Munro was a student there. Munro won a scholarship that enabled her to study at Western for two years, after which she married Jim Munro, whom she met at Western (Thacker, *Alice Munro* 91). Thacker notes that Munro's narrative technique in her early stories "reveals a glimpse of what became her hallmark" ("'Clear Jelly'" 37). That dialectic may be most prominent in her first three books, but her later stories, such as "Gravel," published in 2011 in *The New Yorker* and in 2012 in *Dear Life*, also employ complex narrative techniques that involve time. In "Gravel," a child's voice is expressed by an adult narrator who is explicitly revealed near the end of the story: the narrator looks back upon their trauma, telling their story and trying to make sense of it.

Building on Thacker's work, Ildikó de Papp Carrington argues that "sliding 'up and down the time axis' is characteristic of Munro's technique in both her first-person and third-person stories" (7). As both Thacker and Isla Duncan have noted, Munro's drafting process involves trying out first- and third-person narration in a story until she decides which one is best (Duncan, *Alice Munro's* 1). Her protagonists are often observers of their own childhood selves, and that is true whether Munro writes in first or third-person narration. This narrative technique, Carrington explains in *Controlling the Uncontrollable*, "produces an internal split between the experiencing participant and the observing, retrospective narrator" (7). Munro's "characteristic split point of view," according to Carrington, is "inseparable from her perception of a fragmented and constantly shifting world of disturbing irony, ambiguity, and painfully persistent paradox" (4). Duncan refers to narrative time in her book *Alice Munro's Narrative Art*. She argues that Munro's narration is characterized by "appositeness and coherence of voice, intricacy of structure, networks of connections [and] density of layering" (2). Such layering includes different and overlapping times. Duncan notes that time is part of Munro's narratology: "patterns and connections" in Munro's work "may not be immediately discernible, and may be muffled under layers of time" (5). Time is invoked when Munro uses "subtle modulation of tense" and "the interplay of active and retrospective voices" (5). E.D. Blodgett and Coral Ann Howells also discuss time in Munro's writing. Blodgett explains that Munro keeps the "past and present, not to speak of even more complicated zones of time in between, in continual suspension" (11). Howells, in "The Telling of Secrets / The Secrets of Telling," argues that Munro explores the "limits of knowledge, secrets just glimpsed, the gap between the familiar and the unknown and possibly inaccessible" (39). This space between the known and the unknown, as Howells explains, enables "imaginative transformation and fictive artifice" (*Alice Munro* 4), and it is achieved in part through the manipulation of time: "shifting narrative perspectives...apparent digressions, [and] spatial and temporal gaps" ("Telling" 40). While these scholars have discussed the notion of time in Munro's work, no critic has yet done so in a sustained way, so as to examine time as the focus of scholarship and to delineate how it manifests in individual stories in Munro's corpus of work. *Alice Munro and the Art of Time* aims to do just that, building upon the work of previous scholars while filling this critical gap.

Memory

Time, of course, is intimately related to remembering and forgetting. Memories are past-oriented, fragmented, and unreliable. Munro contemplates remembering and forgetting in her work. As Duncan puts it, "time and memory play immensely important roles in her stories: what is remembered may be consoling, fickle, or fugacious, and what cannot be remembered is replaced by images more bountiful" (*Alice Munro's* 160). In some of Munro's stories, the focus on memory involves the attempt to narrate a traumatic experience from the past. "Miles City Montana," published in *The New Yorker* in 1985 and in Munro's collection *The Progress of Love* in 1986, features a near drowning. As Thacker explains in his biography of Munro, that story has autobiographical elements: Munro's daughter Jenny almost drowned in 1961 (*Alice Munro* 415). The Munros were living in West Vancouver at the time and would move to Victoria to start Munro's Bookstore two years later, in 1963. In the summer of 1961, the family travelled back home to Ontario for a vacation, and that trip "became the basis of 'Miles City Montana'" (125). In *Lives of Mothers and Daughters: Growing Up with Alice Munro*, Sheila Munro, Munro's daughter, writes that "Miles City, Montana" is "one of the most autobiographical of [her] mother's stories" (69), highlighting how Munro writes traumas tied to events in her and her communities' histories.

In her stories that feature drownings or near drownings, Munro emphasizes the protagonists' difficulty narrating their traumas, their struggle to weave the moments they remember into narrative coherence. In "Child's Play," published in *Harper's Magazine* in 2008 and then in the collection *Too Much Happiness* in 2009, Munro's protagonist and her friend drown a fellow camper at a children's summer camp. The adult narrator looks back upon the murderous act she committed when she was a child, trying to piece together this trauma—the implications of which will be discussed later in this book. The story "Gravel" in *Dear Life*—which I do not address in detail in this book—highlights the narrator's inability to piece together what they remember about their sister's death by drowning. "I barely remember that life," the narrator says. "That is, I remember some parts of it clearly, but without the links you need to form a proper picture" (91). Munro writes about trauma as she demonstrates the complexities of memory that are the effects of traumatic events.

Munro contemplates time and memory not only through her protagonists' struggles to remember their traumas, but also through her stories that feature characters with Alzheimer's disease or dementia. She addresses how forgetfulness relates to time, how it creates a fragmented sense of the past and upsets any linear time trajectory or identifying ego. In "Spelling," a story in *Who Do You Think You Are?* published in 1978, the protagonist, Rose, takes care of her stepmother, Flo, who has dementia. The past erupts into the present with Flo's outbursts and cursing—semiotic moments of unconscious desire. Munro highlights the piecing together of narrative as Rose thinks of words for Aunty, another character in the story, to spell. Aunty is based on Munro's great-aunt, Anne Maud Code Porterfield (1878-1976), who also appears in "The Peace of Utrecht," "Winter Wind," and "The Ticket." When Munro returned to Huron County in 1975, she regularly visited her in the home where she lived. The fragments of the past—represented by the letters of the words—are put together in the present like a puzzle. In psychoanalytic terms, Aunty's act of spelling words is a repetition and reversal of Jacques Lacan's theory on the child's entrance into the symbolic order—the realm of understanding the self and the Other in language. For Lacan, the child can enter into the societal world when they enter the symbolic order, but in "Spelling," the elderly Aunty's language breaks down into fragments or parts, letters of words: she performs her occupation of the symbolic order even as that order and her identity have been broken. The child, on the Lacanian trajectory, enters the symbolic order; the elderly woman, on Munro's, leaves it.

Munro further addresses Alzheimer's disease in "The Bear Came Over the Mountain," which was first published in *The New Yorker* in 1999 (Simal 61), and then in a different form in *Hateship, Friendship, Courtship, Loveship, Marriage* in 2001.[2] The disease, as Munro portrays it in "The Bear," "serves as a catalyst for the creation of irony in a narrative that raises questions about remembering and forgetting, fidelity and infidelity, the instability of meaning, the working of ironic discourse, and the abrupt transference of desire" (Goldman and Powell 87). Critic Begona Simal notes that in "In Sight of the Lake," another one of Munro's stories that addresses Alzheimer's,[3] "temporal disorientation is employed to convey the crumbling of the self" (61). Munro often focuses on notions of identity and selfhood in her writing, and this is true in her stories about Alzheimer's, where she portrays the identity of the character who has the disease in relation to what that character remembers and forgets. She demonstrates that "Memory...continues to be central to the Western understanding of human identity," and that "the dramatic erosion of memory, such as that experienced by Alzheimer's patients, necessarily evokes a parallel erosion of one's identity" (64). "The perception of truth and reality as filtered through time," as Simal notes, "has been one of Munro's recurrent concerns" (62). In this book, I apply Simal's observation to selected stories of Munro. While I do not address in detail Munro's stories about Alzheimer's, I highlight the author's and her characters' identities, both personal and public, in relation to how they move and change through time.

Drawing upon the Lockean conception of the self, which "conceives of identity as 'consciousness inhabiting a body,'" Marlene Goldman and Sarah Powell analyze Munro's story, "The Bear Came Over the Mountain" and Sarah Polley's film version of that story, *Away from Her*, in relation to Alzheimer's and identity. "Being a person means being and remaining identical to oneself," they assert. "Thus, forgetfulness, at any age, interrupts both memory and personhood" (82). In many of her stories, including "Lichen" in *The Progress of Love* and "Child's Play" in *Too Much Happiness*, Munro foregrounds the interconnections between corporeality and identity. In "Lichen," published in *The New Yorker* in 1985 and in *The Progress of Love* in 1986, natural environments and eroding landscapes are associated with deteriorating bodies and texts, blurring the boundaries between bodies—environmental and human—and the written and visual texts that represent them. In "Child's Play," Munro examines how one physically identifies with and dissociates from others. Her focus on coming of age and girlhood in that story foregrounds the forging of new gendered identities as they relate to one's own and others' bodies. Memory comes into play, since the protagonist—in typical Munrovian style—is an adult struggling to remember the details of the summer camp she attended as a child and the traumatic event that she participated in there. The idea of "remaining identical to oneself" is explored in "Child's Play"—through memory—though outside of the notion of Alzheimer's or dementia. Can a person "remain identical" to themself if they can no longer remember their recent past, as is the case with dementia? Are they the same self if they dissociate or dis-identify with a heinous act they committed in their past, or a trauma? Munro contemplates such questions in her stories that address disease, disability, crime, and trauma, and she addresses them through remembering and forgetting, complicating time.

It is unsurprising that Munro writes about the elderly and diseases such as Alzheimer's, since her own mother suffered from Parkinson's disease, becoming ill in 1942–1943 when Munro was twelve years of age (Thacker, *Alice Munro* 57). Munro's mother, Anne Chamney Laidlaw, appears in many of Munro's stories in which the author writes about various mother-daughter relationships: mothers who are ill, like Flo in *Who Do You Think You Are?*; mothers who are outsiders, like Ada in *Lives of Girls and Women*; and mothers who are seemingly neglectful or self-interested, like Greta in "To Reach Japan" or the mother in "Gravel." As Elizabeth Hay puts it, "the problem of 'the mother' for a daughter who writes about her is fundamental to Munro's work" (178). In *Lives of Mothers and Daughters*, Sheila Munro says the following about her mother Alice Munro's relationship with her mother, Anne Laidlaw: "From the beginning the relationship between mother and daughter was difficult. Young Alice felt she had to resist her mother's control over her" (150). Sheila Munro further details the many difficulties her mother experienced when her grandmother developed Parkinson's disease. She examines autobiographical elements of her mother's stories, for example, when she writes of *Who Do You Think You Are*: "Rose's attempt to break her engagement, and the self-betrayal and vanity in her capitulation to her need to make Patrick happy, her need to be worshipped, all of this makes me feel as though I have entered into my mother's psyche, that these are her own feelings about her marriage" (10), yet she concedes, "I know I'm on dangerous ground here" (10). The lines between Munro's autobiography and her fiction are blurry, as Sheila Munro articulates. Munro's characters contemplate their pasts through their complicated relationships with their mothers, and through her writing, Munro does the same.

That Munro has been incorporating autobiographical elements into her fiction is well documented by Thacker, first in "'So Shocking a Verdict in Real Life': Autobiography in Alice Munro's Stories," in *Reading Alice Munro, 1973-2013*, and subsequently in his biography of Munro, *Alice Munro: Writing Her Lives, a Biography*. The blurring of boundaries between autobiography and fiction necessarily brings forth notions of selfhood and identity, since "studies in autobiographical and psychoanalytical theory have long held that life writing can express only partial 'truths' or an intention of truthfulness" (Marrone 86). In her article on *Dear Life*, Claire Marrone states, "Prominent in the collection are issues of being and consciousness, crucial to ontology and phenomenology respectively, as well as questions of selfhood explored in autobiographical theory" (85). Building upon seminal essays on autobiography such as Philippe Lejeune's "The Autobiographical Pact," Marrone notes that *Dear Life* presents perspectives from two-time spectrums of human life: that of the child in a story such as "Gravel," and that of an elderly woman in a story such as "In Sight of the Lake." Munro presents both the young child and the elderly woman as holding particular perspectives that involve time and memory. In "Gravel," the protagonist is too young to comprehend fully the tragedy of her sister's drowning, and must work to understand the fragments of her memories of the event later in time. In "In Sight of the Lake," the elderly woman who has Alzheimer's does not know that "her experience of isolation as she enters a nursing home is but a dream" (Marrone 85). In presenting life from its beginnings, through midlife, to its end, this collection highlights *time* in a *lifetime*, as "we ponder the entire scope of our 'dear lives'" (97). In her stories, then, Munro considers notions of time through memory, autobiography, motherhood, and identity.

Narration

Munro uses rhetorical strategies that unsettle any easy progression from beginning to end. For example, she employs intertextuality to bring the past into the present, and to bring both her protagonists and herself—in moments of self-reflexivity—into the literary tradition. In *Lives of Girls and Women,* Munro's literary allusions to James Joyce's *A Portrait of the Artist as a Young Man* and Charlotte Brontë's *Jane Eyre* suggest that the protagonist, Del Jordan, much like Dedalus, will be an artist, a writer like Munro herself. Yet Munro's gender reversal in those allusions to *A Portrait* and *Jane Eyre* emphasize the *woman* protagonist and artist and refer not only to Del, but also to Munro. J.R. (Tim) Struthers, in his article "Reality and Ordering: The Growth of a Young Artist in *Lives of Girls and Women,*" and W.R. Martin, in his monograph *Alice Munro: Paradox and Parallel*, and have noted Munro's literary allusions to Joyce and Brontë. Munro's writing about coming of age and the development of a girl-artist in *Lives* is significant in light of Munro's impending divorce—Alice and Jim Munro separated after *Lives* was published (Thacker, *Alice Munro* 211)—and the fact that *Lives* would become such an important and canonical work of Canadian literature. *Dance of the Happy Shades*, which was published before *Lives,* won the Governor General's Award in 1968, so Munro was already well established as a writer when she wrote *Lives*. Yet, in this period, "Munro's career was entering a new phase" (208). Munro's focus on the development of an artist in *Lives* mirrors her own coming of age as a writer. The publication of *Lives* in 1971, Munro's rising reputation as a writer,

Introduction   XVII

and the significant increase in the production of Canadian literature all happened simultaneously. Fuelled by the country's centennial celebrations in 1967, new Canada Council Grants for artists, and bourgeoning publishing firms in Canada such as McClelland & Stewart, Canadian literature was coming to the fore, and Munro's writing was part of it. Munro applied for a Canada Council Grant three times. She was turned down the first two times, and was successful the third time, in 1973 (237). In *Lives*, Munro compresses time as she creates a character that mirrors herself, blurring the boundaries between writer and character in moments of postmodern self-reflexivity.

Munro both builds upon and resists the legacies of her male literary predecessors to establish her own literary practice. And yet, she does not communicate her feminism in an overt way. "I never think about being a feminist writer," she said in an interview with *The New Yorker* in 2012 (Treisman). Maria Löschnigg argues that "Alice Munro's feminism is implicit and non-programmatic" ("Oranges" 60). She states that it is through Munro's "shaping of her narrative material that her resistance to patriarchal structure and modes of thinking, i.e. her feminist stance, is communicated" (61). In "Images of Women's Power in Contemporary Canadian Fiction by Women," Carol L. Beran compares three of Munro's stories with novels by Aritha van Herk and Margaret Atwood. She examines the female characters in these works of literature in the context of the time in which they were published. Munro's "The Beggar Maid" and "Simon's Luck," both published in 1978 in *Who Do You Think You Are?*, are contemporaneous with van Herk's *Judith*, while Munro's "Lichen," published in 1986 in *The Progress of Love*, falls in between the publication of Atwood's *The Handmaid's Tale* and *Cat's Eye*. Considering how each of these writers portrays female power, Beran concludes that van Herk takes the most strident feminist stance, while Atwood locates female power in creativity and Munro "takes us beyond the issue of male versus female power by presenting images in which forces outside the control of men or women have the ultimate control" (para. 24). Munro's narratives, like those by writers such as van Herk and Atwood, push back against patriarchal structures, which is itself a feminist act; but Munro, unlike these other writers, does not necessarily align herself with what one might call a feminist practice. As Löschnigg puts it, Munro's work is characterized, "above all, by multiplicity, polyphony, digression, and indeterminacy" ("Oranges" 60). This multiplicity and indeterminacy applies to Munro's treatment of time, her practice of upsetting chronology, linearity, and progress to challenge dominant discourses and ideologies.

Munro's literary practice foregrounds how stories are passed from one audience to the next, necessarily layering time. She uses *mise en abyme* as a rhetorical strategy, embedding a story within a story, an image within an image. For instance, Munro layers performances in *Lives of Girls and Women.* The characters of Bert and Clive perform for Del and Naomi, while Del and ultimately Munro perform their writing for their readers. This shift from the boys' acting performance to Del's written one is significant and reflects Del's mother Ada's observation that "There is a change coming...in the lives of girls and women" (165). Del's newfound agency marks an arrival into a time when, as Barbara Godard explains, women see themselves as "a subject of their desires, not as an object of men's desires" (43). Given that *Lives* was published in 1971, the book's demonstration of a movement towards women's subjectivity and creativity is not surprising, since this period was "an era witness to a renewed and vigorous swirl of identity politics as a liberating force" (Lesk 141). Munro further layers literary pasts in "Meneseteung," a story in her 1990 collection *Friend of My Youth* that has received significant scholarly attention and has been frequently anthologized. Munro creates a narrator who in turn contemplates the historical figure of Almeda Roth. As Dermot McCarthy puts it, "the relations between the narrator, the character, and the author in this story are a complex series of mirrorings in which identities slide into each other, are interchangeable" (3). The same kind of "mirrorings" occur in "The Eye," an autobiographical story in *Dear Life.* Young Munro looks at the dead body of Sadie, her babysitter. Sadie's "eye," notably a homonym for "I," winks at Munro, as Munro simultaneously and metaphorically winks at us, her readers, inviting us to believe in the unbelievable. Each performance is a repetition of another; each is embedded within another in a *mise en abyme* that passes through audiences and time. Munro invokes and questions artistic and literary pasts to recreate them and make them new. Typical of postmodern metafictions, her stories are "overtly aware of the twin processes involved in their production: their creation and their reception" (Hutcheon, *The Canadian Postmodern* 45).

Munro's narrative techniques are uniquely her own: they are complex and diverse, and they challenge linear progression and chronological flow. Yet some of the narrative strategies that Munro uses—framing, self-reflexivity, *mise en abyme*—are common in modern and contemporary Canadian literature. In *The Canadian Postmodern*, Canadian literary critic Linda Hutcheon names Munro as a contemporary writer whose work is an example of postmodern metafiction. As well as engaging in the narrative strategies named above, such writers, she notes, are interested in "both the power and the limitation of the printed word to invoke the absent object" (46). Referring to Susan Sontag's work, she explains that the camera, as one example of a technology that invokes absent objects, "records and justifies, yet it also imprisons, arrests, and thus falsifies the fleeting moment" (47). Munro frequently references photographs and photography in her writing—snapshots in time. She does so to complicate and draw our attention to uneasy, ungrounded alignments between art and life. Critics such as Lorraine York and Thomas Tausky have aptly discussed photography in Munro's writing.[4] In the epilogue of Munro's *Lives and Girls and Women*, a mysterious photographer captures the town of Jubilee and its inhabitants in pictures. The epilogue has received considerable scholarly attention, and, as Thacker notes in his biography of Munro, its "few pages are infused with Alice Munro's own life history" (*Alice Munro* 212). The author spent "half as much time writing the epilogue" as she had "writing the whole book" (212). Notably, the epilogue is dislocated in time from the rest of the book. As Atwood points out in her essay about *Lives*, "Epilogue: The Photographer" takes place before the previous chapter, "Baptizing," so in the epilogue, Del has not yet received her exam marks or broken up with Garnet (Atwood, "*Lives*" 112). Here, Munro treats time differently from other writers: she does not adhere to the typical time frame of an epilogue, which usually takes place well after the end of the book.

Whereas in the epilogue of *Lives* Munro considers snapshots of time through photography and writing, in "Lichen," in *The Progress of Love*, the protagonist contemplates and deciphers an old photograph. The photograph is of the character David's naked former lover, Dina, and when David shows it to Stella, she comments that Dina's pubic hair "looks like lichen" (39). Dina's body here is directly compared to an organism in the natural environment, and so Munro conflates human and environmental bodies. The photograph itself, like the natural

XX   Introduction

environment with which the image is compared, is faded and deteriorated. Munro references the photograph in part to explore discourses on the environment and how time affects ourselves and our environments. The author also discusses photographs in her story "Miles City, Montana," in *The Progress of Love.* In that story, the protagonist's husband, Andrew, is constantly taking pictures of her and remarking that she looks like Jackie Kennedy (82–83), which marks moments in time both personally and collectively. With references to photographs, Munro shows arrested moments in time and interrogates how bodies fluctuate and move, how they are consistently becoming or deteriorating, and how they move in and occupy space through time.

Place

Many Munro scholars have focused on the concept of place in her writing, which has more commonly been the subject of Munro criticism than has time. *Alice Munro and the Art of Time* shifts the focus from place to time, and yet the two remain intimately intertwined. Munro's hometown of Wingham, Ontario shares similarities with the fictional town of Jubilee in *Lives of Girls and Women*, and her memories of Wingham make appearances in stories such as "Boys and Girls" in *Dance of the Happy Shades*, as Thacker has pointed out (*Alice Munro* 7). Characters in her stories often reflect settlers of Huron County—the area of rural southwestern Ontario where Wingham is located. When Munro was growing up in the 1930s and 1940s, Wingham was primarily an English and Scottish Protestant town. Indeed, in her autobiographical book, *A View from Castle Rock*, Munro narrates her own ancestors' voyage from Scotland to Canada in the 1800s—a trek that would have been common to many settlers in the region. Starting in the 1950s and 1960s, Munro wrote about her hometown, drawing upon her memories. As critic Marta Dvorak explains, "as nationalism grew in the 1960s, along with the advent of the Centennial celebrations of Confederation, Munro rooted her stories in her native southwestern Ontario Huron County, charting the topography and social geography of her unsung region onto a literary map" (302). In her writing, she plays with boundaries related to both place and time: the modern and the traditional, the "store-bought" and the "home-made," the "town" and the "country" (303). Dvorak states that "Canadian and American readers on the lookout for cultural cartographies of their relation to their home place continue to be drawn to prose refiguring chronotopic spaces thickened by early human negotiations with a primal land still unaltered a few generations ago" (303). Pointing to items that appear in *Dance of the Happy Shades*, such as "oil lamps, drinking pails, chamber pots" (303), Dvorak explains how such items "constitute an index of atmosphere," a "reality-effect" that lends credibility to the narrative while melding the past with the present (304). In this study, I build upon these critical works to demonstrate this coming together of the past and the present, pivoting on Dvorak's work to show how such melding occurs in Munro's writing in various stories from *Lives of Girls and Women* (1971) and *Dear Life* (2012).

Munro contemplates both maps and written histories, displaying the intersections between place and time. In "The Flats Road," the first story in *Lives of Girls and Women*, for instance, the character Benny cannot navigate the city of Toronto and refuses to attain a map to do so, which demonstrates Merilyn Simonds's point that "maps in Alice Munro stories are most often unreadable, unreliable or a matter of dispute" ("Where Do You" 39). In "Heirs of the Living Body," the second story in the same collection, the protagonist, Del, inherits her uncle Craig's written history of Wawanash County, though she has an ambiguous relationship to it and implicitly rejects it. In that story, Del reads a dead cow's hide as though it is a map, which shows Munro's combination of natural, ephemeral time with the desire to order and preserve. Further, Munro shows how place is indistinguishable from its representation and subsequent understanding. In her analysis of Munro's story "Deep Holes," a story that was published in *The New Yorker* in 2008 and in her collection *Too Much Happiness* a year later, Corinne Bigot argues that "Munro's work...demonstrates the impossibility of dissociating place from its inscription in a signifying process" (para. 1). "Real places [Munro] configures," Bigot says, "serve as analogies to the space of fiction, with the emphasis on the works of erosion and fissures evoking gaps in the referential process, allowing for meaning to circulate" (para. 19). The holes of the Ontario landscape where the story takes place are the holes in signification, the breaks in the meaning of fictional works. Munro therefore contests the idea of stability; of place and its representation in ordered documents such as maps; and of time and its representation in written histories. She foregrounds the instability and shiftiness of landscapes and places, the fissures in time, and the gaps in signification that are also productive sites for creating new meaning and change.

Liminality and uncertain positions between here and there, then and now, are evident in Munro's writing. Places are often precarious or deteriorating, and her characters seemingly unsure of their footing in the spaces they inhabit. As Simonds explains, "Place, in Alice Munro, is a chimera: deceptive, implausible, sometimes one thing, sometimes another" ("Where Do You" 26). Place "creates a here and a there. The posibility of travel, of movement into the unknown. And it is in the unknown— there—that Alice Munro's stories reveal their truths" (27). At the outset of *Lives and Girls and Women*, Del, her brother, and Benny are at the riverbank—on the liminal space that is the edge of the land and the water. Benny claims that the bank is his, but Del explains to the reader that "it was ours" (3), meaning her brother's and hers. Munro foregrounds the unsure ownership of the place Del and her brother occupy. Given that *Lives* is about the coming of age of a female writer, the precarity of Del's belonging in her space is akin to the precarity of her place as a woman entering a literary landscape traditionally reserved for male writers. Thomas Dutoit explains that Munro employs "two fundamental and apparently opposed forces, deep geological time and the shallow and ephemeral architectural world, the traces of which she passionately attempts to secure from their disappearance" (77-78). Dutoit's assertion is applicable to stories such as "Lichen," where Munro foregrounds eroding landscapes, bodies, and documents, and to "White Dump," also in *The Progress of Love*, where Munro juxtaposes eroding landscapes with geological time, represented by the silica quarry that the characters Denise and her father Laurence see on their plane ride. Munro's stories exemplify shifts and uncertainties as they portray places and times that are always precarious, always in flow.

As Munro complicates the dynamic occupation of place in time, she often refers to movement through place with references to trains and train tracks, which are recurring tropes in her writing. They signal liminal, in-between spaces and times that exemplify the ambiguous, uncertain subject position of her characters. In "The Flats Road," in *Lives,* Del lives at the end of the road on the edge of the town, near the train tracks. The tracks mark the boundary between the town and the countryside. In "Simon's Luck," from *Who Do You Think You Are?*, Simon hides in the freight car of a train during his escape from the Nazis in the Second World War. His hiding spot is an in-between space that signals temporary safety in a dangerous, transitional time in his life. It also represents his escape and his movement in place from Europe to Canada. In "To Reach Japan," the first story in *Dear Life*, the protagonist, Greta, who is at a crossroads in her life, finds and rescues her daughter, who is caught between two moving train cars. In "A Life in Transit: Spatial Biographies of Alice Munro's Artist Figure," critic Kasia Van Schaik argues that the train car in Munro's writing, and particularly in "To Reach Japan," is a domestic space that is apart from and yet parallel to the home that Munro's protagonists wish to leave. This desire to escape domestic life—or at least to find a time and place to create apart from it—is one that Munro shares with her protagonists. "For Munro, as many writers/mothers of her generation, the problem of interrupted time, affective labour, and maternal guilt remained a critical factor in her development as a writer" (Van Schaik 38). In Munro's stories, "public spaces such as the train carriage or the car might actually afford more artistic privacy than the home" (39). Munro's protagonists move into such spaces to create an alternate life, a narrative apart from the one that features the domestic housewife. Moreover, as Van Schaik notes, "Time...operates differently in these 'unreal' or 'nowhere' spaces... Here on the train [Munro's protagonist] can temporarily—and only temporarily—divest herself from outside responsibilities" (51). Munro mobilizes the symbol of the train in her writing to exemplify uncertain, in-between spaces and temporary, fleeting moments of time.

Alongside Timothy Findley and Margaret Atwood, Munro is among the first writers who come to mind when one thinks of the Southern Ontario Gothic. First coined by Graeme Gibson in his book *Eleven Canadian Novelists*, published in 1972, the phrase refers to writers in the southern Ontario region who employ gothic tropes and are influenced by southern American writers such as Edgar Allan Poe and Flannery O'Connor. Gothic literature scholar John Bowen explains how time relates to the gothic mode. He says, "the gothic wants to see the relationship between the modern world and the past not as one of evolutional development—but of sudden juxtaposition and violent conflict, in which the past erupts within the present and deranges it." Many critics have discussed Munro's stories as overtly gothic.

Wen-Shan Shieh explains that Munro was influenced by Katherine Mansfield's writing and uses innovative narrative strategies to create a gothic undertone. In her article, "The Ordinary Terrors of Survival: Alice Munro and the Canadian Gothic," Karin Berndt states that "the gothic is indeed concerned with the exploration of the fears which enlightened, rational understanding fails to comprehend" (para. 5). She argues that, in this sense, Munro's writing is an example of gothic literature. Munro employed gothic themes in her writing even early in her writing career. Her story, "Time of Death," for instance, was first published in the *Canadian Forum* in 1956 and then in 1968 in her first collection, *Dance of the Happy Shades*. The story is about the tragic death of a child, and the women in the community's coming to terms with it. It has similarities to the later story, "Gravel," including its examination of the complexities and expectations regarding parental responsibility and neglect. Munro sustained the ideas surrounding haunting deaths and gothic modes throughout the years of her writing.

In 1833, the famous English-Canadian pioneer Catharine Parr Traill proclaimed, "As to ghosts or spirits, they appear totally banished from Canada" (139). But in more recent years, critics such as Cynthia Sugars and Gerry Turcotte, in *Unsettled Remains: Canadian Literature and the Postcolonial Gothic* (2009), and Goldman, in *Dispossession: Haunting in Canadian Literature* (2012), have begun to problematize Parr Traill's statement and to analyze the presence of ghosts and haunting in Canadian literature. In direct contrast to Parr Traill's statement, almost two hundred years later, in 2012, Goldman exclaimed that, "the uncanny tropes of haunting and possession pervade contemporary Canadian fiction" (2). Munro employs the figure of the ghost and hauntings in her writing, and the ghost, common in works of gothic literature, disrupts the linearity of the present by inserting the past into it. In "The Flats Road," Benny tells a ghost story about his haunted friend Sandy Steveston, and this story instigates his own pursuit of a wife, Madeleine, who is herself, later in the story, described as both a ghost and as a madwoman. In "Child's Play," a ghost story of sorts, Marlene and Charlene are haunted by their own childhood actions. In "Corrie," a story in *Dear Life*, the protagonist is metaphorically haunted by the past, and her house is like a gothic mansion. The notion of haunting explicitly brings together both place and time, since places are haunted by the presence of the past.

The past violently emerges into the present in moments of unsettling unrest. Munro's stories are gothic, and her protagonists hover at the edges of place and time.

Gothic literature demonstrates a fascination with death and the bodily. Many of Munro's stories associate time with corporeality, linking written documents with natural and bodily materials. This is certainly the case in *The Progress of Love*, Munro's sixth collection of stories, published in 1986, when Munro had just turned fifty-five. Unlike Munro's coming-of-age works, such as *Lives of Girls and Women* and *Who Do You Think You Are?*, the stories in *Progress* consider ageing bodies and deteriorating landscapes. By the time *Progress* was published, Munro had acquired considerable recognition as a short story writer, reflected in the many reviews that the book received. Thacker notes that "reviews of *Progress*, especially those published in the United States and Britain, reveal a level of care and consideration befitting a major author of considerable gifts and power" (*Alice Munro* 424). Some reviews of the work specifically reference time. As Thacker explains, "Munro's handling of time comes in for especial attention, with Heather Henderson in *Maclean's* concluding that in her work 'the past is not a better place— but is part of everyone, demanding acknowledgement'" (425). In "Lichen," Munro links the text of a photograph and the writing of the protagonist Stella's memoirs to environments and bodies. The photograph deteriorates and is no longer decipherable. The paint on a house—like the ink of a pen—is likened to makeup on a person. Each hides that which is ephemeral, that which erodes. In "Lichen," Munro foregrounds the ageing process and deterioration. Munro consistently draws our attention to the movement of time, its marks on the environment and on the body. She thinks of time, in Elizabeth Grosz's words, "through ruptures, nicks, cuts, in instances of dislocation, though [time itself] contains no moments or ruptures and has no being or presence, functioning only as continuous becoming" (*Nick of Time* 5). In "Child's Play," Munro's narrator says, "Every year, when you're a child, you become a different person" (164), which exemplifies the constant "becoming" that the author highlights in her examination of identities through time.

Gender

Munro's writing arguably portrays "women's time," which, according to Kristeva's 1979 article by that title, is aligned with cyclical and eternal time and connected with motherhood and reproduction. Yet it is separate from linear time, "time as project, teleology, linear and progressive unfolding: time as departure, progression and arrival—in other words, the time of history" ("Women's Time" 192). After 1968, Kristeva argues, feminism began to focus on women's difference from men. Since then, she explains, there has been a new, emerging feminism in which women seek simultaneously to insert themselves into linear history, and also to resist it. Kristeva's piece was published some time ago, but it continues to be important in feminist studies. It is relevant to Munro's work, since Kristeva and Munro were writing contemporaneously: Kristeva's "Women's Time" was published just one year after Munro's *Who Do You Think You Are?* Kristeva's work and the work of other French feminists such as Luce Irigaray and Hélène Cixous were highly influential within and beyond literary circles during the 1970s and 1980s, when Munro was writing many of her stories.

Kristevian analyses of Munro's writing continue to be relevant, as we can see from works such as Debarshi Prasad Nath's "Reading Alice Munro's Early Fiction: A Kristevian Analysis," published in 2011, and Jennifer Murray's *Reading Alice Munro with Jacques Lacan*, published in 2016. Murray's study discusses and implicates Kristeva's analysis of Lacan in its reading of Munro and its analysis of concepts theorized by both Lacan and Kristeva, such as *jouissance* and the abject.[5] Much of Munro's writing is written from a woman's perspective that resists linear, teleological time; in that respect, Munro engages in the emerging feminism that Kristeva articulates.

Yet, it is important to recognize the limitations of Kristeva's notion of "women's time," especially from a contemporary perspective. In *Doing Time: Feminist Theory and Postmodern Culture*, published in 2000, Rita Felski analyzes and undoes the binary between linear and cyclical time in her discussion of the concept of "everyday life." She argues that the contemporary concept of "everyday life" is essentially temporal, since it relies on repetition, the repeating of daily chores and habits. Drawing on the work of Henri Lefebvre, she explains that cyclical time, repetitious as it is, undermines the so-called rational progress of modernity. "Repetition" she notes, "understood as ritual, provides a connection to ancestry and tradition as it situates the individual in an imagined community that spans historical time" (83). Felski asks a pertinent question that Kristeva does not: "why are women so persistently linked to repetition?" (82). To answer this question, Felski points to the fact that "women are almost always seen as embodied objects," associated with corporeality (including biorhythmic cycles such as menstruation and childbearing) (82). She also points to the notion that women are "primarily responsible for the repetitive tasks of social reproduction: cleaning, preparing meals, caring for children" (82). While Kristeva's theories concur with Felski's observation that women's experience is one of repetition, including *jouissance*, Felski's more recent theory critiques the gendering of time and shows how it is embedded in the construction of modernity, industrialization, and capitalism, which Kristeva does not.

In *Doing Time*, Felski reads linear (masculine) and cyclical (feminine) time in ways that trouble their apparent division in understandings of modernity. As such, Felski offers a way to discuss how Munro's representations also seem to question and challenge the linear-cyclical binary. For example, in Munro's story, "Heirs of the Living Body," Del's uncle Craig's written history of Wawanash County is a linear, teleological account of time. When Del inherits this document, she hides it in her basement. She keeps her own writing inside the covers of a Brontë novel, and close to her, in her own bedroom. While Del chooses a woman's novel to hold her own writing, rather than her uncle Craig's history, Munro implies that Del's writing also builds upon and is influenced by her uncle's. Del rejects teleological time by rejecting her uncle's history; yet she inserts herself into it by engaging in the act of writing herself, and by aligning her own writing with historical women writers. Her basement floods, ruining her uncle's manuscript; but the flooding also suggests that women's time—that which is associated with maternal fluids, the waters of the womb—washes over the manuscript. Del builds and recreates the very history she rejects. In such instances, Munro works to undo the linear-cyclical binary of time by demonstrating how they meld together.

Munro's writing engages with time that is tied to the body and cycles of birth and death, or the rotation of the earth around the sun. As Kristeva puts it, "there are cycles, gestation, the eternal occurrence of a biological rhythm which conforms to that of nature" ("Women's

Time" 191). Whereas linear time dominates and controls, exerting power over nature's rhythms with mechanical and rhetorical devices such as clocks and maps, Munro's stories seek to resist such domination and foreground the constant renewal of natural cycles. Kristeva associates women's time with the *chora*, a term she borrows from Plato and defines as "matrix space, nourishing, unnameable, anterior to the One, to God, and consequently defying metaphysics" (191). Sigmund Freud argues that the unconscious, like Kristeva's notion of the *chora*, challenges the logic of chronological time, pushing up against it in dreams and presenting the past as though fully present ("Uncanny"). Munro also works to expose and unearth what patriarchy has suppressed. She contests mechanical markers of time, and she moves toward the timelessness of the id,[6] the resistance of the unconscious. Munro constantly draws our attention to cyclical, repetitious time and to the natural and the corporeal. For instance, in *Lives of Girls and Women*, Del traces a dead cow's body with a stick, writing the natural and the corporeal. That the cow is in the river suggests a liminality between land and water. That scene is connected to her uncle Craig's death and her impending attendance of his funeral: the "eyes" are what connects them. Del is afraid to touch the cow's eyes with her stick (43), and later her mother speaks of transplanting the "eyes" when she discusses her uncle's death (47). In "Lichen," Munro emphasizes women's bodies and the rhythms of corporeal time, the cycles of life and death. She explicitly connects women's bodies and natural landscapes, highlighting the ephemerality and renewal of both. Moreover, she incorporates written documents such as histories and photographs into her story, demonstrating their materiality and likening a woman's body to a "body" of written or artistic work. Both, like nature itself, are dynamic and impermanent.

In Munro's "Child's Play," the climactic scene depicts the protagonist, Marlene, and her friend drowning a disabled girl at a summer camp. The scene is horrific and bodily, exemplifying the gothic. It demonstrates the violence of patriarchal, historical, linear time, as the girls perform a domination and extermination of that which they refuse to become. Their murderous act—ironically making themselves the monsters—might be likened to the repression of the unconscious on an individual level, and the collective unconscious on a communal level. The community in which they reside is clearly imperial and patriarchal, as the girls don hats that they call "Coolie hats" (165) and they sing the song "There'll Always Be an England" at their campfire (166). In this story, Munro shows the violence that the protagonist and her friend commit in the name of imperial and patriarchal values, the desire to extricate and abolish that which is Other to them. In Anna Antonova's words, Munro "shows how normative societal beliefs, internalized by the child protagonist, effectively transform so-called 'normalcy' into monstrosity, thus reversing their socially constructed opposition" (para. 2). However, the girls' murderous act in the story might be seen not only as an example of masculine/linear time, but also of feminine/cyclical time, which involves repetition. Felski explains that "visions of the horror of repetition...are distinctly modern" (*Doing Time* 83). "For most of human history," she notes, "activities have gained value precisely because they repeat what has gone before" (83). Marlene and Charlene repeat and therefore work to solidify the horrific imperial values that seek to stamp out all that is Other to the self. In this way, Munro complicates the binary between linear and cyclical time, demonstrating how one is intimately intertwined with the other.

In stories such as "Child's Play," Munro demonstrates how linear, imperial, and patriarchal structures can destroy. The protagonist of that story is embedded within such structures of time, which lead to others' and her own destruction and detriment. In stories such as "Corrie," by contrast, the protagonist eventually finds an alternative to the patriarchal structures in which she is embedded, and she embraces a paradigm that is aligned with women. Interestingly, as we have seen, Munro aligns papers and documents—writing itself—with the corporeal body. Nature, human bodies, and bodies of work, such as writings, are all related to one another for Munro, one folding into another in a humble act of self-reflexivity. Some feminist critics, such as Judith Butler, have suggested that Kristeva's writings are essentialist and equate motherhood with femininity (Söderbäck 65). They suggest that the division of "a presymbolic, drive-ridden, natural, passive, maternal mold or receptacle from a symbolic-logic, cultural, active, paternal force of creation" essentializes along gender lines (67). However, I disagree with such views. As Fanny Söderbäck argues, "Kristeva by no means reduces woman to the function of motherhood. Rather, she returns to the maternal body at least in part to free woman from this very reduction" (65). Söderbäck explains that the maternal body and the *chora* to which Kristeva refers is not only a "*corporal* but also as a *temporal* principle" (66, emphasis in original), and as such it is "moving, displacing, renewing" (65). In this way, Kristeva's theories are applicable to Munro's work. Like Kristeva, Munro shows through temporality a desire to break free of that which orders, defines, and controls.

Munro's writing implicitly rejects "time socialization." According to critic Huebener, time socialization stories are "narratives that reinforce...temporal codes for children and adults alike" (*Timing* 20). The Bildungsroman genre engages in time socialization, since it highlights key moments in a young person's life. Typically, a Bildungsroman depicts the protagonist's movement toward education and spiritual awakening. Coming-of-age novels such as Charles Dickens's *Great Expectations* and James Joyce's *A Portrait of the Artist as a Young Man* feature male protagonists. When such novels host female protagonists, a trajectory of primary education and preparation for marriage and children usually ensues. This is the case, for instance, in L.M. Montgomery's *Anne of Green Gables*, a book that had an influence on Munro. As Thacker explains in *Alice Munro: Writing Her Lives*, Munro read *Anne* when she was nine or ten years old, and was "pleased and troubled" by the book (65). If Montgomery adheres to the conventions of the Bildungsroman, then Munro pushes back against them, which might explain Munro's "trouble" with *Anne*. Munro's two collections of short stories, *Lives of Girls and Women* and *Who Do You Think You Are?*, incorporate elements of the Bildungsroman; however, they also work against conventions of the genre. In so doing, they enact a more woman-centred notion of time, one which, as in Kristeva's work, is against linear progression and teleology. In *Lives of Girls and Women*, Del desires an education, contemplates marriage, and experiences a kind of spiritual awakening. But she ultimately rejects all of these endeavours. Because she spends time with her lover, Garnet, instead of studying, she does not attain the college scholarship she needs and cannot go on to higher education. She rejects Garnet's marriage proposal, knowing that she will not act in the role of wife that he will prescribe for her. Finally, she experiences a sexual rather than a spiritual awakening at the revival meeting when she meets Garnet for the first time—well before his marriage proposal. Therefore, Munro reverses the notion of a spiritual awakening, invoking and repelling traditional conventions of the Bildungsroman genre. She articulates an agency for her protagonist by both adhering to and yet altering the traditional time socialization of the genre. She upsets the expectations of a coming-of-age work and instead engages in gender reversals and gender play.

Canadian Literature

Beyond Munro scholarship, literary experts have addressed time in modern and contemporary Canadian literature. Cynthia Sugars and Gerry Turcotte's *Unsettled Remains* (2009) and Sherrill Grace's *Landscape of War and Memory* (2014) focus on unresolved Canadian settler histories and wars, and the need to return to the past in order to work towards reconciliation. Munro connects personal and collective histories and interrogates grand narratives embedded in patriarchy that inform the Canadian national imaginary. In this book, I explain how Munro mobilizes these conceptions of time to illuminate facets of contemporary Canadian society. I contend that Munro pushes back against linear structures and presents a unique concept of narrative time.

Recent scholarship has considered time in contemporary Canadian literature, but historically Canadian literary scholarship has been primarily concerned with place. From the question "Where is here?"[7] that Northrop Frye poses about Canada in his "Conclusion" to the first edition of the *Literary History of Canada* (1965) [reprinted in *The Bush Garden: Essays on the Canadian Imagination* (1971)], to Margaret Atwood's assertion in *Survival* (1972) that surviving the wilderness is a key theme in Canadian literature, to W.H. New's book, *Land Sliding: Imagining Space, Presence, and Power in Canadian Writing* (1997), scholars have examined and analyzed metaphors of place in Canadian writing. Many literary critics have addressed urban landscapes and the city. Critics who have written about Michael Ondaatje's and Margaret Atwood's writing and place, for instance, have often focused on representations of the city of Toronto.[8] Scholarly critics of western Canadian writers such as Robert Kroetsch and Margaret Laurence, by contrast, have focused on rural landscapes or the small prairie town.[9] Though many continue to discuss place in Canadian literature, there has been an "archival turn" in scholarly criticism in Canada, as Jason Wiens has pointed out ("Archives" 766). Such a turn towards theorizing how and where we preserve the past demonstrates a coming together of place and time. Much of the scholarship on archives focuses on place: where archives reside, and whether the place of that residence is physical or digital. Yet, as Linda M. Morra asserts, "archives move" ("Introduction" 1), shifting simultaneously through both place and time. This melding of place and time—scholarship's focus, that is, on both where and when the archives are—parallels the shift in scholarly criticism from place to time in Munro's work. Munro herself has an acute awareness of how written and photographic documentations of the past—archives—preserve or deteriorate, as she demonstrates in many of her stories such as "Heirs of the Living Body" and "Lichen." Munro showcases the dynamic, not static nature of both conservation and erosion in her work.

In her fiction, Munro began to address time and its relation to place in her early stories published in the 1950s. After Munro won the Nobel Prize in Literature in 2013, she announced that she was retiring from writing, and on May 13, 2024, Munro passed away at 92 years of age. The time trajectory of her writing life is in itself a subject for contemplation. The collections she published in the 1970s, *Lives of Girls and Women* and *Who Do You Think You Are?*, are coming-of-age stories that describe the emergence of a woman writer. Later works address ageing and look back upon a life lived, as the title of her final collection, *Dear Life*, published in 2012, suggests.

It is somewhat ironic that the chapters of *Alice Munro and the Art of Time* are organized chronologically. I argue that Munro contests normative conceptions of time, even as I organize this book in a linear fashion. Each text is considered chronologically in order of the date it was published. As noted, however, Munro works both within and against linear time. The short story form, for instance, is itself a traditional literary and generally linear storytelling form. Yet Munro challenges the conventions of that form. Her stories do not always take place over a few days' time, as many short stories do, and many of them contain an uncharacteristically large number of characters. The stories themselves are often not contained. The first two collections I consider in this book are interconnected short stories or short story sequences. The final four stories of *Dear Life*, since they are explicitly autobiographical, might be read together. To discuss Munro's collections of short stories in the order in which they were published is to show that there is a trajectory within which the author was working: from coming of age, to middle age, to old age. However, as Robert McGill convincingly argues, "Munro's career has been marked more by continuity and recursion than by transformation" ("Alice Munro" 137). McGill explains that Munro criticism has often suggested that the author's work progresses and improves through linear time, yet he cautions against this view. As Munro herself said, "I don't see that people develop and arrive somewhere. I just see people living in flashes'" (quoted in McGill 136). Thus, while Munro works within a linear time frame—as we all work within such traditional frameworks of understanding—she also challenges it in interesting ways, meeting the reader in what is a teleological world in order to push back against it.

The Art of Time

This study analyzes works from six of Munro's fourteen collections of short stories. Chapters three through six focus on only one or two stories in each collection. In the first two chapters of this book, I address Munro's early collections as a whole. I do so because each of these works—*Lives of Girls and Women* and *Who Do You Think You Are?*—are interconnected collections of short stories that feature a single protagonist. *Lives of Girls and Women* is arguably one of the greatest books in the Canadian literary canon. It had immediate success, but its longevity, its persistence in the literary canon, and its recognition as a Canadian classic have solidified its importance over the decades. As Thacker notes, the book "was passed over for the 1971 Governor General's Award, which went...that year to Mordecai Richler, but it garnered new attentions and honours for Munro" (*Alice Munro* 221). *Lives* won other awards upon its publication, such as the Canadian Booksellers Association / International Book of the Year Award (221-22). While there has been much scholarship on this book, *Alice Munro and the Art of Time* addresses it differently by highlighting how time manifests in the book and in relation to some of Munro's other collections and stories. This interconnected collection of short stories addresses time in particularly interesting ways: it challenges the Bildungsroman genre and time socialization, and it plays with gender reversals in this female coming-of-age story.

Like *Lives*, *Who* is also an important book in Munro's career trajectory and within the realm of the Canadian literary canon. Thacker asserts that it "was *the* critical book of Munro's career" (*Alice Munro* 294, emphasis in original). It was written at a key moment in Munro's life, after her divorce from Jim Munro and her move from Victoria, BC, to Clinton, Ontario, which is near Wingham, where Munro lived when she was a child. It was also the first book in which she worked with her long-time editor and publisher, Douglas Gibson, the first book she published with Macmillan, and the first book in which she worked with her long-time agent Virginia Barber (294). The publication history of *Who* is particularly fascinating. As Helen Hoy explains in her article "Rose and Janet: Alice Munro's Metafiction," and as Thacker delineates in his biography, Munro pulled the book from the press weeks before its publication to reorganize and revise it. This textual history has implications in terms of how time is expressed in the collection. Like *Lives*, *Who* reverses tropes and motifs related to time socialization and the expectations of girls' coming of age; it is, therefore, an important work with regard to how the author conceptualizes and portrays time. I have chosen to write about *Lives* and *Who*, but not *Dance of the Happy Shades*, published in 1968, or *Something I've Been Meaning to Tell You*, published in 1974. The reason for this choice, simply put, is that *Lives* and *Who* are more canonical than Munro's other early collections. These two works are Munro's only collections of interconnected short stories, and in them she blurs the boundaries between the short story genre and the novel, which is significant to how Munro treats time in these collections. They are more studied than Munro's other early collections, and works of criticism on them are therefore particularly relevant to students and scholars of Munro's work.

In subsequent chapters of the book, I have chosen to discuss only two or three stories within each collection, and I do not always discuss the title story of each collection. Each story is rich in and of itself and deserves its own critical attention. I have chosen stories that are particularly relevant to the time and place in which they were written, and the times and places in which we live. In chapter three, I analyze stories from *The Progress of Love*, published in 1985, but I do not discuss stories from *The Moons of Jupiter*, published three years earlier in 1982. *The Moons of Jupiter* is an important book, since as Thacker explains, at this time there was a "shift that was still taking place in Munro's writing since returning to Huron County" (*Alice Munro* 369). Further, another story she was working on during this time period, "Working for a Living," was distinctly autobiographical. It was published first in the New York literary review, *Grand Street* (381), and surfaced again in revised form much later in her autobiographical work, *The View From Castle Rock*, published in 2006. However, *The Progress of Love* includes stories that are of interest regarding the notion of time, and Thacker has

Introduction   XXXV

called it "Munro's strongest collection" ("The Way the Skin" 24). Whereas *Lives* and *Who* consider time in relation to time socialization, coming of age, and the Bildungsroman genre, *The Progress of Love* considers time with regard to protagonists who are moving through middle age rather than coming of age. "Miles City, Montana" and "The Progress of Love" are the stories that received the most immediate attention when the collection was first published (Thacker, *Alice Munro* 413). However, "Lichen" and "White Dump," the ones that I consider, intriguingly contemplate middle age in relation to the body and the environment: corporeality and deterioration in relation to time come to the fore. Thacker indicates that every one of the collections of stories that Munro wrote in the 1980s stood apart "as a transforming collection—one in which it feels that the work has become deeper and denser" (413). He names "Lichen" and "White Dump" as stories that demonstrate the quality of Munro's work. My discussion of "Lichen" and "White Dump" in *The Progress of Love* helps to portray how time can be conceptualized not only through the idea of coming of age, as I explain in the first two chapters, but also in terms of the dynamics of the body and the world, and the ever-changing and moving interconnections between these two places in and through time.

In *Alice Munro and the Art of Time*, I move from discussing coming of age, in chapters one and two, to corporeality and ephemerality, in chapter three, to narrative time in chapter four. In relation to narrative time, I limit my focus to two stories in Munro's 1990 collection, *Friend of My Youth*, which was Munro's next published collection after *Progress*. I discuss "Friend of My Youth" and "Meneseteung." Both pieces, and particularly "Meneseteung," have been widely anthologized and are well known. There has been a lot of scholarship on these stories, particular on "Meneseteung," yet I discuss the story in a new light by considering it primarily in relation to narrative time and framing, while also building on the previous chapter's discussion of the intertwinement of corporeality, ephemerality, and time. My analyses of these stories will be useful to scholars and students since these stories are studied frequently in universities. In chapter five, I address two stories in Munro's 2009 collection, *Too Much Happiness.*

I do not address the collections of stories Munro published been 1990 and 2009, such as *Open Secrets* (1994), *The Love of a Good Woman* (1998), and *Hateship, Friendship, Courtship, Loveship, Marriage* (2001).

Open Secrets is an excellent collection that features stories such as "Carried Away," a devastating tale of unrequited love. The title story tells of a missing school girl and a wife brutally treated by her husband. The stories in that collection address that which remains unsaid, those histories that are unrecorded, so to speak, in the name of progress and the march through time.

On July 7, 2024, Munro's youngest daughter, Andrea Skinner, published a piece in the *Toronto Star* newspaper. She wrote that she was sexually abused by her stepfather, Gerald Fremlin, in 1976, when she was only nine years old. In 1992, Skinner told her mother about the abuse, yet Munro stayed with Fremlin until his death in 2013, telling Skinner that she had told her "too late." Fremlin pled guilty to the assault in 2005. Skinner's 2024 story broke a long silence in Munro's family that extended to the public. Munro's status as beloved Canadian writer was suddenly contested as news and social media outlets were flooded with pieces about how to read Munro's writing, given her wrongful and devastating choice not to stand by her daughter. Readers pointed to "Vandals," the final story in *Open Secrets*, which, as I have mentioned, I do not discuss in this book. That collection was published only two years after Skinner told Munro about the abuse. "Vandals" features Ladner, a character who sexually abuses children. The subject of this story, written so close to when Skinner revealed the truth to her mother, might now be read in a new light. Was Munro, in the writing of this story, working through her own knowledge of what had happened to her daughter? It is quite possible that she was. How do we read Munro's stories now, knowing that so much of the darkness within them might have come from her decision to hide a secret of her own? Munro was a brilliant writer, and she was also a deeply flawed human being. Readers continue to grapple with this paradoxical truth.

Ironically, the title of the collection in which "Vandals" appears, *Open Secrets*, was penned at a time when Munro's secret was open within her own family, but still closed to the public. It is telling that the stories in this collection, like so many of Munro's stories, emphasize that which is not said; that which is kept hidden inside, beneath the surface. Munro's stories remain nuanced, detailed, and worth studying, even after learning this new truth. It is important to pay heed to Skinner's voice, acknowledging her story alongside Munro's as we read and study the author in light of new revelations. It is also important to realize that

Munro was celebrated as a literary celebrity, and that her image was created and sustained by readers, fans, and literary scholars—not to mention the Canadian literary institutions of which I/we are a part. We must consider, at this time, the extent to which we create and uphold a kind of heroism for such celebrities, and to realize that while the public can know an artist's work, we can never fully know their personal lives. In the moment of Skinner's revelation, that hurtful secret upset Alice Munro's celebrated public image. Time itself comes into play here. Munro's conscious knowledge of her daughter's abuse was belated, as was the public's knowledge of the same. This delayed awareness draws us back into Munro's writing as we attend to Skinner's and Munro's voices in and through time.

The Love of a Good Woman includes stories previously published in *Saturday Night* and *The New Yorker*, and is exemplary, as it won the Giller Prize that year. While many of the stories in that collection address time, Munro's handling of time in these stories is like her handling of time in previous ones, such as those in *Friend of My Youth*. The same is true for other collections of stories that I do not address in detail in this manuscript, such as *Runaway*, and *Hateship, Friendship, Courtship, Loveship, Marriage*. I have not addressed these collections in this study because I feel that to do so would be to repeat some of the points I make in the first few chapters of the book (on *Lives*, *Who*, *Progress*, and *Friend*).

The progression of the chapters and the choice of the collections I address relate to my consideration of time in Munro's writing. Just as I move from time socialization in chapters one and two to corporeality and ephemerality in chapter three, so too do I move from time and narrative framing in chapter four to retrospection, trauma, and regret—the idea of looking back upon one's past—in chapter five. Having demonstrated the autobiographical impetus in some of Munro's earlier work, I build on that premise to show how Munro creates doppelgängers and thematizes identity in relation to the movement of time.

In the final chapter, I discuss Munro's most recent and final collection of short stories, *Dear Life*, published in November of 2012, and I address three stories in that collection. The first story I discuss, "Corrie," was initially published in *The New Yorker* in 2010. Munro revised the ending of the story, and so the story itself changes through time, as Lee Clark Mitchell explains in his 2019 book, *More Time: Contemporary Short*

Stories and Late Styles. The textual and publication history of "Corrie," though not unusual—since Munro republished and revised other stories too—provides insight into Munro's techniques and emphases. This chapter builds on the previous one, as "Corrie," like "Fiction" and "Child's Play," is retrospective and engages the gothic mode, demonstrating the past's unsettling presence in the present. I also build upon my previous discussion of Munro's themes of identity as I address two of the four explicitly autobiographical works in the collection, "The Eye," and the title story, "Dear Life," and I do so in the context of relevant autobiographical theory and literary theory related to identity and time. This collection brings Munro's work full circle. She aptly calls it *Dear Life*, as though she is addressing and viewing her own life, looking back upon it. I have chosen to focus on *Dear Life* rather than *The View from Castle Rock*, her other autobiographical work, published in 2006. Though *Castle Rock* addresses time through Munro's gesture back to her own ancestral past, *Dear Life* focuses on more intimate autobiographical moments that demonstrate the intricacies between her understanding of time and identity. *Castle Rock* is a brilliant book, and critics such as Morra and Thacker have already discussed and analyzed both its autobiographical elements and its relation to time.[10] It is unique because it addresses the lives of the writer's ancestors. To my mind, *Dear Life* is somewhat more experimental and unique in terms of the autobiographical form, and that is why I chose to write about that collection rather than the other. I felt that to discuss both would be to repeat my points about how autobiographical discourse circulates in Munro's work.

In *Alice Munro and the Art of Time*, I have analyzed only some of Munro's stories that deal with the concept of time. Munro is a prolific writer, and there are many more stories that I might have addressed: she has published upwards of 150 stories in total. The ones I discuss in this book can be viewed as case studies, and they represent the kinds of issues that Munro addressed throughout her long writing career. I only touch upon Munro's consideration of aspects of time related to trauma. Trauma studies and memory studies—both very much related to and indeed a part of time—are vast areas of scholarship in and of themselves. Stories such as "The Bear Came Over the Mountain," in the collection *Hateship, Friendship, Courtship, Loveship, Marriage*, and "In Sight of the Lake," in *Dear Life*, both of which address Alzheimer's disease, are not considered in this book. These stories deserve and have received critical attention, but the theoretical frameworks in which they would need to be addressed here exceed the confines of this study. Thus, I have focused this book on stories that demonstrate a resistance to teleological time, but do not include the inherent complexities of disease or trauma per se.

Munro's writing has received acclaim both within and beyond Canada. Her short stories, among the best in the world, address themes of gender and class. She emphasizes speed and productivity in the late-capitalist period, which have taken and continue to take a toll on human lives and natural environments. This book analyzes Munro's writing to show how the author has been concerned with conceptions of time from 1971, when she published *Lives*, to 2012, when she published her final work, *Dear Life.* Munro employs images and tropes such as the train and train track to mark dominant movements of time. She unsettles such notions of time, emphasizing a more woman-centred conception of it by valuing cycles of birth and death, gestation, and bodily flow. Like many modern contemporary Canadian woman writers, she engages in experimental narrative techniques, while still adhering, to some extent, to the traditional genre of the short story.

This book offers a contribution to Munro studies as it shifts the focus of interpretation from place to time, explaining how the two are intertwined. By addressing how Munro draws our attention to cyclical, repetitious time, and to the natural and the corporeal, I highlight the connections between various tropes in the author's work including identity, ephemerality, and environmental change. This focus is particularly important now, since the contemporary Western world is consumed with the sentiment that there are not enough hours in the day, and the legitimate fear that we are speeding toward the destruction of our planet. While time has always been latent in Munro's writing, *Alice Munro and the Art of Time* brings the concept to the fore and thus allows us to perceive of her work from a new angle.

1

Genre, Narrative, and Time in *Lives of Girls and Women*

MUNRO'S *LIVES OF GIRLS AND WOMEN* (1971) has been described as a Bildungsroman or Künstlerroman, a novel that delineates the life of a person or artist from youth to adulthood. As Maria Luz Gonzales and Juan Ignacio Oliva state, "this work reveals itself as a modern *Künstlerroman*, the portrait and development of the artist as heroine" (181). John Moss implies that the work is autobiographical, since he notes that the protagonist of *Lives*, Del Jordan, "is going to be the writer that Alice Munro becomes" (quoted in Gonzales and Olivia, 181). As I mention in the introduction to this book, critics such as J.R. (Tim) Struthers and W.R. Martin have examined Munro's literary allusions to Bildungsromans written by Joyce and Brontë. In "Alice Munro and Charlotte Brontë," Marjorie Garson further details allusions to *Jane Eyre* in *Lives of Girls and Women*, arguing that Munro was profoundly influenced by Brontë's novel. However, despite its parallels to James Joyce's *A Portrait of the Artist as a Young Man* and Charlotte Brontë's *Jane Eyre*, *Lives of Girls and Women* actively resists alignment with teleological time, which is an aspect of both the Bildungsroman and the Künstlerroman. As such, it does not fit easily into the coming-of-age genre. On the one hand, the book progresses chronologically through time, beginning when Del is a young girl in grade four and ending when she is a young woman and has finished high school; on the other hand, it works against the readers' expectations of a coming-of-age work. By the end of the book, Del has not married, pursued an education, or achieved a spiritual awakening, although she has contemplated all these pursuits.

Munro's challenge to the linear progression of the coming-of-age genre in this collection is important in its relation to gender: she revisits the ways in which girls and women move through time, and she upsets the expectation that girls should attain only an early education, get married, and then have children. In so doing, she "challenges a previous literature which defined women according to a patriarchal domain" and instead engages in a "feminist quest for identity and freedom" (Gonzales and Olivia, 180-81). Thus, Munro's *Lives of Girls and Women* offers a different perspective on time and time socialization. In this chapter, I argue that the book works within the genres of the Bildungsroman and Künstlerroman, but ultimately departs and challenges those genres by pushing back against their traditions and conventions.

Genre

Lives of Girls and Women challenges linear progression through the form of the work, since short story conventions play with time in ways that novels do not. Indeed, it is debatable whether *Lives of Girls and Women* is in fact a novel or an interconnected collection of short stories. While some critics, such as Margaret Harris and Marjorie Garson, refer to the book as a novel, others, such as Roxanne Harde, insist otherwise. She asserts that there are "differences between these short stories and the chapters of a novel," and that the stories "rely on discontinuity, disunity, and fragmentation to depict the realities of women's lives" in ways that novels cannot (58). Critic Suzanne Ferguson notes that the short story sequence or cycle "as we currently think of it is basically a modernist (i.e.: early 20th century) invention" (103), and she cites Joyce's *The Dubliners* as an early example. Reingard M. Nischik has argued that the short story cycle is a genre "especially prominent in North American literature [...that] has sometimes even been considered Canada's national literary genre" (quoted in Berndt, "Trapped" 526). Contemplating the difference in the terms "sequence" and "cycle," Ferguson states that "a cycle by its name should 'go around' something in time, in the consideration of a theme...a sequence should be linked by development... whether in time or theme" (104). This difference in terminology is relevant to the idea of time in *Lives of Girls and Women*. Munro's book may appear to be a sequence, since Del progresses from childhood to adulthood through the book, and yet it is also a cycle, as Munro time jumps and, in the epilogue, circles back to a moment prior to the time of the final story. Genre theorist James Nagel explains that in a short story cycle "each contributing unit of the work [is] an independent narrative episode. There [is] some principle of unification," he notes, "that gives structure, movement, and thematic development to the whole" (quoted in Ferguson 105). The notion of a short story *cycle* rather than *sequence* certainly contests the idea of linear development and progression, and offers a different perspective on time. Munro may be known as a realist writer, as Cinda Gault asserts in "The Two Addies," yet the author complicates the genre of her work: *Lives of Girls and Women* could be a novel, or an interconnected short story collection, or a sequence, or a cycle. Presenting the stories in *Lives* as discreet yet connected, Munro contests what Paul Huebener calls "normative time" (*Timing* 32), which is linear, progressive, and singular.

Munro herself described *Lives of Girls and Women* as "partway between a novel and series of long stories, all [a] 'growing up' sort of thing" (Thacker, *Alice Munro* 211). As Robert Thacker explains, she initially intended the work to be a novel, but decided that it worked better in stories (210). Moreover, the book hovers on the edges of autobiography. A disclaimer to the book says: "This novel is autobiographical in form but not in fact. My family, neighbours, and friends did not serve as models.—A.M." (quoted in Thacker 211). Yet, as Thacker notes, the epilogue of the book, in particular, is autobiographical: "with its focus on Del as an artist and as a young woman, and on Del's own concomitant struggle with the life she finds herself living and the other world she imagines and is drawn to, the epilogue's few pages are infused with Alice Munro's own life history" (212). *Lives*, then, seems to reside in between genres: neither completely a novel nor a set of short stories; neither entirely autobiography nor fiction. Although, in some ways, it seems to fit into the Bildungsroman and Künstlerroman models, Munro seems uncomfortable with those labels too, evidenced by her apology to her editor, Audrey Coffin: "I feel apologetic about turning out this sort of girl-growing-up thing" (212). Her resistance to traditional elements of the Bildungsroman, such as a spiritual awakening and marriage, further demonstrates her discomfort with any easy alignment of her work with this genre. Munro already resists facile or traditional categorizations in her presentation of *Lives of Girls and Women*.

Character

The author challenges normative time through her characters in the work. Uncle Benny, for example, introduced in the first story of the collection, "The Flats Road," does not follow normative time, but functions on a different kind of clock altogether, one by which Del is fascinated. Benedict Anderson notes that in newspapers, we read stories about people who may not know each other but who are still connected in the readers' minds because their stories happened simultaneously and appear together there (26). In *Lives of Girls and Women*, Del's parents subscribe to the town's newspaper, the *Jubilee Herald Advance*, and the *Saturday Evening Post*. While her parents adhere to this notion of time represented by their newspapers, Benny subscribes to an alternate kind of newspaper, one which is "printed badly on rough paper" (6) and has sensationalist headlines such as "Father Feeds Twin Daughters to Hogs" (7). Benny is therefore set apart in time from the other town members and, more specifically, from Del's family. He exempts himself from the logical and chronological time represented in the papers that Del's family reads: his alternative newspapers are "his only source of information about the outside world" (6). The different types of newspapers presented in "The Flats Road" are not only material, but they are also signifiers that point to events or occurrences outside of the material text, and they exemplify different interpretations of those events. In "Synecdoche and the Munrovian Sublime: Parts and Wholes in *Lives of Girls and Women*," Garson explains that "competing discourses jostle with one another in Munro's writing: no thin line can separate off a single word from the textual universe around it" (417). Newspapers in this story are examples of such "competing discourses" (417), and Del is the one who negotiates and evaluates their meanings. As Garson notes, "Munro's style is synechdochal in a...particular sense: she often focuses on 'parts' that call in question the notion of the 'whole' and the relationship of part of whole" (414). The wholeness to which parts are tangential in *Lives* is always on the edge of unravelling or falling apart: languages into competing newspaper discourses; Uncle Craig's dead body into organs, such as the eyes; and Miss Ferris herself into two different lives, the one where she is seemingly happy, and the one where she takes her own life. Even the wholeness of the so-called novel that we read, *Lives of Girls and Women*, breaks down into stories that are loosely held together as one.

Benny is not only apart in time, but also in place, though the two are intertwined. At his house, Del too is immersed in and believes the seemingly unreal, out-of-time world that Benny inhabits. Only when she returns to her own home does she question the truth of Benny's news: "Why was it," she asks, "that the plain back wall of home, the pale chipped brick...should make it seem doubtful that a woman would really send her husband's torso, wrapped in Christmas paper, by mail to his girl friend in South Carolina?" (7). Del's imaginative potential seems to dwindle when she leaves Benny's house. She longs to escape normative time and place symbolized by her parents' newspapers and the banality of her own home. Furthermore, the separation of Benny's home from Del's suggests a disjunction between them in terms of socio-economic class. Critic Katrin Berndt argues that Munro depicts poverty and social mobility through the representation of material objects in her stories, which is relevant given Del's focus on the materiality of newspapers in Benny's home and his collection of old things: "linoleum, parts of furniture, insides of machinery, nails" ("Trapped" 6).

The reference to linoleum is noteworthy, since linoleum has various representational functions in Munro's writing, as Sabrina Francesconi explains in "Alice Munro and the Poetics of Linoleum." On the one hand, as one of Benny's scraps of other people's things, it signals both domesticity and upturning of that domesticity; on the other, it situates the story in place and time, since linoleum was popular in North America from after the Second World War until the 1960s, when vinyl overtook it. That Benny "hoped to patch things up and sell them" (6) suggests that he is interested in these old domestic items insofar as they serve the present market. His interest is economic and demonstrates his desire for socio-economic mobility and prosperity. Joel Burges and Amy J. Elias suggest that in modern and postmodern times, "what seems multiple and diverse is always part of the system, always feeding the logic of capital" (12), and so Benny's things, to return to Garson's argument in "Munro's Synechdochal Sublime," are, in his eyes, useful in terms of their relation to capitalism. The notion that the multiple and diverse are part of the single system of capitalism may seem contrary to postmodern literature's project, which is to resist linearity and to undercut grand narratives. Yet it is worth noting the limits of postmodernity, how what is multiple and fragmentary can be co-opted into the system of capitalism. Munro has said that her family belonged to "the privileged poor" (quoted in Berndt, "Trapped" 524). Del's family home—in contrast to Benny's—is described as "plain" with "chipped brick" (7); and yet, like Munro's own home perhaps, it aspires to be middle-class with its newspapers, artwork, and encyclopedias. Del negotiates these two domestic places, privileging Benny's, with its imaginative potential and fantasies, over her own.

Benny's collection of old things includes both "that of fifty years or so of family life," and "other people's throwaways" (6). The "insides of machinery" and "nails" (6) contrast the domestic image of linoleum and indicate Del's interest in what lives look like on the "insides" (6). Just as Benny desires to fix and build from these old things, so too does *Lives of Girls and Women* build upon the literature of Munro's predecessors. These "throwaways" (6) and Benny's intent to repurpose them might be a metaphor for Del's—and Munro's—methods of writing. Del's act of writing Benny's name recalls Dedalus's act of writing his own name in Joyce's *Portrait of the Artist*; the repetition and revision of the phrase "He preferred not" to "She preferred not" (37) recalls and rewrites that phrase in the feminine from Herman Melville's "Bartleby, the Scrivener."

Munro's references to Brontë's *Jane Eyre*, are, perhaps, the most interesting moments of intertextuality in the collection. In her article, "Alice Munro and Charlotte Brontë," Garson says that Munro "has been profoundly influenced by *Jane Eyre*, particularly by the paradoxes of the Jane/Bertha pairing and by violent scenes dramatizing the power relationships and the occulted allegiances in the novel" (784). Madeleine's act of cutting up Benny's "green suit" (19) is a rewrite and reversal of Bertha Mason's act of cutting up Jane's wedding dress in *Jane Eyre*. Del's act of biting Mary Agnes in "the old part of the house" (52) recalls Bertha's act of biting her brother Richard in the secret part of the attic in *Jane Eyre*, and, as Garson points out, Jane's own attack on her cousin early in the novel. In Munro's references to *Jane Eyre*, subject positions shift: at first, Madeleine is aligned with the mad woman who is Bertha, while Del watches on the sidelines; later, Del herself occupies that same subject position—the mad girl who is both Jane (who lashes out in the Red Room) and Bertha (who bites Richard). Garson states, "Since Del reads Gaskell's *Life of Charlotte Brontë* as she nurses a hangover, and since *Jane Eyre* is a rewriting of that life, as Del's story is of Munro's, *Lives of Girls and Women* invites us to recognize her as such as model" ("Alice Munro" 785). Like Benny, both Del and Munro repurpose old things from their own lives and the literature of others to create their own stories. By turning to the past to depict the present, Munro's stories are both forward and backward looking.

It is significant that Benny's reality is one that resides outside of normative time in his recount of Flats Road resident Sandy Steveston's marriage. According to Benny, Sandy married a widow, but he and his new wife were so haunted by the ghost of her dead husband that finally Sandy demanded that his wife leave. When Del's mother says, "But you don't really believe that, do you?" Benny makes it clear that he does: he gives her a "fierce, pitying look" and explains that he saw the bruises that Sandy got from the ghost poking him in his bed (10-11). In terms of the progression of this story, this recount is future oriented. First, it parallels and foreshadows the upcoming story of Benny and Madeleine's marriage. Like the ghost who haunts Sandy, Madeleine herself is described as a ghost and becomes a legend: she is "thin, white, [and] evasive," and "stories" about her "were being passed up and down the road" (19). Second, the story of Sandy's marriage instigates Benny's marriage to Madeleine. To redirect the conversation away from the story's unbelievability, Del's father tells Benny that he, like Sandy, should look for a rich widow to marry, and Benny says he will (19). Yet Benny's story of Sandy's haunting by his wife's previous husband is also past oriented and demonstrates how Benny resists chronological time. For him, the widow's ghost is not relegated to the past but is very much alive in spirit and part of the present: the past and the present are conflated. The ghost's haunting suggests that the new husband, Sandy, represents "territorial and historical dispossession and inauthenticity" (Sugars and Turcotte ix): Sandy has ousted the so-called rightful former husband. The past erupts into the present in Sandy's home to reveal an "unhomeliness" that "elicits an uncanny or unsettling experience" (19).[1]

Place

The inhabitation of places in Munro's writing is always temporary, always in the midst of sliding out from under one's grasp, always in flux. The ghost of the widow's dead husband in Sandy's own home suggests that Sandy's wife and home are not his, that they have been claimed by another. Similarly, Del notes at the beginning of the story that the riverbank Benny inhabits and fishes at "is not his" (3). Rather, she says, "it was ours"—her brother Owen's and hers (3). Since Del is about to tell the story of her own life, the "it" to which she claims ownership could refer not only to the riverbank but also to her own narrative, intimately intertwined with landscape and place: Del disrupts narrative time by inserting her own story into the historical literary tradition. The inhabitation of the river's edge, moreover, is dangerous. As Garson points out, even as Uncle Benny claims that the riverbank is his, he simultaneously notes that there is a "quicksand hole in there that would take down a two-ton truck" (2), which suggests that he belongs to the riverbank, not that it belongs to him. This kind of danger is repeated in stories like "Deep Holes," in which a family has a picnic on a landscape that is ridden with dangerous holes, or "Lichen," in which the land of the protagonist Stella's home erodes. Munro emphasizes erosion and change through time. As Christine Lorre-Johnston and Eleonora Rao put it, "Homes and landscape metamorphose in a character's perception of them" (3). The various stories where Munro explores drownings, such as "Miles City, Montana" and "Child's Play," further depict characters' environments, natural or not, as dangerous and ephemeral.

In *Lives of Girls and Women*, Munro's attention to who owns or has the right to occupy the riverbank is interesting in light of her position as a settler. Munro is not explicitly an anti-colonial writer, yet we might ask what it means to read Munro today, when settler histories are being questioned and Indigenous ones are coming to the fore. The author's resistance to linear and progressive time is implicitly a resistance to what Huebener calls "imperial time,"[2] the notion that the West is on an ever-progressing and ever-improving timeline. To question who has a right to occupy a particular place is to question who was there before. In the case of Huron County, Munro's home and the model for Del's, the land was occupied by the Anishinaabe and Haudenosaunee peoples.

Though Munro theoretically works against "imperial time," however, there are moments when she eludes Indigenous presence in her stories. Discussing Munro's first collection of stories, *Dance of the Happy Shades*, critic Lorie-Anne Rainville explains that "the title of the opening story, 'Walker Brothers Cowboy,' suggests that the 'Indian' has been forgotten. With its American western ring," she notes, "the title foregrounds the figure of the cowboy and elides that of the Indian" (para. 2). Therefore, in the title of her story, Munro highlights settler rather than Indigenous presences and histories. In *Dance of the Happy Shades*, Indigenous Peoples and even mentions of them are notably absent, yet in *Who Do*

You Think You Are?, published ten years later, that changes somewhat, as Patrick makes derogatory comments about Indigenous Peoples in a university classroom, and a female student challenges him: "Well, there is their own culture, you know" (115). As Rainville notes, Munro's shift here is indicative of the socio-political landscape in Canada at the time. *Who* was published in the 1970s, when Indigenous voices were emerging, "disturbing Canada's collective memory with certain truths" (Rainville para. 5), such as the sixties scoop and the residential school system, both of which took Indigenous children away from their parents. It appears, as Rainville suggests, that Munro represses the memory of colonization in her stories. There are moments, though, such as the discussion of who owns the riverbank at the beginning of *Lives*, and the one that Rainville notes in *Who*, when that repression seems to be exposed. For a contemporary reader, *Lives* invokes Munro and her characters' subject positions as settlers who reside on formerly Indigenous lands.

As Jason Wiens explains, "there are relatively few references to Indigenous people in either Munro's fiction or its criticism" and yet "absences can signify as much as presences, and we might productively read these absences as part of a decolonial critical project ("What Difference" 10-11). Examining drafts of stories in Munro's archives, Wiens traces an episode of Munro's writing that discusses possible Indigenous heritage of one of her characters from a draft of the story "Accident," (the final version of which was published in *The Moons of Jupiter* in 1982), to "Characters," a story that was published in the magazine *Ploughshares* in 1978. In the draft of "Accident" that Wiens discusses, the protagonist, Helena, asks her parents who adopted her "if she could possibly have Indian blood" due to her "thick tan skin" (5). This episode does not make it in to the final version of "Accident." The movement of episodes between drafts of Munro's stories indicates the stories' interconnectivity and the fluid process of writing itself. This dynamic creative process belies linearity and demonstrates change through time. Particularly interesting, however, is the way in which the episode that discusses the possible Indigenous heritage of Munro's character becomes written out of "Accident," though it does appear in "Characters" (Wiens, "What Difference" 2). Ironically, as Wiens further explains, the erasure of the Indigenous presence that the characters of Mr. Cleaver and Dr. Wright in Munro's stories express—"they were wiped out," Mr.

Cleaver said (quoted in Wiens 8)—is repeated in the passage's omission from the final version of "Accident" (10). Wiens's archival work shows how Munro indeed contemplated Indigenous histories in relation to the places where her settler characters reside; and yet, problematically, as her revisions to this episode demonstrate, she sometimes wrote those histories out. Munro's attention to the movement and ephemerality of places in her writing, both historical and geographical, lends credence to the argument that Munro perceived landscapes and places as impermanent, in flux. She resisted the idea that land and place could be owned and sustained in a permanent way. From a postcolonial perspective, however, the infrequent representation of Indigenous people in Munro's stories is notable. Munro foregrounds the dynamics of place but does not often draw attention to the Indigenous Peoples who occupy it.

Del's placement on the riverbank not only unsettles the stability of settler subjectivities, but also gendered ones. The story opens on the riverbank. Del is a name which could be attributed to a boy or a girl. Del herself is with two males, her brother and Uncle Benny, and engages in what might be deemed a "boy's" activity: catching fish. In these opening paragraphs, the reader might question whether Del is a boy or a girl, and thus Munro presents the gendered identities of her characters, as well as the places in which they reside, as slippery, dynamic, and ungrounded. Munro questions gender identity and demonstrates its constructedness in stories well before those in *Lives of Girls and Women*. For instance, in her well-known story, "Boys and Girls," in *Dance of the Happy Shades*, the eleven-year-old girl protagonist says, "A girl was not, as I had supposed, simply what I was; it was what I had to become" (107). It is noteworthy that "Boys and Girls" was first published in *The Montrealer* in 1964 (Thacker, *Alice Munro* 608), just one year after Betty Friedan's *The Feminine Mystique*—a book that questions women's place at home—was published in 1963 (Brandt 33).

The questioning of one's right to occupy a place as home reveals gothic elements of Munro's work, since gothic literature employs notions of what Sigmund Freud calls the "uncanny," the encountering of what is both familiar and unfamiliar, settling and unsettling ("Uncanny"), and what Homi Bhabha calls the "unhomely," a feeling of estrangement in one's own place or home (445). The haunted home is simultaneously a place of discomfort and horror. Munro suggests discomfort in Del's occupation of the riverbank with the attention she draws to who owns it; similarly, she suggests Sandy Steveston's discomfort in his own home, since it seems to be haunted by his wife's former husband. Both instances produce uncanny and unhomely effects. Munro herself has compared her stories to homes, her method of storytelling to the occupation and exploration of those homes. For her, a story is "more like a house" than a road. "I go into it," she says, "and move back and forth and settle here and there, and stay in it for a while" (quoted in Berndt, "Trapped" 521). The author's comparison of a story to a house in which she moves "back and forth" contests linearity in time and place. She haunts the stories that she writes with her presence, which is ghostly insofar as it is behind the scenes, hidden from the reader.

Del states that Benny "could read very well but he could not write" (13), and so Benny asks Del to write a letter for him. The letter is a response to a newspaper advertisement that offers a housekeeper "for a man in a quiet country home." The ad suggests that the housekeeper will marry the man "if suited" (13). Del's act of writing the letter to Madeleine for Benny, like the story of Sandy's marriage, initiates the story of Benny's marriage to Madeleine. When Benny tells Del's parents the story of Sandy marrying a rich women, Del's father says to Benny that he should find a rich wife, which leads Benny to write to Madeleine. Del's writing of the letter initiates the process of Benny finding a wife. Benny asks Del to write down his name and address, which she expands to include "The World, The Solar System, The Universe" (12). It is this moment specifically, as Struthers, Martin, and Ellen McWilliams have explained, that recalls Dedalus's inscription of his address in his geography book, in Joyce's *A Portrait of the Artist as a Young Man*. Dedalus, like Del, includes the world and the universe (Harris 105). That Benny does not engage in the act of writing his own name and address—an expression of his identity—suggests that he is outside of the symbolic order: normative time, language, and law. Rather, he occupies the imaginary realm and orients himself towards what is illusive: the alternative, unbelievable newspapers; the ghost that haunts Sandy. Just as the widow's dead husband haunts Sandy, so too does Del haunt Benny, since she is his ghostwriter, the one who pens his name. She sets his story with Madeleine in motion and symbolically claims authorship of it. As Harris explains, Del "does not intrude herself as author of the text, accepting the role of ministering female, a role which reverses some traditional aspects of female subservience since she has a power, even as a girl-child, which the adult male Benny does not have, the power of the pen and the word" (104). Munro, however, does not simply reiterate Dedalus's act but rewrites and revises it. Whereas Dedalus begins to construct his own identity by writing it, Del begins to construct hers by writing for Benny. She can only enter the predominantly male literary tradition through patriarchy, which is particularly ironic since Benny is outside of normative time. In the same way that she haunts Benny's story as its ghost author, Joyce and other canonical authors haunt Munro's text as authors of its predecessors, and Munro haunts Del's story as the author of *Lives of Girls and Women.* Munro mobilizes the linear history and the tradition of literature and alters it by adding her own voice.

Benny's inability to attain and follow a city map in his search for Madeleine in "The Flats Road" demonstrates a further refusal to adhere to linear, historical time. When Benny first goes to meet Madeleine, Del's father says, "Did you look at that map I gave you?" and Benny replies, "No, I seen some fellow on a tractor and I asked him and he turned me around" (15). Later, when Madeleine leaves and Benny goes to find her in Toronto, he is not successful because he does not attain or follow a map. Just as he does not write, he cannot read the text of the map. He cannot navigate a space that is not his own, unlike the riverbank with which he is so familiar.

If Del aligns herself with Benny and his dissociation from normative time and space, then, by contrast, she refuses to align herself with Uncle Craig in the second story in the sequence "Heirs of the Living Body." Right from its beginning, the story invokes imperial time and situates Craig alongside it. In other words, Munro summons and resists the notion that what is important happens only in relation to a single time and place, namely, the imperial centre, and that "alternative visions of nationhood and collective temporality" are "impossible, abhorrently stagnant, or non-existent" (Huebener, *Timing* 30). Craig's alignment with the town's colonial history is marked by the "Red Ensign" and "Union Jack" on his front veranda, and his position as the clerk of "Fairmile Township" (28). It is also marked by the pictures displayed in his den: photographs of "the Fathers of Confederation...the King and Queen," and "a log house which had stood on the site" (28). These objects are metonyms for the British Empire and signal Canada's relationship to it. Critic Christine Prentice states that "through Del Jordan's narrative, we see...story making processes construct the world in which she lives and simultaneously construct her as part of that world" (29). Del notes the items that represent Britain and understands that she is a part of that national heritage, even as she rejects it. Karin Brendt explains that "Munro aestheticizes material objects to draw attention to individual and communal mechanisms of socio-cultural participation and exclusion" ("Trapped" 523). Del's negotiation of Craig's material items that signify Canada's historical alignment with Britain are those "communal mechanisms" that suggest his and Del's "socio-cultural participation" in them—even as Del attempts to exclude herself. As Gault notes, in the early 1970s, when *Lives* was published, feminist and national political initiatives were occurring at the same time: second-wave feminism, and the movement towards repatriation of Canada's constitution from Britain ("Two Addies" 442). Situated in this context, Munro's work might be seen as both feminist and nationalist. Del's assumption that Craig is one of the men in the picture of the log house, which existed much before his time, is the first indication in this story that Del refuses to adhere to normative and imperial time. Craig "was displeased with me" Del states, "not on account of any vanity about his age, but because of my inaccurate notions of time and history" (29).

Similarly, Del does not accept Craig's written history of Wawanash County on the expected terms. When her two aunts, Elspeth and Grace, upholders of patriarchy and order, offer her Craig's manuscript after his death, Del carries it "awkwardly under her arm" (59) and then puts it in her cellar, which floods (60). Her "awkward" relationship to the manuscript and her placement of it away from her contrast her intimate relationship to her own writing, poems and part of a novel that she keeps under her mattress and her bed (59-60). Her own writing is "folded inside a large flat copy of *Wuthering Heights*" (60): it is symbolically embedded within the female literary tradition. The "mistake" (28) she refers to at the beginning of the story—the misrecognition of the time of Craig's photograph—recalls the "mistake" (60) she makes at the end—the placement of Craig's manuscript in the cellar. Neither are indications of being wrong but rather of being resistant, of her refusal to adhere to notions of normative time. Finally, her writings are secretive, tucked in or under her bed and folded between the covers of another book, unlike Craig's writings: he "did not question that he was part of...

Genre, Narrative, and Time in *Lives of Girls and Women*   13 public events, of politics" (30). Del's observation here might be read as feminist, insofar as she implies that she and other women, unlike Craig, might question their part in public and political discourse. That she feels both "remorse" and "unblemished satisfaction" at the destruction of Craig's manuscript suggests that she at once mourns the loss of normative time represented in the male literary tradition, and relishes a new, alternative time represented in her own writing and in the continuation of a female literary tradition.

Corporeality

In "Heirs of the Living Body," Munro draws a parallel between the corps, the body itself, and a corpus of writing. This comparison is evident in Del's experience of seeing a dead cow on the edge of the Wawanash River. The dead cow might be likened to other gothic and corporeal images throughout the book: the rape by "five boys" of Mary Agnes, mentioned only a page before (42); the bodily and sexual "torture" of Del's mother by her younger brother (73); the suicidal drowning of Del's teacher, Miss Farris—in the same river at which Del finds the cow; and Uncle Craig's dead body, discussed right after the cow scene (44). Of these, Munro depicts the strongest association between the dead cow and Craig's dead body. Del notes, for instance, that one of Craig's "eyes was blind" (29), and she is fascinated by the unseeing eye of the dead cow (43). But she also describes the dead cow specifically as a text, a map: "the brown could be the ocean, the white the floating continents" (43). As though she wields her own pen, she "traces" (43) the shapes on the cow with a stick. Like Craig's manuscript, which later rests in Del's cellar, wet from a flood, the cow is soaked in the water of the river. Just as she would read and write literature, Del "reads" the cow's body, trying to figure it out as she "writes" on it: "Tracing the outline of a continent again, digging the stick in, trying to make a definite line, I paid attention to its shape...as if the shape itself were a revelation beyond words" (43-44). Thus, Del negotiates the "corps" of the cow as she does the "corpus" of the settler literary tradition—literature that emerged out of settler-colonialism—of which Craig's history is a part. Her "contempt" (43) for the dead cow mirrors her contempt for Craig's wet, dead manuscript at the end of the story. Her own story will both derive and depart from it.

When Del studies and traces the cow, she also studies the world and herself. She not only sees the shapes on the cow as continents on a map, but also "pay[s] attention" (43) to them as if they are "real continents or islands on real maps" (43-44). To write about the world around her, she must first seek to understand it. The stick Del holds when she traces the colour on the cow's hide is like a pen, and so her tracing of the "map" is a foreshadowing of her future career as a writer. Indeed, like a writer, Del writes on the cow—the world—that she contemplates. In so doing, she strives for accuracy: "With my stick I traced [the continents'] strange shapes, their curving coasts, trying to keep the point of the stick exactly between the white and the brown" (43). Del contemplates the cow-world in which she lives and questions the legitimacy of her own place in it. When she gets to the eye, she becomes shy, as though she is not sure she has a place on this map: "I tapped the face. I was shyer about touching the face. I was shy about looking at its eye" (43). Mary Agnes is with Del in this scene, and unlike Del, she is not shy about touching the cow's eye ("she laid her hand—she laid *the palm of her hand*—over it, over the eyes" [44, emphasis in original]), which may suggest that she is open to life and death, while Del desires clear boundaries between the two. In terms of her own writing, Del will not simply trace the maps of the past, such as her uncle Craig's history, but will have to face the eye and add herself—her own I—into her writing.

Munro puns on the homonyms eye/I: when Del studies the *eye* of the cow, she simultaneously contemplates the *I* who is herself. The eye of the cow is likened to Craig's blind eye, and so we can deduce that Del's *I* is also related to and associated with Craig's. The cow's body is a map, as is Craig's manuscript and Del's story. She will read and negotiate those who have gone before her in order to write her own story. Rather than repeat her predecessors' stories or follow the linear, progressive time that is expected of her, Del, and implicitly, Munro, works within and against what has come before. In this way, Del fundamentally departs from what her aunts, Elspeth and Grace, expect of her. Her aunts covet Craig's manuscript after his death, worried that someone "might get hold of it and bring it out as if it was their own" (58); paradoxically, they also tell Del "that the manuscript was [hers]" (59). Though she is its "heir," she refuses to "own" the manuscript. Rather, she does with it exactly what her mother, Ada, says they can do medically with bodies, use parts but not the whole: "someday these parts will be used!...Transplant them! For instance eyes" (47). Del sees the world around her with her eyes and appropriates the *I's* of the literary past to construct and write her own.

"Heirs of the Living Body," then, is inherently about time: history and the part Del might play in relation to it. It is clear that Del strategically resists progress and growth represented by Craig and his revered manuscript depicting the past of Wawanash County. Munro repeatedly invokes the notion of the heir, a rightful owner and inheritor, but she also disbands it, exposing its error and invalidity. Del witnesses but rejects colonial history and the heirs of the King and Queen she sees in Craig's photograph at the beginning of the story, just as she ultimately refuses the ownership of Craig's manuscript. Instead, she reads the past to assert her own agency and follow her own sense of time: fragmented, disunited, and partial.

Del's aunts are full of contradictions. On the one hand, Elspeth and Grace are aligned with normative time and "the linear notion of progress," which, according to Huebener, intertwines with "powerful social emphases on punctuality [and] productivity" (*Timing* 24). On the other hand, however, there are instances where they exemplify Kristeva's notion of "women's time": they resist the symbolic order and embrace the semiotic.[3] That they are aligned with normative time is clear when Del notes that "their house had a chiming clock, which delicately marked the quarter hours" (61). They embrace those mechanical markers of time that dominate over cycles of nature. It is through such normative concepts of time that "the prized concept of firstness and the more ambivalent concept of newness are claimed by certain people and denied to others" (Huebener, *Timing* 24). Del's aunts clearly uphold the patriarchal order, suggesting that settler men such as Craig are the ones who should be the "first" to write history. Del notes that they draw "the dearest line" between men's and women's work, and that "any stepping over this line, any suggestion of stepping over it, would meet with...light, amazed, regretfully superior, laughter" (32). The settler and patriarchal order they uphold is also the symbolic order. They believe in, protect, and revere Craig's written history, his perspective on history, which is consecrated in language. While they consider giving Craig's manuscript to Del's brother Owen, "because he's the boy" (59), they ultimately decide to give it to Del, "because she is one who has the knack for writing compositions" (59). Del breaks their "trust" (58), since she keeps it in her cellar, which floods. She strategically refuses to preserve the patriarchal and symbolic order. While Elspeth and Grace suggest that Del "get the feel of Uncle Craig's way of writing" and "copy his way" (59), she does nothing of the sort. Rather, aligned with Munro herself, she rewrites it completely, working within and against it not to repeat his story, but to write her own. As critic Jędrzej Burszta explains, Del is relieved when the manuscript is destroyed by the flood, since that event "frees her from the fixed and constricted identity transmitted through tradition, here imagined as some useless heritage, a set of dates, names and events entirely removed from her own life" (26). Munro's *Lives of Girls and Women* invokes the Bildungsroman and Künstlerroman genres, but ultimately defies them by not buying into their conventions. Likewise, Del now owns a copy of Craig's manuscript, and is influenced by it; and yet, she does not repeat his words and ideas but reinvents them.

Elspeth and Grace exemplify their superiority with regard to race, as they engage in offensive practical jokes and performativity. In the stories that they tell one another, remembering the past, Grace dresses up as a "darky," and they scare the hired man, an Austrian (32-33). They position themselves as better than both the Austrian they scare and the Afro-Canadians they role-play. The offence they take to the Austrian hired man's language highlights their haughty attitude: "the flood of foreign cursing, it would freeze your blood...Till I made up my mind I'd show him" (33). Playing the Other upon which settler identity depends, the aunts reveal their sense of racial superiority as they haunt the hired man in a moment of gothic sensibility. As Cynthia Sugars and Gerry Turcotte explain, critics such as Alan Lawson and Stephen Slemon "highlight aspects of ambivalence, liminality, mimicry, boundary dissolution, and epistemological destabilization that characterize the negotiations that occur in [contested] locations" (viii). In this scene, Munro arguably destabilizes the settler-invader narrative that claims Canadian spaces as settler ones, showing that the aunts are determined to dominate in the settler region that they believe to be their own. It is notable, here, that Del takes distance from her aunts, watching their behaviour and listening to the stories they tell. With her representation of the aunts and Del arm's length from them, Munro demonstrates both racial diversity in settler regions and settlers' racist attitudes towards it.

Elspeth and Grace's alignment with settler and patriarchal values is not straightforward. They also resist these values. They "respected men's work beyond anything," but also "laughed at it" (32). Del explains that they "told stories" (32). But the stories they tell are only for each other. "It did not seem as if they were telling them to me, to entertain me," Del states, "but as if they would have told them anyway, for their own pleasure, even if they had been alone" (32). Indeed, Elspeth and Grace's language, at times, seems closer to the semiotic than the symbolic. Kristeva asserts that "there is a general social law, that this law is the symbolic dimension which is given in language and that every social practice offers a specific expression of that law" ("System" 25). The semiotic, by contrast, contests that law "wherever there is a transgression of systematicity" (29). Elspeth and Grace defy the symbolic order and systematicity with their "ridiculously complicated language, where true news of the outside world was not exactly forbidden, but became more and more impossible to deliver" (57). This seems to be a women's language, full of pleasure or the *jouissance* of which Kristeva writes, and apart from the "world of public events, of politics" ("System" 30) in which Craig believes. Their separation from the "outside world" mirrors Benny's separation from it, indicated by the bizarre newspapers to which he subscribes, "his only source of information about the outside world" (6). The stories the aunts tell each other seem to establish a communal identity between them. The form of Munro's writing in such instances demonstrates how the aunts' identities fold into one another. In the conversation they have about the joke they play on the hired man, for example, Munro makes it difficult to decipher who is saying what. Elspeth's and Grace's voices are blurred together, as though they are one.

In "Princess Ida," Del says that for her mother, Ada, "scenes from the past were liable to pop up any time, like lantern slides, against the cluttered fabric of the present" (70). This story is about the discomfort of the past rubbing up against the present, evident in the disjunction between Del's mother's recount of her childhood and Del's perspective of her Uncle Bill and his version of the past. In Del's mother's gothic depiction of her childhood, her brother "tortured" her (73). Yet Del cannot reconcile her present estimation of her uncle, whom she has just met, with the stories her mother has told about him; she cannot understand how her uncle can be the boy from the past who tortured her mother. Moreover, while her mother describes her grandmother as "a religious fanatic" (71), her uncle describes her as a "saint" (81). In "Changes and Ceremonies," Del says of her teacher Miss Farris's death that she can no longer think of her teacher's past moments without thinking of the most recent one, her suicide: "if the last one is true then must it not alter the others?" (133). Likewise, in "Princess Ida," she cannot easily match the stories of her mother's past to her present. In other words, Del does not seem to be able to link people and events in a linear, narrative sequence through time. As Huebener notes, referring to and quoting Henri Bergson's work, "duration is the experience that occurs when we comprehend a note in a song in relation to the notes that surround it...[It] 'is made up of moments inside one another'" (*Timing* 9). This is Munro's view of time as depicted in "Princess Ida." She resists it "as a linear sequence—a discrete movement from A to B" (9).

The title of the story, "Princess Ida," is a reference to Del's mother, Ada, and the story centres around that mother-daughter relationship. Del "attempts to understand her mother and to decode her through the enigmatic signs that are attributed to her" (Murray 41). Munro mobilizes the figure of the mother throughout her short stories, and these figures range from the "'wicked stepmother' side of the maternal figure seen in 'Royal Beatings'" to the "mother in her own right as an autonomous subject," seen in "Princess Ida" (41). As Jennifer Murray explains, critics have addressed the autobiographical impetus behind Munro's mother figures (41). Munro's complicated relationship with her own mother was punctuated by Anne Laidlaw's death in 1959 from Parkinson's disease. She wrote about her relationship with her mother and her mother's disease in the autobiographical story, "The Peace of Utrecht," which was first published soon after her mother's death, in the spring 1960 issue of the *Tamarack Review* (Thacker, *Alice Munro* 150). With regard to her process of writing *Lives*, "After years of...repeated attempts," to write the book, Thacker explains, "*Lives of Girls and Women* came together during 1970." Munro began with the writing of the section on "Princess Ida" (210). In a 1994 interview, Munro said, "The material about my mother is my central material in life, and it always comes the most readily to me. If I just relax, that's what will come up" (quoted in Murray 42). That Munro's own mother played such an important part in her life and her writing indicates that mother figures in her writing are worthy of our attention. In terms of Munro's writing process, it is notable that she frequently revised and republished her stories. Often, they appeared first in journals such as *The New Yorker* and then later, in revised versions, in her story collections. Murray explains how elements of "Princess Ida" were reworked to appear again in "The Progress of Love," a story that Murray calls "a variant of...'Princess Ida'" (153). Munro's mother figures are based at least in part on her own mother and are slippery, changing; likewise, her stories, including "Princes Ida," are themselves unfixed and move dynamically through time.

Mothering

Time is explicitly related to how Munro constructs Del's relationship with her mother. As is typical of Munro's narrative technique, Del "is split between the child's naive perspective and that of the more reflective, remembering adult she has become" (Murray 44). As Murray puts it, Del "is both the preadolescent girl still partially in the thrall of the all-powerful mother of early childhood, but nevertheless beginning the process of adolescent self-differentiation *and* the adult narrator trying to use the perspective of time to re-evaluate both her mother and her own expectations of that mother" (44, emphasis in original). In psychoanalytic terms, the return to the mother is the return home, a movement backwards in time and place, back to the womb. Critic Brian Diemert notes that "the cave is a recurring image in *Lives of Girls and Women* and is emblematic of the womb/ tomb configuration" (122), which emphasizes Munro's focus on the movement to the mother figure and the female body. Referring to the moment when Del comes out of the funeral home basement with Mary Agnes, Diemert further explains that "it is Del's emergence from this cavern that marks her own birth into story and into family history" (122). This birth also recalls the story that Del's uncle tells in "Princess Ida" about the butterfly emerging from the cocoon, a transformation. Kristeva states in "Stabat Mater" that "we live in a civilization where the *consecrated* (religious or secular) representation of femininity is absorbed by motherhood" (161, emphasis in original). To focus on one's relationship with the mother, then, is to interrogate one's relationship to femininity itself—a project that is implicitly one of Del's missions in this feminist Bildungsroman. The focus on the mother figure in "Princess Ida" is a movement toward the past, not only toward Del's mother, but toward Del's mother's mother, who is also implicated in the story. Murray convincingly argues that the story "concerns a daughter focusing on her mother and on the mother's pain, a hurt that reaches back to that mother's relation to her own mother" (153). The pain and indeed the traumas of the past that both Del's mother and her maternal grandmother experienced are not named but hinted at in the story. Such moments signify the "return of the repressed" (149) and are connected to Del's uncle, even though we don't know the details of what he did to Del's mother. Just as Sandy Steveston's wife's former husband returns to haunt him in the story that Benny tells in "The Flats Road," so too does the past "torture" (73) that Del's uncle inflicted on her mother return in "Princess Ida." In each case, the past is not put to rest but erupts in uncanny moments of pain and *jouissance*, that which can be felt but remains unnamed, unspoken. Time is important in "Princess Ida" because the author addresses how traumas from the past persist in the present and shows both the pain and silence implicit within them.

Munro's focus on the complexities of mother-daughter relationships can be read in a different light when considering Andrea Skinner's revelation about the abuse she experienced at the hands of her stepfather. In "Princess Ida," it is clear that Del cannot reconcile the portrait of her uncle that her mother has painted for her, as her torturer, and the person that Del now sees before her. Likewise, the outward appearance and reputation of Skinner's stepfather, Gerald Fremlin, might have been disjunct from his concealed identity as a pedophile. The layers of pain and trauma that are invoked in this scenario in "Princess Ida" are interesting, since Munro only hints at them, demonstrating how carefully they are hidden. They cannot be fully named or known, even within the story. The story invokes the traumas of Del's mother and Del's mother's mother, highlighting the power of intergenerational trauma, but the readers and Del herself never come to know the details. Munro's writing of *Lives of Girls and Women* occurred before Skinner was assaulted by Fremlin. Munro and her first husband divorced in 1972, one year after *Lives* was published. The ways in which Munro depicts the pain and power of family secrets in this collection are prescient.

Del contemplates the past in the present when she discusses a painting that her mother created in "Princess Ida." The painting, which hangs in their kitchen at the farm, shows "a stony road and a river between mountains, and sheep driven along the road by a little girl in a red shawl" (68). About the painting, Del says, "long ago I had believed that the little girl was really my mother and that this was the desolate country of her early life. Then I learned that she had copied the scene from the *National Geographic*" (68). That Del indicates that she had such thoughts "long ago" shows that she no longer holds the same perspectives about her mother's past that she once did. That she initially believes that her mother is the girl in the picture—only to find out otherwise—shows that she tries to see and to understand her mother's past, but Ada and her past remain beyond Del's grasp. Del's revelation that the painting is copied highlights the literary and artistic histories that *Lives of Girls and Women* invokes. Just as Munro and Del build upon historical and literary pasts—Uncle Craig's history and the Brontës' novels—so too is Ada's painting derived from a painting or photograph that existed prior to it. Del finds that her mother is not the girl in the picture, and also that her mother does not cherish the painting: "I don't want it where people will see," her mother says (68). As Murray states in *Reading Alice Munro with Jacques Lacan*, "Del has romanticized [the painting] into an original creation by an artistic mother, painted in early marriage" but Ada "has no such romantic notions: 'That one? Do you want that one in here?'" (45).

Ada negotiates the past in images such as the one in the *National Geographic* and creates her own art in relation to them. If she puts herself into her art, as she implicitly does with the girl in the red shawl, she does not intentionally do so. Only when the artwork is read by others does that interpretation arise. Such might be the case in Munro's own stories. Munro puts herself in her fictional works, but she remains somewhat hidden or different there, her writing exemplifying both the fictional and the autobiographical. Munro layers histories of artworks and complicates their interpretations while also demonstrating that Del cannot fully know or understand her mother: her mysterious past eludes her. It is noteworthy that Ada copied the picture from *National Geographic*, a magazine that is historically aligned with the Western gaze (Lutz and Collins). Del and Munro are writers in a new age that both arise out of and resist patriarchal structures. Ada too is contained within patriarchal and imperial systems, as a subject in *National Geographic*, but also participates within those systems as the artist who created the very painting within which she appears.

Near the end of "Princess Ida," Uncle Bill tells a story about when he and Del's mother were children, and they saw a butterfly come out of its cocoon: "It was a yellow butterfly, little spotty thing. Its wings all waxed down. It had to work some to get them loosed up...Takes a little fly. First time it ever used its wings" (84). The "yellow butterfly" (84) is linked metonymically to Del's uncle, that "yellowish man" (83). The butterfly looks entirely different as a butterfly than it did as a caterpillar. Likewise, in Del's eyes, her Uncle Bill seems different as an adult than he must have been as a child. The mismatch between the caterpillar and the butterfly is akin to the mismatch between the stories Del has heard about him and his present self. Right after we hear about Bill's story of the butterfly, Del learns that Bill "is a dying man" (85). Like the butterfly, who will not live long because it has transformed in the house while there is a blizzard outside (84), Bill is not long for this world. Munro employs the symbol of the butterfly to demonstrate the disconnection between the past and the present. She contests the flow of linear time and shows that the past is not linked to the present in a clear and straightforward way.

Yet the butterfly is also metonymically linked to Ada, Del's mother. Like the goddess Isis, who Del mentions at the end of the story, Ada is a mother with "sheltering wings" (Cotterell and Storm 290). Her royal pen name, "Princess Ida," is related to Isis, since that goddess "is sometimes regarded as a personification of the throne" (290). Moreover, the butterfly relates to Del herself, as do the "adolescent" frogs at Uncle Benny's riverbank, mentioned on the first page of the book (3). Like the butterfly and the frogs, Del undergoes change and transformation, in her case, from a girl to a woman. Through its "wing," the butterfly is metonymic for the sense of hurt Ada feels, described as a "wing": "there was something in the room like a down flash of a wing or knife, a sense of hurt so strong, but quick and isolated, vanishing" (86). The sense of hurt is acute but fleeting. It is an example of how moments from Ada's past— in this case her torture by her brother—"pop up at any time" against the present (70). A moment of hurt from the past erupts into the present: temporary but singular and real. Finally, the caterpillar's transformation into a butterfly has religious connotations, since it takes place on Easter. Metaphorically, the butterfly could be a symbol for the resurrection of Christ, or it could signify Del's uncle's impending transformation from material body to ethereal spirit. The body outlives its mortal time to become an immortal soul.

Huebener discusses women's experiences of "waiting, of being left out of the linear progressive project" (*Timing* 137). In the second last story in *Lives of Girls and Women*, "Baptism," Del's friend Naomi engages in the act of "waiting," apart from the linear and progressive march of time. She waits for marriage and prepares herself for that pursuit: "She went around to various stores and had them put things away for her, which she would pay for at so much a month. In the hardware store she had a whole set of pots and pans put away, in the jewellery store a case of silverware, in the Walker Store a blanket and a set of towels and a pair of linen sheets" (170). Her waiting is specifically time and future oriented: she has been given days of grace to pay for her marital items. Naomi exists in an in-between time, neither young girl nor married woman, occupying a place of stasis. Yet Naomi also falls from grace. She gets pregnant before her time—that is, before marriage—and so she not only "waits" but is also "in waiting." Here, despite her preparations, Naomi unintentionally defies the normative and social time progression that is expected of her: first marriage, then pregnancy. As Munro demonstrates, in the modern Canadian society of Del's world, that misalignment with normative time comes at a price, exemplified by references to the society's disdain and Naomi's sadness and regret (218-20).

Feminism

"Baptism" opens with a distinct statement about normative linear time. Munro situates Naomi within that time, and Del both within it and apart from it. Whereas Del continues her academic studies in "Latin, Physics, Algebra," Naomi moves to the third floor of the school where "typewriters clacked all day" and there were signs on the wall "preparing one for life in the business world" (166): *Time and Energy are my Capital; if I Squander them, I shall get no Other*" (166, emphasis in original). Del's studies are grounded in what are conventionally masculine domains, and Naomi's studies support businessmen, and so both Del and Naomi are inside of patriarchal time. The statement that pronounces itself at Naomi's section of the school is an example of the notion of "singular time beholden to capital" (Burges and Elias 3). Time must be used efficiently and productively, that is, to serve the status quo under capitalism. In terms of Munro's book and Naomi's position here, that status quo is the business world of men, and Naomi plays a woman's role in relation to it. Unlike Naomi, however, Del resists this notion of time, of "the real and busy world" (166) and women's place there. Del has "ink on [her] bare red hands" (167), unlike Naomi, whose "nails are coral" (166). Del's hands are stamped with "purple ink" (174) as she enters the community dance that they attend. The ink suggests that Del is already marked as unfeminine and as a writer. In addition, those markings set her apart from others, particularly Naomi and her coworkers, who Del fears "are looking at her [Del]" unadmiringly (167). Thus, "Baptism" at once posits Del alongside patriarchal time, yet also asserts her status outside of it and as a writer and artist, typical of a Künstlerroman. The story defies the normative trajectory and path through which its female protagonist achieves the status of an artist.

Del continues to be separate from normative time and society's expectations. When she dances with Clive she seems misaligned with the symbolic order. She learns his name only after they dance, and while dancing she is unable to understand what he says and how he expresses himself in language. "I heard the words," she states, "but could not figure out the meaning" (175). She cannot be what he seems to expect, "somebody small, bright, snappy, flirtatious" (175), and her failure to do so is expressed specifically in terms of time: "But everything I did, every movement and expression with which I tried to meet him, seemed to be too late; he would have gone on to something else" (175). Her separation from the feminine roles she is expected to play subsequently becomes a series of escapes: from the hotel room with Bert, Naomi, and Clive, for instance, and from her "baptism" by Garnet French. In each of these instances, she refuses to be Other to the boys who attempt to define her. Rather, she must tell her own story and in her own way.

In "Lives of Girls and Women," Del feels that Mr. Chamberlain's penis during his masturbatory performance "did not seem to have anything to do with [her]" (159). As Smaro Kamboureli notes in her feminist and Lacanian reading of that story, the scene is a "parody of the phallus as the privileged signifier" (36). Mr. Chamberlain's discourse ("Lucky for you? Eh?" [159]) "demands that the feminine beholder reaffirm the phallus's privilege" (Kamboureli 26), which Del will not do. In "Baptism," Bert and Clive perform for Naomi and Del. Clive "jump[s] around the room, shadow-boxing, illustrating his jokes," and Clive and Bert "[pretend] to be fighting" (178). Clive and Bert's childlike performance is more for each other than it is for Del or Naomi. Once again, it has "nothing to do" (159) with Del. In both Mr. Chamberlain's and Clive and Bert's performances, then, she is not the appreciative audience member she is expected to be. She strategically resists a women's place in the male trajectory of narrative.

Moreover, Del's friendship with Jerry Storey in "Baptism" demonstrates her complicated relationship to patriarchal time, and ultimately, her resistance to it. Del and Jerry compete for the top marks at school. While Del says that Jerry's "IQ was the highest ever seen in Jubilee" (182), she also says that she beat him sometimes because of his impatience and forgetfulness with French, History, and English literature (182). Both Del and Jerry believe that each is superior to the other: "I thought that Jerry was a thousand times more freakish, less attractive than I was, and it was plain that he thought putting my brains and his in the same category showed no appreciation of categories" (183). Jerry's feeling of superiority over Del has to do with gender. He tells her, for example, that she has a "first-rate memory, not unusual feminine gift for language, fairly weak reasoning powers and almost no capacity for abstract thought" (183). Jerry positions himself alongside intellectual capacities that he views as particularly masculine—reasoning, abstraction—and overtly eliminates her from those capacities. Boasting about his own intellect, Jerry says that "there is still time to get the Nobel prize" (183). Yet, again, he explicitly eliminates Del from that same possibility: "most great breakthroughs are made by men under thirty-five" (183).

That Munro won the Nobel Prize in Literature in 2013, forty-two years after she wrote *Lives of Girls and Women*, makes Jerry's comment here particularly ironic. Autobiographical aspects of Munro's work, as Linda M. Morra suggests in "It Was[n't] All Inward," are often hidden. If this coming-of-age story is autobiographical, then Munro inadvertently forecasts her own fate, projecting her own future. In so doing, she both inserts herself into patriarchal time—she receives the previously male-dominated institutional honour of the Nobel—and excludes herself from it, since she wins the award not for advancement, as Jerry Storey imagines for himself, but rather for what Jerry calls the "feminine gift of language" (183). In "Baptism," just as Del escapes from Clive and Bert's and Garnet's attempts to confine her to a woman's role, so too does she escape from Jerry's attempt to do so. Del agrees to let Jerry see her naked, but just as he does so, his mother arrives home, and

Jerry puts Del in the cellar so that his mother will not find out about her. Del's comment, "I was all by myself on the back of the cellar stairs, locked in, naked" (191) represents Jerry's—as well as Clive and Bert's and Garnet's—confinements and limitations of her to what they deem appropriate for her gender. Yet Del escapes the cellar, after Jerry gives her clothes back to her, just as she escapes the confines of the other boys' expectations.

Critics have weighed in on Del's sexual relationship with Garnet French in "Baptism." In the story, Del loses her virginity to and has an ongoing sexual relationship with Garnet in her senior year of high school. She breaks up with him, however, when he suggests marriage. More specifically, she rejects him when he tries to baptize her in the river, all while he explains to her that she will have to convert to his religion if they are to marry. The baptismal scene invokes drowning, which recalls other stories in which Munro features drownings or near drownings: "Miles City, Montana," "Child's Play," and Miss Farris's drowning in the Wawanash River in "Changes and Ceremonies," in *Lives of Girls and Women*. "I thought that he might drown me," Del says in "Baptism." "I really thought that" (223). Yet this baptismal scene also suggests that Del's transformation is more an individual awakening than a religious one. As Sue Thomas explains, Carol Ann Howells reads Del's story of her affair with Garnet and her ultimate rejection of him "as a romance of 'woman's transformation through sex'" ("Reading" 108). For Howells, Del's sexual relationship with and ultimate rejection of Garnet signifies "a triumph of the liberal ideals of egoistic self-sufficiency and rationality" (108). On the other hand, as Thomas also explains, critics such as Kambploureli and Barbara Godard endorse a reading of Del and Garnet's sexual relationship that is more aligned with French feminism. Godard argues that the affair signifies "a rebellion against the textual disembodiment of women in male precursors, and a giving 'birth to the text (corpus) and to her body (corps)'" (quoted in Thomas 109). As we have seen throughout *Lives of Girls and Women*, Munro consistently draws parallels between human bodies and textual ones. It follows, then, that Del presents herself as the subject of her own sexual desire rather than an object of Garnet's. She comes into her own sexual awakening as she begins to create her own identity and write her own story. Her ultimate rejection of Garnet is not unlike her rejection of Craig's manuscript. She does not copy Garnet's or Craig's way because to do so, she must objectify herself as Other to him. By contrast, she comes into her own as she writes and identifies her own self—her agency and identity.

Del's refusal to be baptized by Garnet is the refusal to follow the linear progression of patriarchal time. Indeed, Garnet has written her into his story. As in the stories that Mr. Chamberlain and Clive write of her—where she is supposed to be an appreciative audience member rather than an actor—she will not be written. On the underside of a roof beam of a porch, Garnet has inscribed the names of his previous girlfriends in chronological order. He adds Del's name and then says, "I think I've come to the end" (210), describing his love life like a story. Del recognizes herself as a character in his story: "It was my name" (210). This is an uncanny moment,[4] a moment of doubling. Munro draws attention to herself as Del, folding into her protagonist, the boundaries between them blurred. If this conflation of author and protagonist is not immediately clear, it is when reader comes to the epilogue, when Munro contemplates herself and Del—like the photographer—as a writer-artist who confronts but cannot accurately or definitively represent reality. In an interview with Struthers, Munro said about the epilogue that without it the book "was not the story of the artist as a young girl. It was just the story of a young girl" (quoted in Thacker, *Alice Munro* 212). Since *Lives of Girls and Women* incorporates autobiographical elements within it, the moment in which Del sees herself as a character might mirror one in which Munro hints at her own self in Del. Likewise, the moment at which Del recognizes her name in the inscription might be like readers recognizing themselves in the characters of Munro's story and in literature in general. "A dynamic of intimacy," to use Morra's phrase, is created between the writer, the narrator, and the reader ("It Was[n't] All Inward" 205). It is a distinctly postmodern, self-reflective moment in which Munro sees her former self in her own stories, and in which the reader is brought into the text in a moment of relatability between the reader and the narrator. In terms of the patriarchal timeline that Garnet has created with the names of his girlfriends, in this moment Del understands that Garnet has defined her as his, and she knows that she will not be what he wants. Her refusal to be his wife is enacted in her resistance to his baptism of her. She rejects the expected chronological order of things—baptism, marriage, children. She will not be the "end" to his story (210). The end, in fact, is that which both Del and Munro reject, and so, once again, linear chronology is rejected as the so-called "end" is actually Del's beginning, her launch into a life that is uniquely her own.

Conversely, Del has also written Garnet as who she wants him to be, and he, like her, does not match that definition. As Margaret Atwood puts it, Del "does not want the real person; she wants only the version she has made of him, and that we have witnessed her making during the story about him that she's been telling us" ("*Lives*" 111). Del's true baptism, rebirth, or awakening in this story, then, is this knowledge. When Del and Garnet swim in the river, Garnet expresses his interest in marrying Del. When she refuses to get baptized so that he can marry her, he pushes her head down into the water, "bobbing [her] up and down," at first, playfully, but then, "with less and less gentleness" (221), until "the wide, determined, painful grins on [their] faces hardened" (222). This near-drowning is metaphorical for Garnet's restriction and confinement of Del to the womanly role he wants her to play. That she emerges from the water "shaking, gasping, drinking air" (223), shows that, though she has rejected Garnet's baptism of her, she is, nevertheless, born anew. She comes to understand and know herself—that true to her new identity as a writer, she "meant to keep [Garnet] sewed up in his golden lover's skin forever" (222), and that all along she was acting "in play" (222). As a metanarrative, this scene emphasizes that Del is Munro's fictional creation. The author does not reiterate her own so-called real life, but rather rewrites and revises it with a difference. Del the character is not "real" but "in play." Just as Del does to Garnet, Munro "sew[s] up" Del in a fictional character's "skin" (222). The scene also emphasizes Del's new role as an artist who will not follow patriarchal chronology or stay in the place the symbolic order has deemed right for her.

According to Anne McClintock, "The male ritual of baptism—with its bowls of holy water, its washing, its male midwives—is a surrogate birthing ritual, during which men collectively compensate themselves for their invisible role in the birth of the child and diminish women's agency" (29). Relevant to "Baptism," Del's refusal to be baptized by Garnet is a reclamation of her own female power, a rejection of the masculine appropriation of birthing, and a manifestation of her knowledge that "all the powers [she] granted him were in play" (222). Her rebirth will be of her own making. This reclamation of her own power is also evident in her recount of her loss of her virginity. Del and Garnet first have sex against Del's house near a bed of peonies, symbolic of her "deflowering" (Kamboureli 37). The next day, Del "look[s] at the peonies," finds blood there, and then tells her mother that there is blood at the side of the house, stating that she "saw a cat there...tearing a bird apart" (212). Her literal story of losing her virginity is transposed onto a metaphorical one, and so it is significant that she does not simply retell her story to her mother as it happened. Rather, she rejects repetition in favour of invention and creativity. As Kamboureli puts it, "she does not represent in the mimetic sense of the word. Hers is a representation belonging to a discourse that *presents* what the Father insists is absent" (37). Del shows women's authorship and agency as her body writes her story.

Epilogue

The disjunction between the so-called reality—normative time and chronological narrative—and the inventive representation of it is evident in "Epilogue: The Photographer." The epilogue focuses on Del's plan to be a writer and her fictional reconstruction of the town of Jubilee and the Sheriff family. It begins with the contrast between Del's own views of the town and her mother's. Del admits that her fictional reconstruction of the town and the Sheriff family in the novel she plans to write does not match the truth: "I changed the family name from Sheriff to Holloway, and the dead father from a storekeeper to a judge...[I]n my novel I had got rid of the older brother, the alcoholic" (228-29). Moreover, as Atwood explains, "In the epilogue, Munro does something that she will do again and again in later stories: she time jumps" ("*Lives*" 112). In "Baptism" Del says that she has received her exam marks and did not get the scholarship to go to university (220), but in "Epilogue: The Photographer," she is still waiting for her marks (232)—thus, the epilogue takes place before "Baptism." On Atwood's reading, Del has the strength to reject baptism and break up with Garnet because she already has another fate in store: her writing career. Additionally, Atwood notes, in the epilogue Munro time jumps again, when "Del tells us that in the future—her future as a writer—she would, like Uncle Craig writing his formerly disparaged history, try to make lists of everything in the town" ("*Lives*" 113). Del laments that the "hope [for] accuracy," both Craig's and her own, is "heartbreaking" (236) since it can never be fully realized. She, like the fictional photographer in her novel, captures moments but must sift through the inventory of images to interpret them, and to express the so-called truth, which is always an approximation. Throughout the epilogue, Del begins to understand the challenges of perceiving her outer and inner worlds and representing them in language, in the symbolic order.

Perhaps the most interesting part of the epilogue is when Bobby Sheriff invites Del into his house, and she realizes not only that he is different from how she has fictionally represented him, but also that she does not know him. Her encounter with Bobby highlights the maturity that Del has reached at the end of this coming-of-age story and signifies an epiphany, much like the one Del has when she rejects Garnet's baptism. Bobby's invitation for Del to enter his house and join him for cake and lemonade is reminiscent of the wicked witch inviting Hansel and Gretel into her candy house. Here, once again, Munro alludes to previous works of literature and builds upon them. "'Could I persuade you to step into my yard and try a piece of cake?'" Bobby asks, while opening his gate for Del to enter (232). When Del enters Bobby's home, she realizes he is not someone to be feared, even though he has spent time in a mental asylum. Unlike the other boys she has met—Clive and Bert, Jerry, and Garnet—Bobby does not expect her to conform to his or anyone's expectations. He sees her not as the girlfriend of Garnet, but rather as "the girl who's going to university...a clever girl" (234). He does not get that quite right—she has not yet received her scholarship—just as Del has not got him right either. Yet he sees her for who she is and who she wants to be, rather than who anyone might expect her to be.

Bobby's statement to Del, "Believe me...I wish you luck in your life" (236) is a blessing—a reversal of the curse of the wicked witch. It is at this moment that Bobby seems to be a muse figure for Del—again a reversal of gender roles, since, traditionally, muses are female figures for male writers. Bobby himself performs femininity in this final scene. His femininity, at the end of the book, contrasts Del's boyishness at the beginning of the book, when she catches frogs with Uncle Benny in "The Flats Road." Bobby's wish of luck to Del is an act of grace that is extended within and beyond language when Bobby rises "on his toes like a dancer, like a plump ballerina" (236). Munro herself marked this moment as especially significant. As Thacker explains, Munro revised the epilogue extensively and was undecided about whether to keep it in the book: Munro "continued wavering about the epilogue until Bobby Sheriff's pirouette came to her ('he rose on his toes like a dancer, like a

Genre, Narrative, and Time in Lives of Girls and Women 31

plump ballerina'; an act that 'appeared to be a joke not shared with me so much as displayed for me'). The pirouette 'turned it around...When that came to me I knew I could leave it in'" (*Alice Munro* 215). For Del, the action seems "to have a concise meaning, a stylized meaning—to be a letter, or a whole word, in an alphabet [she does] not know" (237). The book ends with Del's acceptance of this act of grace: "yes, I said, instead of thank you" (237). The book thus ends "at the threshold" (Atwood, "*Lives*" 114) of Del's new life as a writer, with an act that defies interpretation and incorporation into linear time itself.

In *Lives of Girls and Women*, through form and character, and most prominently through her protagonist, Munro belies normative time on various counts. As Neil Besner asserts in "Remembering 'Every Last Thing,'" "Del's voice invites us to migrate easily with her across the borders between past, present, and future, so that our sense of what happens to her becomes more episodic than strictly linear" (159). Del resists imperial time by positioning herself against the chronological, historical narrative of Uncle Craig's inclusive history of Wawanash County, though the absence of Indigenous characters and histories in *Lives* might indicate the limitations of that resistance. Munro challenges historical time by indicating that the inclusive history of Craig's making, upon which there is a "whole solid, intricate structure of lives supporting us from the past" (31), does not work. Rather, as Del discovers at the end of the book, the "whole mysterious and as it turned out unreliable structure" (234) of so-called reality upon which fiction is based is fragile and indeterminate. Munro, through Del, revises the male literary tradition by inserting her own work into it. The author shadows her protagonist as her creator in the same way that other literary authors shadow *Lives of Girls and Women* as Munro's predecessors. In this book, ghosts appear to become a part of the present: the ghost of Sandy's widow's husband; the ghost of the disappearing Madeleine and her mysterious past; and the ghosts of Munro's literary predecessors, and Munro herself in her writing of Del. In much of contemporary Canadian literature, as Marlene Goldman notes, ghosts and haunting show "uncanny threats to national and individual identity" (*Dispossession* 4). While *Lives of Girls and Women* is no exception, the book additionally mobilizes such tropes to unravel and disassemble the structures that uphold time as linear, progressive, and singular.

2

The Past and the Present in
Who Do You Think You Are?

IF MUNRO RESISTS NORMATIVE TIME in *Lives of Girls and Women*, then in *Who Do You Think You Are?* (1978), she does so more specifically by depicting the past as consistently a part of the present. For Munro, history is not relegated to what has already happened. Rather, it continually erupts into the present, in both senses of the word: the past is *now* and it is *here*. In Munro's writing, personal and collective histories are not improved upon in a progressive march toward the present. They are intertwined with and inseparable from the present, which is no better than the past. Memories, portrayed by the author as shifty and dynamic, are a constant reminder of what has gone before. Neither memory and history nor the personal and collective are static; they are in constant revision and renewal. Like *Lives of Girls and Women*, *Who Do You Think You Are?* might be described as a Bildungsroman. Yet, in the latter text, the author not only complicates the genre's neat linear teleology—the movement from girlhood to womanhood—but also the ideas of personal development and progression. As Sara Jamieson explains in "Surprising Developments," unlike *Lives*, *Who Do You Think You Are?* follows the protagonist, Rose, beyond her teenage years and into middle age. "Rose is around forty when, in the last two stories, she returns to her hometown of Hanratty to assist her stepmother Flo in moving to an old age home" (54). Jamieson further notes that *Who Do You Think You Are?* "foregrounds the ages of its characters in a way that both registers and resists the process whereby the number of a person's years has become a defining aspect of identity in twentieth-century culture" (54).

33

Munro challenges the "assumption that chronological age functions as a natural and universal measure of human development" (54). Time socialization, therefore, comes to the fore in the collection, and Munro demonstrates her resistance to it in the stories Rose hears and tells, and in the narrative of Munro's *Who Do You Think You Are?* itself.

Munro's process of writing *Who Do You Think You Are?* and the publication history of the text are relevant to the discussion of time in her writing, since the publication history shows Munro's continual revisions through time. For Munro, texts—just like her treatment of history and memory—are dynamic rather than static. The original version of the book—before Munro pulled it from the publishers to revise it— had two protagonists, Rose and Janet, whereas the final version has only one, Rose. The draft of the manuscript "contained six third-person stories about Rose, all retained in the published collection, and six first-person stories about Janet, three of which—'Connection,' 'The Stone in the Field,' and 'The Moons of Jupiter'—were deleted and published in *The Moons of Jupiter*. It did not include 'Simon's Luck'" (Hoy 59). That story was initially written in three parts, and each part focused on a different woman's relationship with Simon. The final version, which was eventually included in *Who Do You Think You Are?*, had been revised and reduced, and the three women were rewritten as one, Rose (64-65). In Munro's revisions of *Who Do You Think You Are?* from a work about two heroines to a work about one, from a book written in both first- and third-person narration to one written solely in third person, the development of a character *through time* is of the essence. Munro eventually realized that "Rose and Janet were the same person" (59). Central to Munro's revisions was the successful development of a single character from childhood to middle age. This development, despite Munro's challenge to normative, linear time, was best achieved by unifying the central character and following her through a significant portion of her life.

The most intriguing part of Helen Hoy's study on Munro's writing process is the revelation that the character of Janet had written the character of Rose. This detail, which Munro revealed at the end of the draft manuscript, made the original work explicitly metafictional. Munro asked in a letter to her agent, "What do you think of using *Who Do You Think You Are?* as a title rather than *Rose and Janet?* In which case this story, which is slight but important, could come at the very end. What do you think of its revelation that Janet has written the Rose stories?" (quoted in Hoy 74). As Hoy points out, this revelation, situated at the end of the collection, functions similarly to the epilogue of *Lives of Girls and Women*: both reframe the previous stories and highlight the centrality of the artist-writer and the artifice they create. As Hoy puts it, "Just as the epilogue transforms *Lives of Girls and Women* into a *Künstlerroman*, foregrounding what was previously inconsequential, so 'Who Do You Think You Are?' belatedly transforms the parallel stories of Rose and Janet into metafiction" (74). Yet, Munro ultimately published *Who Do You Think You Are?* as a collection solely about Rose, eliminating the metafictional revelation at the end. Despite this change, Munro retains various metafictional aspects of the text. Rose's career as an actress foregrounds the theme of performativity and the creation of characters who are always dressing for another part, always in flux. Rose is an actress, and Janet, like Munro, a writer, and so Munro, in the draft version of the book, blurs the boundaries between the creator and created; the subject who is doing the creating and the object that is being created. It is noteworthy that even once *Who Do You Think You Are?* was back in production, Munro continued to revise its stories for the American version, which Norton was to produce. There are, therefore, differences between *Who Do You Think You Are?* and the American version of the collection, titled *The Beggar Maid* (Thacker, *Alice Munro* 336–44). To this effect, Munro invites autobiographical readings of her characters and conflates herself as a writer with the characters she writes, resisting "any simple dichotomy between reality and illusion, truth and fiction" (Hoy 79).

Who Do You Think You Are? is an important collection in Munro's career as a writer. In 1976, only a year before Munro published the collection, she secured an agent, Virginia (Ginger) Barber, from New York. As Thacker explains in his biography of Munro, Munro had been submitting stories to *The New Yorker* since the 1950s, but it was only after she started working with Barber that her stories were accepted there, and these acceptances were due to "the quality of [Munro's] work, Virginia Barber's abilities, good timing, and a bit of luck" (*Alice Munro* 318). Subsequently, Munro experienced great success with the magazine: "Between April 1980 and December 1984, she had nine stories accepted by *The New Yorker*...By June 2004, forty-seven Munro stories first appeared in the *New Yorker*, under four different editors in chief"

(317). Therefore, *Who Do You Think You Are?* signals a turning point in Munro's career, since it was at this time that she reached significant success as an author both in Canada and the US. It is also an important collection for personal reasons. Between the publication of *Lives* and *Who Do You Think You Are?*, Munro moved back to Huron County to live with Gerald Fremlin. "Her return to Huron County and her renewal of her imaginative connections there," Thacker notes, "meant that the stories Munro wrote during 1976 were imbued with a more immediate sensibility and also a different imaginative relation to her subject matter than she had previously displayed" (327). At this time in her life, Munro launched into national and international success as she simultaneously returned home. As Thacker notes, *Who Do You Think You Are?* is "*the* critical book of Munro's career" (128, emphasis in original).

Violence

The first story in the collection, "Royal Beatings," was published in 1977 in *The New Yorker*. Journalist William French "called attention" to the story in an article in *The Globe and Mail* a week after it appeared, "offering a progress report on her current writing" (Thacker, *Alice Munro* 331). The title of the story inaugurates the trope of royalty that is ironized in the work: Rose is reminded of and haunted by the poverty of her childhood, which is far from royal.[1] Munro invokes Canada's colonial ties to Britain, then, and undermines them, contesting imperial time, which is "closely tied to homogenizing meta narratives associated with progress, growth, and development" (Huebener, *Timing* 29). The beatings in the title of this story refer both to the ones Rose receives for perceived insolence toward her stepmother, Flo, and the one that Mr. Tyde receives from three men for the hearsay of his violence toward his daughter Becky. Rose's father's beatings of her, which Flo inaugurates, are followed by Flo's royal treatment of Rose: Flo brings Rose a tray of appetizing delicacies (25) to absolve herself from guilt.[2] Mr. Tyde's beating is also followed by a royal treatment, though not for the victim, who has died, but for one of the perpetrators of Mr. Tyde's beating, Hat Nettleton: years later, Rose hears Nettleton interviewed on the radio, revered as the town's centenarian. In his case, not only is he absolved of guilt, but he is upheld as a model citizen: "Photographed on his birthday, fussed over by nurses...Oldest resident. Oldest horsewhipper. Living link with our past" (30). In critic Lawrence Mathews's interpretation, the ending of "Royal Beatings" "changes our understanding of the story" (188). In this way, it is like the epilogue of *Lives of Girls and Women*, which reframes the stories as metafiction through the role of the photographer, and the draft manuscript of *Who Do You Think You Are?*, which reveals Rose as Janet's invention. At the end of "Royal Beatings," Rose says that "years later, many years later," she heard Hat Nettleton on the radio, revealing a disjunction between what Flo told her about him in the past and how he is represented on the radio in the present, and leaving us to question the essence of that character. In typical Munrovian style, the story moves between two time periods. In the first, Rose is a young protagonist, and the story is about her relationship her stepmother, Flo, and her father, who beats her. In the second, Rose is a middle-aged adult who remembers those beatings and contemplates the violence she suffered as a girl and the violence of the small town itself.

In "Royal Beatings," the townspeople have covered up or ignored Nettleton's violent past—his beating of Mr. Tyde—and replaced it with a more respectable history. Nettleton's beating of Tyde is not an uncontested truth, but a story Rose hears from Flo ("I shouldn't even be telling you this stuff" [10]); likewise, Tyde's beating of his daughter Becky—the reason Nettleton and the others beat Tyde in the first place—is hearsay ("The story being…The stories persisted and got added to…Then people said" [9]). "Royal Beatings" thus demonstrates how the past exists in the present through narrative. The present version of the past is always inaccurate, an approximation. On the one hand, Tyde's violence toward his daughter is represented in public gossip about violence in a private, domestic setting: the gossip itself may be spoiled through narrative. On the other hand, the public discourse surrounding Nettleton's so-called respectable history may hide his violent past, and so it too is clouded and altered for public consumption. In "Private Scandals/ Public Selves," Brian Johnson explores how gossip functions in *Who Do You Think You Are?*, asserting that the work "is neither a Bildungsroman as some critics maintain, nor even a *Künstlerroman* as others have argued, but a *Klatschmaulroman*: a novel of the education of a gossip" (417, emphasis in original). He suggests that Munro employs a "gendered representation of gossip by revisiting an old stereotype of the crone in the character of Flo," and that identities—those of Flo and Rose— are "formed in the heat of gossiping about the other people's private

The Past and the Present in *Who Do You Think You Are?*   37 scandals" (419). In *Who Do You Think You Are?*, stories—including Flo's about Nettleton beating Tyde—are ever-present in Rose's memories and are juxtaposed against the town's official history, which is deemed glorious and celebratory. However, neither the story about Nettleton as a violent perpetrator nor the radio's hero-like depiction him of are necessarily accurate, though their invocation in "Royal Beatings" raises questions not only about domestic violence, but also about private lives and the representation of those lives in public discourse.

Sherrill Grace notes that "history is like a field hiding stones/stories that continue to surface and, as they surface, they *change* the story... make room for more stories...allow us to see forgotten memories" (31, emphasis in original). When Rose hears Nettleton interviewed on the radio, she "[longs] to tell somebody" (30) but does not. We might interpret Rose's knowledge (through Flo's storytelling) of Nettleton's beating of Tyde as a powerful disruption of the town's so-called respectable history, just like—to use Grace's metaphor—the "stones/stories" of history that surface in a field. However, since Rose does not tell anyone, that disruption remains only a possibility and is not actualized. Therefore, Munro seems to question the possibility of challenging the historical status quo. And yet, if we take into consideration that "Royal Beatings" is a published work that has itself entered the public realm, then we can interpret Munro's story as a challenge to those of small-town Canada. Munro draws attention to what is not said—note that Becky Tyde's perspective is absent—and suggests that stories that could challenge the status quo too often remain untold. The movement through time in the town of Jubilee is violent: the alleged violence of Tyde against his daughter, and later, the violence of Nettleton against Tyde. Yet these narratives, which move from Flo to Rose, stop there and do not disrupt the violent, linear, and patriarchal progression through time. Moreover, they exist only as hearsay and gossip, and so they do not represent the "truth" that stands in opposition to the language that covers or hides it. Munro exposes the disjuncture between the public's representation of Nettleton in the radio interview and Flo's in the medium of literature; the story itself. The author "allow[s] us to see...forgotten memories" (Grace 31) that disgrace and mock the town's sense of moral superiority, and yet she also raises questions about those very memories by situating them in gossip. We cannot get to the essence of Nettleton, who we can either read as a violent perpetrator or a model citizen; likewise, we cannot get to the essence of Rose or Munro, since Rose, in the draft manuscript, is a character originally written by Janet, who was in turn written by Munro.

In "Royal Beatings," Munro challenges the trajectory of personal progress and chronological age. Ages are confused, as adults are described as children, and vice versa. Images in the story are simultaneously associated with birth and death. For instance, Rose's mother's death is configured in the image of an egg, which is typically associated with birth: "'It's like a boiled egg in my chest, with the shell left on.' She died before night. She had a blood clot on her lung" (2). This image is repeated when Rose explains that her father and Flo did not keep much by which she might remember her mother: "[Rose] had nothing to go on but some *egg* cups her mother had bought" (2, emphasis added). Just as the stories of Nettleton's violent past go unreported by the radio interviewer, so too are the stories of Rose's mother ostensibly forgotten. Furthermore, the image of the egg is metonymically linked to Becky Tyde when Flo tells Rose that Becky, like the seeming eggshell in Rose's mother's chest, "had not cracked" (8). This association of Becky with an egg—not yet born, or childlike—is apt, since Flo describes Becky as though she is still a child, who, due to polio, "had not grown any taller" (8). Becky's stagnancy in time is reinforced in Flo's story about her. According to the townspeople, Flo explains, Becky was "kept of out sight" and became pregnant by her own father, who "disposed of" Becky's child (9). Here, Becky is physically and sexually abused and prevented from progressing from child, to woman, to mother. Jamieson states, "Interrogating the role of chronological age in the production of identity adds a new dimension to the discussion of midlife in Munro's work, which has so far focused on the body as the primary site of resistance to the cultural devaluation of the ageing self" (56). In the recurring image of the egg, however, Munro invokes the female body to upset the chronology of age. An egg is part of a young woman's body, and Munro envisions it as part of older woman's body too. Rose's mother describes the clot on her lung by saying that it feels like an egg in her chest. Munro, therefore, calls upon images of the body to interrogate "the role of chronological age." Choosing a symbol that represents the potential for new life demonstrates how Munro turns chronological age upside down. She at once invokes the body and contests the notion of ageing solely in and through it.

Skinner's revelation might be taken into account when reading "Royal Beatings." The public reception and celebration of Nettleton is thwarted by Rose's knowledge that he engaged in a violent beating. That beating was in the name of so-called justice, but in this story, Munro questions the ethics of revenge and shows how violence can lead to further violence. Munro herself, of course, received recognition, accolades, and celebration for her writing, her status as a literary celebrity upheld within and beyond Canada. Yet, underneath, there was a hidden truth that indicates that she engaged in delusions, denials, and complicities with regard to the abuse of her daughter. Munro, perhaps, writes herself into her own fiction through the character of Nettleton as she experiences public recognition in her own life, while concealing dark and hurtful secrets. Fremlin was the perpetrator of the violence toward Skinner, and Munro compounded that violence by keeping that secret, uncannily mirroring in her own life the compounding effects of violent acts.

Jamieson argues that Munro's work "repeatedly stages the conflict between the impulse to fix someone's age to a precise number and the inability to do so" (58). In *Who Do You Think You Are?*, Flo seems to have reverted to childhood at the end of her life when she is in the "Home" for the elderly, thus demonstrating Munro's challenge to common perceptions of chronological age. Rose's father and Flo put Rose in her childhood "home" in which she receives "royal beatings"; and Rose puts Flo in a "Home" late in Flo's life. Rose "lies on the bed" (24) of her room after the beating, silenced. In a similar vein, Flo sits "in a corner of her crib" (30) at the "Home": "she had stopped talking" (30). Thus, Rose, a child, is conflated with Flo, an older woman—the two seem to become one. Munro's characters "resist constrictive social categories of time" (Huebener, *Timing* 20), with mixed implications. Flo's silence means that she will not be able uphold the status quo and reinforce sites of power, such as Rose's father's beatings, but it also means that she will no longer tell stories that sometimes disrupt official, public narratives. In *Who Do You Think You Are?*, there is a tension between Flo's upholding of the patriarchal order and her disruption of it, which is similar to Del's Aunts Elsbeth and Grace in *Lives of Girls and Women*. Flo and Rose's stories are often just beneath the surface, waiting to emerge. As is the case in her story of Nettleton, Flo's stories keep the past present, even as that past is distorted. After Rose's father beats Rose, "Flo says she never recommended a *hiding* like that" (24, emphasis added). That "hiding" might be interpreted as both the beating that Rose receives and the concealment of some stories in favour of others. The double meaning of "hiding" here is significant because it highlights the danger and violence implicit in secrecy or pretence. Del may not tell anyone about her father's beatings, but secrecy disregards the truth and privileges the hiding of it. Yet, feigning or pretending, in another interpretation, can enable the creation of new identities. In the draft manuscript, Janet creates the character of Rose, while Munro creates the characters of both Janet and Rose, "hiding" aspects of her own life behind them. John Orange asserts that "Munro...explores the secret selves inside the roles and public masks we wear only to discover even deeper and often unfathomable depths to the human personality" (87). This is precisely what she does to challenge common perceptions of chronological age in *Who Do You Think You Are?*

Royalty is mobilized as a trope not only in "Royal Beatings," but throughout *Who Do You Think You Are?* In fact, the title of the book as a whole subtly refers to that trope, since it implies that Rose might think herself royal—or others might think she is acting royal—when she is not. In the second story in the collection, "Privilege," Rose, later in life, "queen[s] it" (31) over others by telling them about her impoverished past: Munro mocks Rose's "privilege" over those who "wished they had been poor, and hadn't been" (31), a statement tinged with irony. Whereas poverty invokes shame, here, that shame is reversed, and Rose displays it proudly. As Goldman notes, "reflecting on their experience of shame, Munro's mature narrators literally parade their shame" ("Alice Munro's" 80). In "Royal Beatings," various beatings are interconnected: Rose is beaten by her father, which recalls Becky's beating by her father Tyde, which in turn instigates Nettleton's beating of Tyde. The victims of the beatings, including Rose herself, experience shame, whereas the perpetrators, such as Nettleton, are celebrated. In her analyses of *Who Do You Think You Are?*, Goldman suggests that Munro subverts the dynamics of shame in part through non-heteronormative subject positions, such as the one that Rose takes towards Cora in "Privilege." Such subversion, she notes, "primarily entails challenging the violent and repressive patriarchal, heterosexual modes of reproduction that support the nuclear family and the sex-gender system" ("Alice Munro's" 88). Munro exposes physical and emotional violence in so-called daily life—repetition through time—to challenge norms and the status quo.

Sexuality

In "Privilege," Rose, as a child, admires Cora and the other two older girls at school who will write the entrance exam to high school: "Three queens. But when you looked closer, a queen and two princesses" (40). Yet Cora does not fit that royal description, as Rose's stepmother, Flo, makes clear when she mocks Rose: "'There goes your idol!' she would say, seeing Cora go by the store after she had started high school" (48). In opposition to the British queen, for whom lineage is of utmost importance, Cora is "illegitimate" (41) and does not personally progress but becomes a failure (49). Moreover, the school in the fictional town of Hanratty, Ontario, is a parody of a castle: Cora calls Rose from above, not from a castle's tower but from the school's "fire escape" (42), and Rose learns to avoid the school basement, which, like a dungeon, is "black, dripping like a cave" (37). The scene from the fire escape at once alludes to Shakespeare's *Romeo and Juliet* and the fairy tale *Rapunzel.* Like Juliet calling to Romeo, Cora calls to Rose in an act of love. Like Rapunzel, who is trapped in a tower, Cora and Rose are trapped in the small town of Hanratty. Paradoxically, the school later both loses its castle-like qualities and showcases the town's new post–World War II prosperity, which demonstrates ephemerality and the movement of time: the castle "dwindled" (49), while the school "got fixed up" (50).

"Privilege" parodies the notion of the small Canadian town as royal and the people in it as noble, and it also rejects what Huebener, in *Timing Canada*, calls "time socialization"—the notion that a young person should engage in particular behaviours to prepare for the future as an adult. Yet the story in *Who Do You Think You Are?* surpasses *Lives* in that respect because it also contests the time socialization of middle-aged women. Time socialization in this story and in the collection as a whole is interconnected with class. As Jamieson notes, Dr. Henshawe, Rose's professor, is described as youthful: "Rose feels able to borrow a raincoat from the much older woman because the garment attests to the latter's 'classical youthful tastes'" (59).[3] "Compare this with Flo," Jamieson states, "who, while still in her early thirties, wears the same 'print housedresses' that 'a woman of fifty, or sixty, or seventy might wear'" (59). Munro shows how "chronological age" might "have very different meanings in different social contexts" (59). Munro's rejection of time socialization is also a rejection of age-specific expectations for women, since her protagonist in *Who Do You Think You Are?* is female, as is typically the case in her stories. Her rejection of these age-specific expectations for women marks the book as feminist. Wendy Robbins et al. point out that "gossip suggests that Dr. Henshawe may be lesbian" (55). In "The Beggar Maid," Patrick expresses his worry that Rose has been influenced by Henshawe's ways: "I know who's been talking to you," he says. "Some people don't have a very high opinion of her. They think she has an influence on girls" (122). Patrick implies both that Henshawe is a feminist, and that feminism—at least to him and to his own position—is dangerous. Henshawe's deviation from the so-called normal trajectory of a woman's life, from schooling to marriage to children, threatens the status quo to which Patrick adheres and which he represents. This resistance to linear, progressive movement through the time of a woman's life adheres to Kristeva's and other feminists' notions of time: they incorporate the cyclical and the corporeal. Munro's focus on an alternative time and her rejection of linear process are important. She clearly sees the injustices and confinement of women's roles in Canadian society and wants to work towards liberation. As Del's mother, Ada, puts it in *Lives of Girls and Women*, "There is a change coming I think in the lives of girls and women. Yes. But it is up to us to make it come" (164). Arguably, Munro's literary work itself contributes to that change.

In one interpretation, the movement through time in the story "Privilege" brings progression and prosperity. After the war, not only does the school get updated, but people "[move] away to take war jobs" and those who stay are "better paid than they had ever dreamed" (49). In another interpretation, however, the passing of time results in deterioration. Cora herself deteriorates she "[turns] into a dark sulky-looking girl with round shoulders" (49). She passes the entrance exam but fails at high school (49) and so rejects the "centrality of time discipline and its associated values of punctuality...efficiency, and future planning" (Huebener, *Timing* 107). Rose's love for Cora, like the school, loses "all its evil energy, its anarchic spirit, its style" (48). Munro perverts the expectation, according to traditional time socialization, that a girl should have a crush on a boy. Instead, Rose has a crush on a girl.

Cora's painting of Rose's fingernails on the fire escape is like a sex scene during which Cora dominates Rose. "Spread your fingers out," Cora states. "There. Relax...Hold steady like a good girl. You don't want me to go all crooked on you, do you?" (43). Munro states outright that Rose's love for Cora is "sexual" (44), and Rose explains how "outlandish" that idea would be to Flo (48), who often—though not always—supports systems of power and normative time. Queerness, then, interrupts linear time and upsets and challenges traditional time socialization for women, even as non-heteronormative subject positions can repeat patriarchal power relations and reinforce roles of the dominant and the dominated—as we see in the relationship between Rose and Cora. In Munro's allusion to *Romeo and Juliet*, Cora plays a role that is spatially above Rose, on the fire escape, and she physically and emotionally dominates her in the painting of her nails as a quasi-sex scene. Drawing upon both Kristeva and Luce Irigaray, feminist philosopher Elizabeth Grosz notes that "if bodies are to be reconceived, not only must their *matter and form* be rethought, but so too must their environment and *spatio-temporal location*" (*Space* 84, emphasis in original). Although Munro challenges heteronormativity, the place and space in which that challenge occurs does not allow a full unravelling of the status quo. The school and the people stay the same temporally, too: "progress" is valued, and patriarchy continues. However, the qualification of "progress" changes—the people might dwindle or fail, but they simultaneously disrupt and regenerate.

Stefan L. Brandt argues that "'queer' themes [are] prevalent in Alice Munro's fiction" (30), and he articulates those themes as "a narrative awareness of identity and behavioural options that deviate from the norm (28)." This "queerness," he explains, "is not necessarily to be equated with homosexuality, although it may well include it" (29). It is noteworthy that, as Brandt points out, "Munro's appreciation of otherness did not always match the dominant discourse in Canadian literature," and that "before the Quiet Revolution of the 1970s, Canadian society, in general, was not exactly accepting of minorities" (31). *Who Do You Think You Are?* was published in 1978, but it was not until the 1980s that "the U.S. and Canada saw the emergence of...*queer sensibility*, namely an awareness in literary and cultural practice regarding non-normative behaviour" (31, emphasis in original). The term "queer" itself did not emerge in Canada as one that signalled sexuality until the early 1990s, when queer theorist Eve Kosofsky Sedgwick "proclaimed that the use of the word 'queer' was groundbreaking" (Brandt 31). While the term originally referred "to things regarded as odd, strange, or vaguely peculiar, the term suddenly epitomized an altered understanding of life as being complex and diverse as opposed to linear and normative" (32). Munro's consideration of "queer" themes in her writing "points to a new understanding, an awareness in which diversity and heterogeneity trump conformism and tradition" (32). In "Privilege," then, Rose's sexual attraction to Cora works both within and against traditional discourses of sexuality, and in this regard, Munro was well ahead of her time. While Cora's position on the top of the fire escape mimics the spatial location of Juliet in Shakespeare's play, a heteronormative and canonical literary work, Munro reverses it. Cora is the dominant, masculine figure, yet she is in Juliet's place. The love depicted is between girls rather than a girl and a boy, which suggests an alternative to the heteronormative discourse of sexuality. Indeed, Munro troubles "gender categories that support gender hierarchy and compulsory heterosexuality" (Butler, *Gender Trouble* viii) and suggests the possibility of an alternative, woman-centred epistemology while simultaneously foregrounding performativity.

Rose's love for Cora "dwindles" (49) like the school's castle-like aura. Interestingly, Rose, through the narrator, expresses a tone of nostalgia for the loss: "Nobody from the school could reach over and get their lilacs...Cora's grandfather had to retire" (50). In "Royal Beatings," as we have seen, Rose notices the mismatch between Flo's story of Hat Nettleton and the radio announcer's, but has no one to tell. Similarly, in "Privilege," Rose feels sexual love for Cora but cannot tell: that love, ultimately, is not actualized but lost. The one time that Rose attempts to express her love for Cora, by giving her candy, Cora exposes her by telling Flo (47). The gesture of giving her candy aligns Rose with Flo, who works in a candy store, and with the wicked witches or strangers who tempt others with their sweets. Because Flo upholds the patriarchal order and normative time, Cora's action squelches the possibility of consummation. On the one hand, Munro rejects the conventions of the "time socialization story" in this "narrative of youth" (Huebener, *Timing* 104–05): Cora defies age expectations by getting less attractive in her teens and by failing at school (48); Rose defies social expectations by loving a girl rather than a boy. However, just as Rose is unable to upset the official historical narrative of Hat Nettleton, so too is she unable to upset the normative conventions of time socialization in "Privilege," since her love for Cora is never fulfilled but instead deteriorates. Therefore, Munro gestures towards alternative time but suggests that it may not yet be brought to fruition. Often, the inability to bring forth change, in Munro's stories, is due to shame. As Goldman notes, referring to Luna Dolezal's book, *The Body and Shame*, body shame "springs from an individual's perceived inability or unwillingness to mimic the norm" ("Alice Munro's" 81). Rose's shamed body—due to being beaten by her father and her deviation from heterosexual normativity—may result in her own sense of shame that keeps the beating or "hiding" (24) hidden.[4]

"Wild Swans," like "Privilege," is future oriented: "Privilege" depicts a movement toward deterioration rather than progression; "Wild Swans" demonstrates Flo's foresight, yet Flo sees Rose as a victim of an unseemly future. "Wild Swans" begins with Rose's recount of one of Flo's stories, a warning to Rose about what she might encounter when she ventures, for the first time, from the small town of Hanratty to Toronto. Her suggestion that someone "wicked" (75) might offer her candy to kidnap her recalls Rose's offering of candy to Cora in "Privilege." It also alludes to the wicked witch who offers Snow White a poisonous apple, and it suggests dissemblance, the hiding of a so-called wicked identity within a kind and generous one. In "Wild Swans," Flo situates Rose as the innocent victim who might be duped into accepting such enticement from a malevolent stranger; in "Privilege," by contrast, Rose herself is the malevolent one who offers Cora enticement into what would be considered an illicit sexual relationship between two girls. Furthermore, Flo describes herself as "wicked" (75) to one of her customers at the store where she sells candy, as though she is the witch in Hansel and Gretel who tempts and lures others. With Flo's warning, Munro suggests Flo's alignment with time socialization and the assumption that young girls are innocent and must guard themselves to remain so until they become mature women. Yet Munro resists time socialization by suggesting that both Rose and Flo, at alternate times, also play the role of the "wicked" (75). She challenges the expected order of events and refuses to adhere to the conventions of the Bildungsroman genre, which delineate the progression of a young girl—and a "good girl" (43)—from innocent childhood to experienced adulthood. Munro's push back against time socialization for girls and women is a feminist gesture: she explores the problematic connotations around "goodness" and "wickedness" that an entrance into women's sexuality, according to the patriarchy, entails.

The portrayal of Rose as both innocent and wicked, but neither fully both, might be read in a new light since Skinner's revelation. "Wild Swans" addresses sexual assault thematically, which is noteworthy, considering Munro wrote this story shortly after the assault on her daughter occurred. The story could, therefore, be seen as Munro's attempt to work through the knowledge of Fremlin's pedophilia by questioning the innocence of girls, though it is speculation whether Munro knew about her daughter's abuse at the time of writing. When Skinner told her mother about the abuse years later, Fremlin stated that Skinner was "looking for sexual adventure" and compared her to Lolita in Vladimir Nabokov's novel (Skinner)—an accusation that is as ludicrous as it is alarming. Munro's apparent denial of the innocence of girls in her treatment of Rose, however, troubles a feminist reading of the story, since we might now read it as an apology for the perpetrator or an accusation of the victim's complicity.

Ironically, Flo's story comes true. Her past warning or prediction is infused into Rose's present experience when a man sexually touches her on the train to Toronto. Rose escapes her home in Hanratty, where her she must endure "royal beatings" from her father; yet ironically the train is no safer than her own home, since she is sexually assaulted there. As Rao explains, in Munro's writing, "home is a place of violence and nurturing; a place to escape to and to escape from" (42)—a relevant statement when we consider Fremlin's assault on Skinner. Rose's first trip to Toronto, the one she took as a child, is associated with her present one, through the metonym of her coat. Here, the past is again infused into the present. During Rose's first trip, she drinks a sour glass of chocolate milk and vomits on her coat: "All day long she was afraid people in Toronto could smell vomit on her coat" (76). During her second trip, "a corner of [the man's] newspaper," which she later realizes is his hand, "touched her leg, just at the edge of her coat" (80). In both instances, Rose's coat, associated with herself, is tainted or spoiled. In the first instance, she unwittingly drinks spoiled milk; in the second, she experiences sexual touching without her consent. Although Flo warns Rose that she might be violated, her story and Rose's experience are somewhat different. Flo warns Rose, in particular, about people "dressed up as ministers," who she says "are the worst" (80); the man who touches Rose says he is a minister, though he is dressed in regular attire (79). Later, Rose wonders whether he is a minister at all (85). The layers of semblance are worth noting here. "Dress[ing] up" recalls Rose's school that was "fixed up" after the war, covering its disrespectable history. It also relates to Rose, who is an actress and therefore dresses and acts like someone else as part of her job. Yet this man says he is a minister but is not dressed as one. His "saying" is also a dressing up, an act or semblance of "goodness" that he clearly belies when he sexually touches her. That he says he is a minister brings up the notion of religion in the text; however, unlike *Lives,* as Josephine Kealey asserts, religion is not prominent in this collection of stories. "Religion and its offerings are finally no longer useful," Kealey explains, "to the Munrovian young woman on the brink of adulthood and artistic maturation" (208). The invocation of the minister, then, does not so much highlight the theme of religion as it foregrounds performativity, the constructed roles of "goodness" or "wickedness" that one plays and that one becomes. The interchangeability of "minister" and "father" here also suggest a parallel between this scene and the one in Munro's real life, in which Skinner was assaulted by her [step]father.

Rose cannot be reduced to an innocent girl who might be unwittingly enticed, since she also plays the role of the enticer when she offers Cora candy. Likewise, this man has no fixed identity: each of his roles easily slips into another. Like the man's elusive identity, Flo's past prediction or warning does not remain static and unchanged, but instead erupts into the present, reinterpreted and revised. Even though Rose has left Flo at home, her presence is still with her. Not only does Rose recall Flo's warning when the man touches her on the train, but she is consistently reminded of her: "She couldn't stop getting Flo's messages" (85). In this instance, the train represents a liminal space between Rose's childhood and her adulthood, between the town of Hanratty and Toronto, between Rose's past and her future. Flo is Rose's stepmother, and so Rose does not fully separate from her but is continually tied to her, thus defying the psychoanalytic and Lacanian time progression from oneness with the mother to separation and alienation from her.[5]

Semblance

Lee Garner and Jennifer Murray explain how Munro invokes theatricality or role playing "where the limits of socially acceptable behaviour are transgressed" (1). In such instances, theatricality "illustrate[s] the acting out of transgressive moments through a discourse which allows for a distancing gesture within the narration" (2). This "distancing gesture" (2) is evident in the sexual scene between the man and Rose on the train. For example, Rose reduces the man and his actions to a hand: "But what if it was a hand? What if it really was a hand?" (81). The hand is further reduced to "the hand's pressure" (81). Like Rose's coat, a metonym for herself, the hand or its pressure is a metonym for her feelings of disgust and sexual pleasure, the latter of which she calls upon later in life: "he remained on call, so to speak, for years and years" (84). Francesconi explains that in Munro's stories, "the search, recovery and appropriation of things past are systematically textualized" (343). Rose's later "call" upon the memory of the man touching her on the train, to experience sexual pleasure, is an appropriation of that experience. The "referent of memory," Francesconi notes, "is far from a given and defined essence" and is "instead an irreducibly procedural, interpretative and dialogic process" (343). Just as Del repurposes the past to write herself anew in *Lives of Girls and Women*, so too does Rose repurpose and recall the past to take ownership of her past and present experiences in *Who Do You Think You Are?*

Trains in Munro's writing often signify transitions, movements from one part of the protagonist's life to another. Munro mobilizes the train as a mechanical marker of time and place to demonstrate movement and change. Mechanical markers of time have overridden natural ones in contemporary Western society. Yet, in "Wild Swans," Munro invokes mechanical time with the train to suggest natural time in Rose's life. In the story, Rose's trip on the train from Hanratty to Toronto signifies her transition from girlhood to womanhood, even as Munro mocks and unsettles any easy movement from one to the other. As Rao states about Rose's trip to Toronto: "Here the train that takes Rose elsewhere becomes a pathway, a liminal space, a 'line of flight' between class and cultural differences: her working class background, to which she does not want to belong, and the upper-middle-class environment she will eventually get to know" (50). In Munro's description of the train ride, place and time become conflated, each a part of the other: movement through space is simultaneously movement through time. The train ride marks Rose's sexual awaking; yet Munro describes that awaking with reference to the landscape through which Rose moves. Space is time accelerated as Rose travels toward an "earlier spring (77). The "landscape" (77) becomes "tenderer" (77), like Rose's body, in patriarchal discourse, as she approaches womanhood. Carol L. Beran notes that Munro "ironizes [woman's] identification with the beautiful land" ("Beautiful" 154). Rose is not "empty of desire and void of sexual agency" (McClintock 30), like the so-called empty land that colonials imagined, or as patriarchal discourse would expect her to be. In a description of her own sexual arousal, couched in terms of the landscape and scenery, a flock of birds, "wild swans, even" (84), like Rose's legs, "fl[y] apart in celebration...exploding...taking to the sky" (84).

McClintock explains how patriarchal and colonial narratives have historically associated women with an eroticized landscape. Munro ironizes and reverses this situation, associating the landscape with the licentious man. His actions are displaced onto the scene Rose observes outside the train window: "suburbs where bedsheets and towels used to wipe up intimate stains flapped *leeringly* on the clotheslines...children seemed to be frolicking *lewdly*" (84, emphasis added). Just as Del distances herself from Mr. Chamberlain's masturbation in "Lives of Girls and Women," so too does Rose distance herself from this man by displacing his actions onto the landscape in "Wild Swans." W.H. New notes that "*land* can function not just as the revelation of the status quo, but also as the *space* or *place* or *site* of challenge to the accustomed borders of power" (6, emphasis in original). Munro's description of the landscape, related to Rose's sexual arousal and the man's actions, is both dynamic and subversive: dynamic because it signifies change and the movement of time; subversive because it challenges and reverses the notion of the eroticized feminized landscape. Thus, Munro upsets imperial time and progress, suggesting an alternative, anti-imperial mindset, and contesting women's association with the landscape that imperialism attempts to dominate.

Munro challenges preconceived notions of the scenery or setting in "Wild Swans" and in "The Beggar Maid." Drawing once again on the trope of royalty, in the latter story, Rose's university library is a parody of a castle, where Rose plays the part of "damsel in distress" when she meets her lover, Patrick Blatchford (99). The library, like a castle, "had casement windows, which might have been designed for shooting arrows through" (97); the arrows, like Cupid's, might have shot Patrick, who first meets and falls in love with Rose in the library. Incidentally, the architecture of the library described here is like the one at Western University, where Munro herself attended classes. Rose, a "scholar" according to Dr. Hanshawe (96), misses university parties and sports events because she works in the library. Like Rapunzel in the fairy tale, Rose resides in an (ivory) tower and looks down upon those who attend the university's social events: "the cheers and songs were idiotic, if you listened to the words" (97).

While Rose configures herself as a "damsel" (99) and haughtily sees herself as superior to some of her peers, Patrick deems her the "beggar maid" (101) and a "white goddess" (105). Alluding to Edward Burne-Jones's Pre-Raphaelite painting of *King Cophetua and the Beggar Maid* (1884) and Alfred Tennyson's poem "The Beggar Maid" (1842) (101), Munro emphasizes a rags-to-riches tale and configures those historical works of art as a part of the present, representative of a life that Rose and Patrick repeat. Patrick's reference to Rose as the "white goddess" (105) adds another layer to their contractedness, whereby they play the parts of King Cophetua and the beggar maid. Patrick says, "There's a book I have called *The White Goddess.* Every time I look at the title it reminds me of you" (105). The book, first published in 1948 by Robert Graves, is about myth-making. With this reference, Munro highlights the construction of storytelling: Rose and Patrick perceive each other as characters and their romantic relationship as legend. It is interesting that the story of the king and the beggar maid is an appropriation of an African story, and that both the Raphaelite painting and Tennyson's poem were published at the height of European colonialism in African countries. With this in mind, we might read Patrick's association of Rose with "the beggar maid," and with the "white goddess" as an alignment with imperial time and values, especially as the word "white" in relation to the goddess suggests race. The story of the king and beggar maid has been invoked in numerous literary and artistic works, including Lewis Carroll's most famous photograph, "Alice and the Beggar Maid." The "Alice" in Carroll's photograph is Alice Liddell, but we might think of Alice Munro here, since the two share a first name. Seeing as Munro discusses photography regularly in her work—in "Epilogue: The Photographer" in *Lives*, for instance—and considering she was familiar with Carroll's work, it is likely that she would have known this famous photograph. As such, we might read Munro as hiding behind the various literary and artistic interpretations she presents. She, like Rose, might be interpreted as the "beggar maid": Rose came from a working-class background, but with her marriage to Patrick, moved into the middle-upper class; likewise, Munro came from a working-class background, but with her marriage to Jim Munro, also entered the middle-upper class. Munro's fiction and autobiography collide in such references to literary and artistic works in this story. Near the end of "The Beggar Maid," the narrative shifts to a later time, after the end of Rose and Patrick's ten-year marriage. Rose's personal history of courtship and marriage to Patrick, like the painting and poem, have become story. Just as Burnes-Jones and Tennyson repeat and reinterpret an older tale about an African king and his beggar-lover, so too does Rose repeat and re-envision her own story about her marriage to Patrick—which may very well be, in part, a repetition and re-envisioning of Munro's own marriage to and departure from Jim Munro.

In *Lives of Girls and Women*, Munro self-reflexively draws attention to that book as a literary work and inserts her own voice into the literary canon, occupied by writers such as Charlotte Brontë and James Joyce. Similarly, in *Who Do You Think You Are?*, she patterns her story in relation to previous ones told by Burne-Jones and Tennyson and explicitly foregrounds reinterpretations and revisions that continue to occur through time. The story of Rose and Patrick's love and marriage, it is worth noting, does not follow the previous ones upon which it is based. Unlike the painting, the poem, and the tale from which they borrow, Patrick and Rose's love does not last. Munro invokes literary and historical time with her allusions to previous works, but she also envisions an alternate time—another story—that ultimately departs from them. Re-envisioning a new kind of narrative time and employing a *mise en abyme*, Munro refuses to repeat stories in which the woman serves the man. Rather, she envisions a new, female literary tradition that embraces women's time and offers ambiguous endings that suggest independence over subservience.

History

Munro theorizes history itself in "The Beggar Maid," demonstrating its problematic denial and repression. Munro's rejection of traditional historical time is a call for systematic equality—not only to include women in history, but to tell the stories of history from feminist perspectives. Munro's theorization of history in "The Beggar Maid" exposes this bias and seeks to right it. In "The Beggar Maid," Patrick is an aspiring historian, but ultimately gives up that career path to work in his father's department store business, a "mercantile empire" (102), in the words of Dr. Henshawe, the retired professor with whom Rose boards at university. "Patrick's father [did not] care for this concern about the past" (113), and his sisters mock him for his scholarly interest in history (114). Rose feels both out of place and out of time when Patrick's mother gives her a tour of the grounds of their home. As Rao puts it, she "experiences a confusion, a distorted perception of seasonal time: "Patrick's parents lived on Vancouver Island...About half an acre of clipped green lawn—green in the middle of winter; March seemed like the middle of winter to Rose" (52). Rao writes about place and home in Munro's writing, but here place intertwines with time, as the place of her wealthy soon-to-be in-laws feels not quite right, out of seasonal time.

Patrick's mother refuses to discuss the past—"she hated people being *reminded*" (113, emphasis in original). In fact, she explicitly rejects the community's and her family's histories. When Patrick asks her, for example "what steamers went up the coast, what year was the settlement abandoned, what was the route of the first logging railway," she says, "irritably, 'I don't know. How would I know about that?'" (113). Likewise, when Rose questions her about her family's history, she says, "'No. I don't think they were stonemasons.' Something like fog went out from her: affront, disapproval, dismay" (112). Patrick's mother's comment here exposes her class bias as it suggests her "disapproval" for what she considers to be lower class professions, such as stonemasonry. Given Rose's working-class background, Patrick's mother's judgemental attitude might be extended to Rose herself. Patrick's family associates with the business class and the department store chain they have built, so we might interpret his family's denial of history as aligned with the "time discipline" that E.P. Thompson suggests is an aspect of "mature capitalist society" (quoted in Huebener, *Timing* 10). On such a view, "all time must be consumed, marketed, put to *use*" (Thompson quoted in Huebener 10, emphasis in original). This pragmatic "time discipline" is certainly indicative of Patrick's mother's perspective: "Any interest beyond the factual consideration of the matter at hand—food, weather, invitations, furniture, servants—seemed to her sloppy, ill-bred, and dangerous" (113). Through her characterization of Patrick's family members, who not only reject history but also display contempt for one another, Munro critiques modern capitalist society. Public versions of history often focus on politics and military affairs, traditionally male realms. Even though Patrick's mother upholds patriarchal time, history is "dangerous" (113) because it exposes a possible a working-class past, and it shows the possible meaninglessness, emptiness, and precariousness of the wealthy business class of which she is a part. In "Obsolescence/Innovation," Burges explains that the logic of late capitalism assumes constant renewal, a shedding of the old in favour of the new. This temporal movement, however, makes its players in the past obsolete. It is this fear of becoming obsolete that stokes Patrick's mother's anxiety. To expose her family's past is to reveal the "unreliable structure" (234) upon which her own family wealth resides.

The denial of history, however, is not limited to Patrick's family, but extends to Dr. Henshawe and Rose, though more subtly. Although Dr. Henshawe is "in her seventies" (88), as Jamieson explains, she "almost never appears without her leitmotif of girlishness" (58). Rather than playing the part of a mature lover, Rose, when she is with Patrick, acts youthful: she "[feels] a need to be continually playful" (108). This act of playing the part of a child at the very moment she is supposed to be an adult is repeated in "Mischief," when Rose and her new friend Jocelyn, in the maternity ward, act like children: "The nurse said, 'Wasn't it time for them to grow up?'" (136). Munro disrupts the notion that age corresponds to expected actions and behaviours. While Judith Butler focuses on gender performativity in her work, Butler's early theories are applicable to Munro's troubling of age. Munro challenges age as a "foundational category of identity" and exposes it as a "[production] that create[s] the effect of the natural...and the inevitable" (Butler, *Gender Trouble* vii). Munro similarly challenges traditional time socialization, which is usually marked in the Bildungsroman genre, and she contests expectations for girls and women to behave in particular ways during stages of their lives. In so doing, she upsets foundational gender categories upon which identities are based. On the one hand, women expressing "girlishness" (Jamieson, 58) might adhere to the patriarchal order, which infantilizes as it dominates; on the other hand, playing such "girlishness" when one is a grown woman pushes back against time socialization and expectations for women to behave in so-called "proper" ways. As Butler puts it, "gender is a kind of persistent impersonation that passes as the real" (*Gender Trouble* viii). To perform "girlishness" (Jamieson, 58) is a kind of play, a performance that both adheres to and resists gender normativity and the status quo.

In "Simon's Luck," Munro demonstrates time's shiftiness, the notion that events are not easily situated in concrete or fixed moments in time. By suggesting a disconnect between events and moments, Munro contests "the relationships between time, power, and everyday life" (Huebener, *Timing* 233). Although "Simon's Luck" was not initially included in the Rose stories, Munro phoned her agent, Virginia Barber, on the twelfth of December 1977, to indicate that there would be a united collection of ten Rose stories. "The anticipated stories," as Hoy explains, "included a Rose version of 'Simon's Luck'—'...I'm sure she's bound to meet Simon—that's Rose's luck,' wrote Barber in her response to the phone call" (62). The story begins with Rose attending a party in Kingston, Ontario, where she teaches drama, and the party's attendees are college faculty members. There, she sees Simon, a Jewish professor with whom she has had brief affair. She goes home with him again after the party and resumes her affair with him. Much of the story juxtaposes the recall of events with their retelling, though the memories and the stories that represent them never quite match. For example, at the party, Rose explains that her cat died in her dryer that day, though "it had happened last week" (208). The time referent changes from Rose's experience to her act of telling the story: she has the power to tell and revise the time of the event. In another instance, Rose cannot recall, until later, the name of her former student, David, who she sees at the party. She eventually recognizes him as her former student, but does not remember anything else about him. David is rude to Rose at the party: "up yours Rose" (209), he says. Yet Rose cannot figure out why. The person and the event that mark their connection to her are not easily reconciled. Already, in "Simon's Luck," Munro challenges traditional narrative time and the idea that events can be easily remembered and configured into sensical language. Munro unravels the match between the event and its retelling to show that any narration of an event necessarily limits and restricts. Certain details are remembered and retold, while others are left out or approximated. In so doing, she exposes the limitations of linear, normative time.

Rose finally recalls the context of her relationship with David right after Simon tells her how he escaped the Nazis in World War II. David "sprung out of the floor" (212), as Simon was hiding on the floor of a freight car on a train during his escape (215). As Rose is seemingly accused by David at the party because he might not have received a grant, so too is Simon accused by the Nazis, for no reason other than his Jewishness. The telling of David's story is intertwined with the telling of Simon's, the two indistinguishable from one another, complicating linear, narrative time. Later, when Rose tells Simon about what it is like for her to live in the countryside, she explains how she used to walk on deserted country roads. One time, while doing so, she heard shots being fired, then saw people in a car "shooting out of the windows" (219). Yet, when she told the lady at the nearby store, Rose explains to Simon, you "could tell she [the lady at the store] thought going for walks by yourself was a lot more suspicious than shooting groundhogs" (219). Just as Rose is seen as at fault when she is the victim, not the perpetrator, so too is Simon when he hides on the train, though under more formidable circumstances. Once again, Rose's story becomes intertwined with Simon's, even as the two are vastly different. While Rose is seen as suspect, simply because she is a woman walking on a road alone, Simon is seen as suspect due to his Jewishness. Remnants of Simon's past story of escape are subtly though powerfully infused into Simon's and Rose's lives, erupting into the present and continuing to haunt them. Munro pushes back against both patriarchal time, that which blames women, and imperial time, which, in this case, blames Jews, to expose the wrongness and unfairness of both. Munro situates these instances within both place and time: Simon's hiding takes place in Europe and invokes the time period of World War II; Rose's instance takes place in Canada in the present narrative of the story. While pushing back against both imperialism and patriarchy, Munro suggests that returning to our understandings of victims and victimhood in place and time can lead to altered perspectives on history.

However, Rose and Simon are accusers or perpetrators themselves. Even if unintentional, Rose might be deemed responsible for her cat's death in the dryer. Likewise, Simon's statement about David's presence at the party—"I don't know how he got in. I said no bloody students. There's got to be some safe place for them" (211)—ironically recalls the language of the Nazis and the "safe [place]" (215) of the freight car where Simon hides. In "Simon's Luck," just as the cat hides in what, ironically, the cat deems the "safe place" (211, 215) of the dryer, so too does Simon hide in the freight car of the train. In this interpretation, Rose, who is implicated in the cat's death, is aligned with the perpetrator, the "French and German voices" (215) who did not find Simon. While the cat might be likened to Simon due to their search for hiding spaces, the cat might also be likened to Rose, a "pleasure [seeker]" (208) who "[seeks] warmth...love" (209), and who is associated with domestic duties such as doing laundry. The ambiguity of Rose and Simon's subject positions is important here, and it recalls Flo's and Rose's characters as alternately "good" and "wicked." Munro resists defining characters in bounded ways, and instead she reveals their complexities and contradictions, their acts of performativity and transformation.

The cat is a symbol for memories themselves, those to be retrieved by Rose, of her student, and by Simon, of his escape on the train. Grace states that "inconvenient stories about the wars were pushed aside... [but] they have always haunted the dominant Canadian narrative, waiting to surface, waiting for us to pay attention, waiting, even for resurrection" (10). The dominant Canadian narrative that Munro pushes back against is the idea that war was glorious and did not result in widespread death and trauma. Official historical narratives engage in a collective forgetting of the atrocities and horrors of war. In "Simon's Luck," Munro gestures towards both personal and collective memories that go against the grain and reveal hidden, unwanted truths. In "Royal Beatings," she shows how citizens of the town of Jubilee hide violent local truths such as Nettleton's beating of Tyde; in "Simon's Luck," she exposes how the nation also hides violent truths, such as the violent ways that Jews in Canada were treated during and after World War II. Munro critiques how progress is revered while atrocities are kept concealed. That Simon hides on a train—a mechanical marker of time's so-called progressive movement—shows that there is an ugly and hidden side to the march of progress that war so readily and problematically celebrates.

Rose finally retrieves from her memory the story of her student, and she also retrieves the cat from her dryer. In both cases, she is too late.

She has already written a reference letter for David for a grant that was, perhaps, not successful, and she has already neglected to check her cat's presence in the dryer, which has led to the cat's death. Thus, there is a disjuncture between Rose's memories and the clock time within which actions related to those memories are embedded. The retrieval of the memory and the action related to it do not properly coincide. Of course, Rose does not understand the results of her actions until later, since, as Burges and Elias explain, "The present is usually illegible to itself, and its assumptions can be glimpsed only by hermeneutics other than its own" (2). But Munro clearly foregrounds this disjuncture to contest and complicate any notion of normative time. Goldman comments on the uneasy relationship of memory to troubling histories: "Remembering is not easy. On the contrary, it can be a tremendously unsettling experience. In Canadian literature, haunting and possession are powerful tropes for highlighting this tension between the desire to face the past and the fear of what skeletons may emerge from the familial and national closets, if we engage in this uncanny process" (*Dispossession* 5). "Simon's Luck" foregrounds the difficulty of facing the past, even if that difficulty is ironized. The story shows the belatedness of memory retrieval, how the realization of the past's significance often happens too late. By demonstrating such belatedness, Munro contests narrative time that assumes a clear, linear progression, an easy and straight movement through time and the telling and retelling of stories. Rather, she suggests that realizations, though often after the fact, are legitimate and valid. It is important to pay heed to such belated moments and refrain from dismissing them because of their deferral. Only by doing so, Munro seems to suggest, will we work toward an understanding of the past and liberate both others and ourselves.

When Simon leaves Rose and does not come to see her on a weekend when they have plans together, the lady from the store comes to tell Rose's fortune. She says that she "can't locate [Simon]" (223) in Rose's future, recalling both Simon's act of hiding in the freight car, where the authorities can't find him, and Flo's foresight of Rose's future in "Wild Swans." However, Simon—his influence and his memory—continues to be present in Rose's life. His acts of starting a garden for Rose (220) and insulating her house (221) metaphorically suggest that he helps to build her life anew and begin a self-sufficient life apart from Patrick. His suggestion that Rose "start some things [for the garden] indoors"

(220) implies renewal not only within her home but also within herself; and his suggestion that she start "from seed" (220) implies that the renewal will involve going back to her origins, to her beginning. Ajay Heble points out that "the following two chapters [after 'Simon's Luck'] deal with Rose's return to Flo and Hanratty" (115), which suggests that Rose's renewal of identity involves going home. Unlike a conventional Bildungsroman, *Who Do You Think You Are?* concludes with a return to the past, a movement back home rather than away from it.

The title of the story, then, refers not only to the luck Simon receives, not being caught by the Nazis, but also to the luck he gives to Rose, the gift of releasing her into her own, renewed identity. Like the luck that Bobby Sheriff gives to Del at the end of *Lives of Girls and Women*—"I wish you luck in your life" (236), he says—the luck that Simon gives to Rose is a blessing that enables her to live her life anew. The train ride that Simon takes from occupied to unoccupied France is like the journey that Rose takes, by car, from Toronto to Vancouver, during which she feels "calm and clear-headed" (229) and realizes that "love removes the world from you" (230). It is as though she is leaving her past behind her and is unburdened by it at the very moment that she will begin to turn back to it. Her movement from one place to another, from east to west, is also a movement through time. When she arrives in Vancouver to take a new acting job, the producers have to use makeup techniques to make her look older: "Some special make-up techniques, ageing techniques, had to be used on her face" (231). Rose is born anew, and thus looks younger. Her journey through place has resulted in a movement back through time, yet that backwards movement, for Munro, is not regressive but refreshing. The makeup that makes her looks older is just an appearance, hiding, this time, not what is ugly but what is new.

Critic David Peck suggests that Simon passes his good luck to Rose (135). The fate that befalls Simon is not only good, since, at the end of the story—when the story jumps to a year later—Rose finds out that Simon dies of pancreatic cancer. One day when Rose is working as an actress and filming on the deck of a ferry boat near Vancouver, she meets a woman whom she had met in Kingston a year ago, at the party with which the story opens. At first Rose does not remember her, but once the woman begins "to talk about Kingston, the couple who had given the party, even about the death of Rose's cat" (232), Rose recognizes her. She recalls that the woman had told Rose at the party that she was working on a paper about "the suicide of female artists" (212), and Rose had thought at that time that she looked like "a prime candidate [for suicide] herself...emaciated bloodless, obsessed" (212), though now, belatedly, Rose sees she was mistaken: "she didn't throw herself into the sea" (233).

Knowing now that Simon dies of cancer, the earlier image of Rose seeing "him naked peering down the cellarway" (221) is rich with implications of the past and the future. Rose had spent the night at Simon's after the party, and in the morning, naked after his night with Rose, Simon looks down the cellarway because he needs to fix the furnace. This naked image of Simon, however, also suggests the indignity of the Nazi death camps that Simon escaped, and it foreshadows his coming death by cancer: "naked" (221) and all body, we might interpret this image as one of Simon peering into his own grave. The ending of the story, in fact, is rife with ambiguity and is not only about good luck. The unnamed woman with whom Rose speaks on the ferry deck wonders "if they [Rose and the other actors] were going to be shooting any more scenes" (232). "Yet the woman's question for Rose—"whether they will be shooting any more scenes" (232)—is also a question for Munro. Rose and the author who writes her are here conflated into one. Rose may be shooting a few more scenes; in a similar vein, Munro may be writing a few more scenes. Rose will continue her acting career and Munro will continue her writing one. The woman's perceived desire "to get into the background or even the foreground of these scenes" (232) refers both to the play that Rose acts and to the story that Munro writes—Munro, that is, hides behind the protagonists she writes, and does not wish to show herself. The "somebody" that calls Rose "to go back to the scene" (233) could be Munro herself, calling her character, Rose, back into place. The "girl who didn't throw herself into the sea" (233) is at once the girl who Rose's character watches to make sure she does not take her own life, and the woman who was writing the paper on suicide and was a "candidate" herself. She is also Rose, and the cat who "seeks warmth... love" (209) in the dryer but who in this case is spared from death and can start anew. Unlike Simon, who, Rose muses, dies unfairly ("It was preposterous" [233]), Rose remains alive and well. The story ends metafictionally, musing on its own construction. The detail of Simon's death, Rose muses, "should have been left out" (233), and yet it is not; it is left in full view. Munro resists a narrative teleology that would suggest "hiding" those details that do not make sense, that are "a kind of disarrangement" (233) in favour of leaving such details on the table, exposed. In so doing, she asks us to face those aspects of the past that have been left behind—that have been untold—to expose what is underneath, to start anew.

Home

The story "Spelling" examines language and storytelling, extending and deepening the self-reflexivity apparent throughout the collection. In a similar vein, the story examines Rose's confrontation and understanding of herself: she returns to the place of Hanratty and to the time of her past. Hoy's study of Munro's process of writing *Who Do You Think You Are?* identifies the importance of the story "Spelling" within it. Two early manuscripts of the collection, both focusing on the Rose rather than the Janet stories, incorporate the story "Spelling" differently than how it ultimately appears in the book. The first draft of the manuscript was written in first-person narration, and the second was rewritten in third-person narration. In the first draft, "Spelling" preceded the other stories, while in the second, parts of it were interwoven throughout the collection (Hoy 61), a method that she abandoned halfway through (80). Munro's experimentation with weaving the story throughout the collection highlights its importance, and as such, it is worth examining in relation to time and textuality. The story itself emphasizes two letters that Rose receives. Near the beginning, letters stating that Flo can no longer live on her own are sent to Rose and her half brother, Brian. Later, Rose remembers a time when she received a letter from Flo in which Flo expresses her disapproval of Rose showing "a bare breast" (250) in a recent film. Each letter forces Rose to examine her past and herself. The first instigates Rose's return to Hanratty and to Flo, whom she had not seen in two years (239). The second—albeit earlier—letter results in an epiphany for Rose: "she had a fresh and overwhelming realization" (250). Rose suddenly understands Flo's earnestness and realizes that to mock Flo, as she does when she reads her letter aloud to others, is to repeat Flo's actions that are "painfully, truly meant" (250). Despite her unwillingness to accept it fully, Rose also seems to understand Flo's role as an uncaring mother: the "bare breast" (250) that Flo rejects has sexual connotations as well as nurturing, motherly ones. As readers of *Who Do You Think You Are?*, we receive written communication from Munro, which are the stories she tells in the book. Similarly, Rose is the recipient of written words of communication, but in the form of letters rather than stories. Unlike Brian, who receives the first letter but does not return to visit Flo, she assumes the responsibility of listening and responding to them.

Rose remembers a time when Flo arrived, unannounced, at a Toronto award ceremony where she was receiving an award for her acting. Flo has an outburst and makes a racist comment in the middle of the ceremony, creating a scene and embarrassing Rose.[6] Flo's outburst is an eruption of Rose's past into her present. It is precisely what Bhabha calls an "unhomely" moment. For Bhabha, "the unhomely is the shock of recognition of the world-in-the-home, the home-in-the-world" (445). Flo's outburst exposes Rose's unseemly origins at the very moment Rose is recognized for achievement and for transcending these origins. It is a belated repetition of the discursive and physical violence she experienced and witnessed as a child. Flo's racist language, for instance, mirrors the sexist language against Becky Tyde and Franny McGill in "Royal Beatings" and "Privilege," respectively. Sugars and Turcotte explain that "'unhomely' or 'spectral' legacies of imperialism... [appear] in the form of unresolved memory traces and occluded histories" (vii). Those histories, they note, are often "readily figured in the form of ghosts or monsters that 'haunt' the nation/subject from without and within" (vii). In "Spelling," Flo is the monster and a spectacle at the awards ceremony, with her "thick, gray-blue wig" (250). She haunts Rose by unearthing unacknowledged personal and communal histories with her outburst. Flo and Rose can no longer poke fun at the woman in the home whose hair had "grown out like a haystack" (234): they too now wear that "wig" (250, 252). Generations conflate: Rose realizes that Flo is a part of her—she "stuck [the wig] on her own head" (252)—and that they are both at one with the elderly, unhinged women of the past. The hair that "had just pushed up through" the rotten hat on the old woman's head (235) is none other than history itself. It is the presence of women of the past "[pushing] up through" the "hat" (235) Rose now wears, the person she now is.

In "Spelling," Munro puns on the word "letter." Letters are both those sent through the mail and those of the alphabet. In so doing, she draws attention to the act of writing in relation to memory and

62   ALICE MUNRO AND THE ART OF TIME

communication. On the third floor of the seniors' home, where some had "given up speaking...moving" (245), Rose meets an elderly woman who spells the words she hears. Rose and this woman, called only "Aunty" (245), collaboratively create: they textualize meaning and emphasize the bodily, materiality of words. Aunty, for example, "strain[s] forward, grunting to get the word" (246). Initially, Rose can only think of words that are "obscene" or "despairing," and Aunty says and spells her own word, but suddenly, Rose thinks of the word "celebrate," and Aunty spells it (246). Grace explains how the act of narration is paramount to memory: "The *narrative*—the forming of stories and history, of myths, and discursive formations—is the crucial step in creating landscapes of memory" (29, emphasis in original). This scene is indicative of Rose's return to her memories, but it also demonstrates her writing of them.

Rose's act of saying a word for Aunty to receive and spell mirrors Munro's act of writing the text *Who Do You Think You Are?* for her readers to receive and interpret. Aunty, like Munro's readers, participates in both the creation of the word and its interpretation. Rose's realization that she has the artistic power to act and to write her memories is something to "celebrate," despite the "obscene" or "despairing" (246) histories that those memories bring. That Rose does not write her memories by herself but rather in collaboration with an older woman powerfully suggests the coming together of old and new generations. This eruption of the past into the present helps to make and sustain meaningful stories and human connections through time. At the end of "Spelling," Flo's past is her present. Suffering from dementia and thinking she is in the hospital rather than the home, she wants to show Rose the gallstones she had removed, but cannot find them. That "they were in a bottle" (252) suggests that the gallstones represent part of Flo: like memories, they are messages in a bottle. Flo expressing relief when Rose assures her that she "took them home" (252) corroborates that interpretation. Flo knows that part of herself, which lives on through Rose's memories, is safe with Rose. Those memories will be passed down to the next generation, the stories continually retold and reinterpreted. It is significant that Munro uses a part of the body, Flo's gallstones, to signify memories and stories. For the author, who is aligned with women's time, memories and stories are very much a part of the body, even when they are separated from that body. Stories are corporeal bodies of work that cannot fully be separated from their artistic creator. They both exist apart from and within that creator. They circulate beyond the body but can also be brought back home.

The final story in the collection overtly demonstrates the past within the present. As W.R. Martin explains, "most of the story is a filtering of the past—and especially of memories of Milton Homer and Ralph Gillespie—through Rose's consciousness" (122). There are three distinct times in this story. The first is late in Flo's life, during the same time that "Spelling" takes place, when Flo goes to the seniors' home and Rose speaks with Brian about the arrangements: the story begins and ends here. The second is when Flo is not yet in the home, but she has already "[given] up the store" (268). During this period, Rose visits Hanratty and questions Flo about former classmates and townspeople, such as Milton Homer (269), and then reunites with Ralph Gillespie at the legion (271). The third is Rose's childhood, to which she frequently returns in this story through memory. The story moves in and out of these three times. In the story "Who Do You Think You Are?" Rose physically travels back to Hanratty and metaphysically travels back in time to her memories.

Just as Munro writes an enactment of a curtailed baptismal scene in *Lives of Girls and Women*, so too does she write an alternative baptism in *Who Do You Think You Are?* When Rose is a child, Milton Homer blesses newborn children in their homes. Unlike a pastor, he does not "call on the Father or the Son to do any business with water" (255); rather, he does "all of this on his own authority" (255). As Kealey explains, Milton's "aunts were members of the socially powerful Methodist church, whose influence eventually dies...the passing influence of that church seems to have gone hand in hand with Milton Homer's garish antics" (214-15). Since Rose is one of the babies who Milton "pick[s]...up" (254), we might determine that he passes luck to Rose, right after her birth, in the same way that Simon does in "Simon's Luck," later in her life. Yet Milton's blessings on newborn babies in Hanratty also recall the evil witch Maleficent's visit to the Princess Aurora in the fairy tale *Sleeping Beauty*, during which the witch curses rather than blesses the child, and this allusion adheres to the trope of royalty in the text. That Milton Homer's ritual can be interpreted as a curse is evident in Rose and her brother's unfavourable reaction to the idea that it might have happened to them: "Rose...began to tell Brian a story she thought he wouldn't like"

(254), and "Rose [knew] it was likely [that he picked her up too], though she hadn't been going to mention it" (255). The story therefore invokes a return to Rose's origin—the moment of her birth—and ambiguously suggests that either a blessing or a curse was set upon her.

Milton's ritual of visiting newborn babies, like almost everything Rose knows about him, might be hearsay: Rose "didn't really know if she remembered Milton Homer holding Brian, or had been told about it" (255). She is able to imitate Milton because she has heard Ralph Gillespie do so, though she has not heard Milton himself (256). Thus, we are introduced to mimicry and simulacra in this story.[7] In a sense, Ralph and Rose are reflections or mimicries of one another. Through the narrator, Rose notes the similarities between her and Ralph: the "alphabetical closeness" of their names; their "family" likeness in "habits or tendencies" (266). Likewise, her observation that Ralph's imitation is very good—"he was so successful that Rose was amazed, and so was everybody else" (267)—could equally be applied to her own success as an actress. Most interestingly, Ralph shows Rose that in his schoolbook he "stroked out the word *Chapman's* [in the title of Keats's poem] and inked in the word *Milton*, so that the title now read: *On First Looking into Milton Homer*" (260, emphasis in original). While Ralph's action of changing the title is itself a form of imitation—like his mimicry of Milton—it is also an act of creation: he alters the poem's title to write his own. Similarly, Rose's act of reciting a poem for her teacher, Miss Hattie (who is Milton's aunt), is an act of imitation and creation: she copies by reciting and creates by doing "memory work" (262).

Just as Milton's act of picking up newborn babies might be a blessing or a curse, so too might Ralph's writing of a new title and Rose's recitation be interpreted as either moments of brilliance or as mistakes. The brilliance or error lies in the disjunction between the text and its representation. Milton lived with his two aunts, his mother's twin sisters. One is Miss Hattie, Rose's high school English teacher. Rose memorizes a poem more quickly than her classmates, and when she says she has completed the memorization, Miss Hattie does not believe her and asks here to recite it for the class. When Rose does, Miss Hattie warns Rose about "her boast" (262). After class, Miss Hattie says to Rose, "Who do you think you are?" (262). Rose notes that lesson—not to strive or show one's smartness too much, especially as a girl—is the lesson the teacher feels is most important of all (263). Yet Ralph and Rose, like other artists, never quite get it right: "both of them were sloppy with ink, subject to spilling and blotting mishaps" (266). Their artistry and their error are one and the same. Rose's statement that "many other people believed she needed" the lesson not to show too much intelligence (263) is a feminist statement about the limitations set on girls and women. Rose feels she is impeded or limited because she shows her intelligence and therefore steps outside of what is deemed to be a girl's place.

At moments, Ralph is like Milton, whom he imitates, and the line between himself and the person he acts is blurred. Flo tells Rose that "half the time" he imitates someone who new people in the town do not know, and so "they just think it's Ralph being idiotic," and Rose replies, "Like Milton Homer?" (271). In the same way that Ralph becomes his subject, so does Munro: Rose and Munro are conflated into one. Rose laments that she is sometimes ashamed of her work, but not for the reasons that the public believes she is. It is not because of the "bare breast" (250) that she shows on film, but rather because she can't quite get her character right: "there was always something further, a tone, a depth, a light, that she couldn't get and wouldn't get" (275). Similarly, Munro might not have been ashamed of the sex scenes that appear in her books and the censorship that ensued, but rather that—in her estimation—she did not achieve her characters and her writing to their fullest: "everything she had done could sometimes be seen as a mistake" (275). Rose imitates others and recreates the text, the story out of which she acts, and so does Munro. Just as the poet John Keats is in awe of the Greek poet Homer (in translation by George Chapman), exemplified in his poem, "On Looking into Chapman's Homer," so too is Munro in awe of the poets John Milton and Homer, as Ralph's revised title and the character name suggest. She sees them and responds to them with her own literary text, *Who Do You Think You Are?* Ralph and Rose's ability to "look into" Milton and Homer in ways that others cannot or do not— they examine and recreate poetry—results in Rose's sense of closeness to Ralph: "she felt his life close, closer than the lives of men she'd loved" (277). The tradition of poetry that might begin with Homer is continued with Milton, with Chapman's translation of Homer and with Keats's poetic interpretation of it. That tradition is extended by Ralph and Rose, who read, interpret, and reenact it, and finally with Munro, who writes her own works of literature. The literary past pushes into the present and becomes part of it, reimagined and rewritten.

As Thacker has noted, *Who Do You Think You Are?* marked a major moment in Munro's life and in her work. Of Munro's revisions of the manuscript, Thacker says, "Certainly among the most celebrated episodes in Canadian publishing history was Munro's decision during the fall of 1978 to take *Who Do You Think You Are?*, then in production, off the press and restructure it" ("This Is Not" 21). Munro wrote and published her collection of stories, *Something I've Been Meaning to Tell You* in 1974, after the publication of *Lives* and before *Who*, and that book, her third, was "a pastiche volume made up of reshaped older material and new stories" (21). After attempting a manuscript entitled "Places at Home," which she eventually abandoned, she turned to the stories in *Who Do You Think You Are* (Thacker, *Alice Munro* 289). It was her father Bob Laidlaw's death, according to Thacker, that enabled Munro to write "Royal Beatings," the first story in the collection, since it was her own father who administered the beatings about which she wrote ("This Is Not" 23). At the time that she was writing *Who*, she had already left Jim Munro and was living with Gerald Fremlin, and had moved from Victoria, BC, back to Huron County, Ontario. It was this return home that sparked her writing of this collection. As Thacker puts it, Munro "settled back deeper into Huron County, becoming once again more comfortable with its immediacies—its scenes, presences, ways, and culture—using its detail in ways new for her was something she *had* to do" (23, emphasis in original). Out of these circumstances came *Who Do You Think You Are?* Along with *Lives of Girls and Women*, it is arguably one of Canadian literature's most important collections of stories.

Throughout *Who Do You Think You Are?* Munro infuses the present with the past, showing how history is always and continually a part of the present. The book undermines royalty in various ways, evident in the title of the collection. This theme is repeated in its last story, when Miss Hattie warns Rose against haughtiness or ambition by asking her who she thinks she is. Munro plays with the notion of time socialization and age expectations in the collection, as Flo sometimes reverts to childhood and Rose seemingly becomes her mother, each a part of the other.[8] Through Rose's love for an older girl at school, Cora, Munro debunks the common chronology of romantic love and the Bildungsroman. She further upsets the conventions of those genres and reveals unwanted or untold pasts by depicting Rose's sexual experience as one of a man sexually touching her on a train without her consent. Importantly, *Who*

Do You Think You Are?, like *Lives of Girls and Women*, incorporates intertextuality to exhibit the continual unfolding of history, the existence of the past in the present. "The Beggar Maid," for example, invokes a work of art by Edward Burne-Jones and the story of King Cophetua as told in poetry by Tennyson. The story "Who Do You Think You Are?" invokes the ancient Greek poet Homer and the English poets Milton and Keats to demonstrate how historical literary works influence contemporary artists. The collection also cites historical events, such as the incarceration and genocide of Jews during World War II. References to World War II, in fact, infuse the text and show how the past is a part of many Canadians' present lives and identities. For example, the school in Hanratty is renovated after the war and the character Ralph Gillespie was a naval officer who was injured during the war. Finally, the text is self-conscious and self-reflexive. Munro depicts herself in her protagonist and draws attention to Rose as a constructed character. The book as a whole makes a powerful statement about the importance of historical and literary pasts and suggests that the present is undeniably reliant on and determined by them. Though the book exhibits an unearthing of "obscene or despairing" (246) personal and collective histories, the continuation of the past in the present, when reworked, revised, and reimagined, Munro suggests, is to be "celebrate[d]" (246) as life itself.

3

Time and Corporeality
"Lichen" and "White Dump" in *The Progress of Love*

MUNRO'S COLLECTION OF SHORT STORIES, *The Progress of Love*, highlights and ironizes the idea of progress and considers middle age, the ageing process, and corporeality. Between the publication of *Who* in 1978 and that of *Progress* in 1986, Munro continued to write for literary magazines such as *Saturday Night* and *The New Yorker*, among others, and in 1982, she published the short story collection *The Moons of Jupiter*. During the 1980s, as Thacker explains, the opportunities Munro received increased, "owing to Munro's growing reputation" (*Alice Munro* 373). Publishers such as Jack McClelland from McClelland & Stewart sought to publish her work. Her agent, Virginia Barber, wrote to Munro and said, "Tell me which house you want. I'll let the lucky devils know, and then create a glorious contract" (quoted in Thacker 382). But Munro stayed loyal to her editor Douglas Gibson and the publishing house Macmillan. That changed by the time *Progress* was published. Gibson moved to McClelland & Stewart and Munro followed him there, only after lengthy negotiations between Macmillan and McClelland & Stewart that were facilitated by Munro's agent and McClelland's executive vice-president Linda McKnight (417-20). During those years, *The New Yorker* increasingly sought to publish Munro's stories and the first accession of her papers was received by the University of Calgary. Thacker's *Probable Fictions*, the first scholarly book of criticism on Munro's writing, was released (382). *Moons* received many excellent reviews and was an important collection in the author's career, but when *Progress* was published, David Macfarlane of *Saturday Night* explained that the collection "is probably the best collection of short stories—the most confident and, at the same time, the most adventurous—ever written by a Canadian" (370). Thacker notes that the stories in both *Moons* and *Progress* "seemed to have a different, deeper quality" than some of her previous ones (413). He says that "Miles City, Montana" and "The Progress of Love" stand out as exemplary in *Progress*. Certainly, those two stories are important works and have been frequently anthologized. Yet, "Lichen" and "White Dump," as Thacker suggests, are also among the best stories in this collection (413).

I turn now from an analysis of two of Munro's most important books, *Lives* and *Who*, both coming-of-age works, to these two stories from *The Progress of Love*. I build upon the existing scholarship and focus on time, identity, and the body. My analyses of "Lichen" and "White Dump" follow Munro's shift from writing about coming of age to writing about ageing and show how the author contests linear, progressive time through notions of women's identity and corporeality. I analyze these particular stories because they provide a unique perspective on time in the author's work. They highlight the connections between time and place—in the concept of erosion, for instance—and problematize how Western art and culture have associated women's bodies with nature. "White Dump" appears at the end of *The Progress of Love*, suggesting a kind of closure to the collection and, as Thacker indicates in "The Way the Skin of the Moment Can Break Open," this story, along with the title story, indicates "the direction Munro was moving in the 1980s," a direction that was both fictional and personal (24).

Recent scholarship has examined Munro's treatment of the ideologies that conflate feminine bodies and natural environments. In "Putting it Down to Experience," Elizabeth Barry builds on the theories of Simone de Beauvoir, Elaine Marks, and Kathleen Woodward. She argues that "ageing is often perceived and presented as (an) unmediated 'experience' not conducive to theorization or even analysis" (13). Old age can function, she says, as an "other to symbolization, a kind of Lacanian Real" (13). If, as both Jean-Paul Sartre and de Beauvoir suggest, women in Western society "are inescapably associated with the material, their bodies an obstacle to transcendence and to symbolization" (13), then the ageing woman is "doubly disenfranchised by her association with bodily materiality" (13), an argument, Barry explains, that Susan Sontag makes in her 1972 essay, "The Double Standard of Ageing" (13). Barry convincingly argues that midlife for Munro's women "represents an experience that resists theorization and eludes the cultural imaginary just as advanced old age has often been thought to do" (14). She maintains that Munro explores "the insights offered by the experience of ageing and its distance from the cultural symbolic, even when these do not translate into recognizable forms of 'wisdom' or rational sense" (15). In short, Barry maintains that ageing women in Munro's writing are both associated with materiality and increasingly separated from patriarchal representations of that materiality. Yet, Munro re-evaluates the connection between women and their bodies and environments: the body is not Other to the self but an integral part of it.

In "Stories in the Landscape Mode" critic Claire Omhovère considers the ways in which Munro's stories envision "the tension between spatial containment and temporal flow" (82). She examines the connections between Canadian painting and literature when she suggests that Munro invokes landscape "to probe the political and poetic implications of the feminization of the land, which has been one of the constants of Canadian painting and literature since their inception" (82). Omhovère explains that in "Lives of Girls and Women," "Walker Brothers Cowboy," and "Lichen," "landscape triggers moments of recognition when rarity of insight is mitigated with irony, grotesquerie, or even, sometimes, humiliation" (82). She analyzes the ways in which the female nude appears in and among landscapes in Canadian painters Edwin Holgate's and Kathleen Munn's work and argues that Munro similarly includes the figure of the nude in some of her stories to examine Western representations of women's bodies in landscapes, even as she contests those representations. As Omhovère puts it, "the narrative distributes space into a basic topography through which a small town is contrasted with the surrounding countryside, codes of conduct are opposed to unrestraint, and Scots-Irish settlements stand out against a diffuse aboriginal presence that endures in the local geography and some of its toponyms, such as the Wawanash River in both *Dance of the Happy Shades* and *Lives of Girls and Women*" (86). Barry's and Omhovère's scholarship is relevant to my discussion of time in "Lichen" and "White Dump," since these critics highlight the intersections between women's bodies, Canadian landscapes, ageing, and ephemerality.

In *The Progress of Love*, Munro's writing is more experimental in form than it is in *Lives* and *Who*. She plays with shifting narrative perspectives and increasingly employs time jumps, moving back and forth between the past and the present. She addresses the ageing body and ageing itself more than she does in her previous works. Characters' experiences and conceptions of time, and time's intertwinement with corporeality, are central to *The Progress of Love*. The body as dynamic and ephemeral is highlighted in all of the stories in the collection. The title story, for instance, begins with its protagonist, Euphemia, visiting her ageing father in a seniors' home and coming to terms with his ageing body and his impending death. "Miles City, Montana," another story in the collection, considers discrete moments in time and imagines them differently in the face of the near-drowning of the protagonist's daughter—a bodily, near-death experience. "Lichen" and "White Dump" show explicitly and implicitly how Munro conceives of time in relation to the ephemerality of the body. They demonstrate the eventual deterioration of both people and things as well as the inevitable regrowth and renewal that results from that deterioration. As in *Lives of Girls and Women* and *Who Do You Think You Are?*, Munro contests linear notions of progress and defies normative conceptions and societal assumptions regarding time. In so doing, she attempts to free women's identities from the frameworks through which patriarchy has defined them.

"Lichen"

Mary Jarrett notes that "the passing of time is notoriously Alice Munro's preoccupation" (83). In "Lichen," a story that was first published in 1985 in *The New Yorker* and then in 1986 in *Progress*, that passing of time is linked to ageing and the body, primarily but not solely of women. Jean Mallinson explains, "The metaphor implicit in the image of lichen in the story draws on the very old analogy between woman and landscape" (55). Along similar lines, Marianne Micros argues that Munro ironically invokes the pastoral, which "idealiz[es] the love object, the landscape, or love itself" (44). She does so not only by likening women's bodies to so-called natural landscapes, but also by using "a subtext of allusions to...pastoral poems and love sonnets" (44). I argue that Munro's act of connecting women's bodies to natural landscapes in the story is not only ironic: the author also foregrounds corporeality to work against the Cartesian mind-body split. Grosz explains that "as soon as knowledge is seen as purely conceptual, its relation to bodies, the corporeality of both knowers and texts...must become obscure" (*Volatile Bodies* 4). "Lichen" contests such obscurity and does not disavow but rather reaffirms the centrality of the body to the self.

The story's protagonist, Stella, is a woman who is presumably in late middle age and spends her summers at her beach house, where the story takes place. It begins with her former husband David's arrival, and takes place over the days of his visit. At the story's opening, we find out that Stella was married to David for twenty-one years, but has now been separated from him for eight. David always comes to visit Stella on her father's birthday, which already highlights the theme of ageing and the passing of time. On the day of David's arrival, her father is turning ninety-three years old. Each year David brings the same gift for him, "a bottle of scotch-whisky" (32), and he and Stella visit her father in his nursing home. This year, David has brought his lover with him, Catherine, who he describes as "a hippie survivor...who doesn't even know those days are gone" (38). At the beginning of the story, it seems that Catherine is his current lover, yet soon he tells Stella that he has a new lover, Dina, about whom Catherine does not yet know. The story is told in third-person narration, and it moves in and out of David's and Stella's minds in a shifting limited-omniscient narrative perspective. It is clear that David is sexist, since he often comments disparagingly on his current and former lovers. He also continually replaces his lovers with younger women. He suggests that his current girlfriend, Dina, is childlike, noting that she plays with wind-up toys (44). Munro ironically undermines David's condescending and sexist tone toward the women in the story, highlighting and interrogating the intersections between ageing bodies and landscapes as well as their rejuvenation and renewal.

Early in the story, Munro draws our attention to the materiality of natural landscapes and human bodies, foregrounding their ephemerality and renewal. Stella's summer house overlooks Lake Huron and is built on "clay bluffs" that are "steep" and "not so substantial" but have "held so far" (30), suggesting their eventual decay. At the beach by the summer house, there are "baskets of wire, stretching out into the water...to protect the beach from erosion" (37). Yet the landscape not only deteriorates but also proliferates: Stella, who lives there, has a garden where she "grows vegetables," and at her house there is a "jungle of wild blackberry bushes" (30). Stella herself seems to be part of the landscape in which she resides. In her first appearance in the story, when David arrives at the beach house, she "steps out of [the black-berry] bushes, holding a colander full of berries" (30). Like her natural environment, she too ages over time, according to David, who notes her "natural deterioration" (31). Alongside her environment, she shows signs both of ageing and of growth and renewal. On her first appearance, David sees that "there is nothing underneath [her] clothes...to support or restrain any part of her" (30). Just as her garden grows, so too does Stella "sprout" (31), her "warts" and "facial hair" like the "thorn bushes" that David thinks should be "cleaned out and burned" (32). David suggests that the ageing Stella "burst[s] out of [her] female envelope" (31), implying that David compartmentalizes women, particularly women's bodies. Right from its beginning, "Lichen" articulates the movement of natural landscapes and bodies through time. Additionally, it highlights David's attempt to confine bodies and emphasizes Stella's corporeal resistance to such confinement.

The story draws parallels between David's three successive women: his first wife and the protagonist of the story, Stella; his current lover, Catherine; and his new girlfriend, Dina. At the beginning of the story, when David and Catherine arrive at Stella's beach house, David comments to Catherine that Stella has "turned into a troll" (30). Catherine states, "Well. She's older" (30), and David replies, "Older than what, Catherine? Older than the house? Older than Lake Huron? Older than the cat?" (30). It is clear to the reader that Catherine means "older than herself," and wants to differentiate herself from David's former wife. Yet David's questions suggest that he may not differentiate between the two women, and Munro highlights this notion of similarity or copy. As Barry notes, "Catherine, nearing forty, is on the cusp of a transition from youth to middle age" (20), and as Stella's description of her indicates, she could be either "a young woman at the peak of her childbearing potential, or a youthful older woman advertising the products of the next stage of life" (20). "In either case," Barry explains, "her existence (and her projected acts of consumption) are unimaginably determined by her biology" (210). For David, Catherine replaces Stella and Dina replaces Catherine in a pattern that is repeated through time. Just as Stella appears to be part of the natural surroundings—emerging from the berry bushes (30)—so too does Catherine: "The blackberry bushes catch [her dress] everywhere, and Catherine has to keep picking herself loose" (31). "Codes of conduct are opposed to unrestraint" (Omhovère,

86), as Catherine metaphorically tries to disentangle herself or "[pick] herself loose" (Munro, "Lichen" 31) from that restraint, from the definitions of femininity that David imposes upon her. Like Stella, Catherine too strives to break free of David's feminine definitions and confinements. Both seek to "burst out of that female envelope" (31) that is the Western patriarchal discourse that limits them.

In Stella's description of Catherine sitting on the lakeshore, she conflates the impending erosion of the landscape with the ageing of women. Catherine sits on "long, low walls of rocks that have been stacked in baskets of wire, stretching out into the water. They are there to protect the beach from erosion" (37). That Munro uses the rare word "groins" to describe these walls suggests her association of them with the groin of a body (Omhovère 93). Stella observes that Catherine's dress is made "of cobwebby cotton...with scores of tiny, irregular pleats that look like wrinkles" (31). That Stella uses the word "wrinkles" to describe the pleats of Catherine's dress suggests a subtle commentary on Catherine's ageing skin. Stella again refers to the image of a cobweb to describe the walls that prevent the erosion of the beach: "those groins are going to have to be rewired entirely"...since they are "worn to cobwebs" (38). Here, Stella once again clearly associates the eroding landscape with Catherine's ageing body.

Barry notes that Stella observes Catherine "with a mixture of sympathy and jealous contempt" (20), and that mixture of emotion is seen in Stella's description of Catherine when she first arrives at Stella's cottage and on the groin of the beach: sympathy and jealousy in the youthful description of her with the "lake breeze blowing her filmy dress" (37), and contempt in the description of her dress as "cobwebby" (30). In her seminal article, "Visual Pleasure and Narrative Cinema," first published in 1975, Laura Mulvey argues that in cinema, females are sexualized under the male gaze, and that male subjects are aligned with viewers in objectifying sexualized female objects. What is particularly interesting, if we read the story with Mulvey's argument in mind, is that Stella does not see Catherine with her own eyes but through the lens of patriarchy, repeating the male gaze on a female body, and she does so by likening Catherine's body to the landscape she inhabits: the pleats of her dress like wrinkles of the skin; the walls that strive to prevent the erosion of the beach like the groins of her body. Mulvey argues that the male spectator engages in a harmful power dynamic that objectifies and denigrates the female subject, and this is precisely what Stella does when she gazes at Catherine, looking at her as though "she could be posed for a picture" (37). It is not only David with whom Stella is momentarily aligned, but also with a long line of male artists of the female nude. The female nude in nature was portrayed by Canadian painters such as Holgate, as Omhovère observes, and in European paintings from the sixteenth to the early twentieth centuries. In "Lichen," Stella occupies a subject position which vacillates between the female object of the male gaze and the masculine subject who is aligned with it.

Barry notes that "most insistently in [Munro's] narratives, women are still unable to connect knowledge with social or emotional power, caught by their circumstances in a trap in which self-reliance and femininity seem to be incompatible qualities, bodies active or beautiful but not both" (22). After Stella gazes at Catherine sitting near the beach, she asks David if there is something wrong with Catherine's eyes: "Her eyesight. It's just that she doesn't seem to be quite focussing, close up. I don't know how to describe it" (37). On the one hand, Stella repeats patriarchal discourses in her description of Catherine and frames her as an object of beauty. As such, she cannot seem to recognize Catherine as an agent of her own action; she is the object of Stella's gaze but cannot return that gaze or "look back." On the other hand, it is Stella, not Catherine, who does not seem to be able to focus. When David puts "a Polaroid snapshot in front of her eyes," showing her a photograph of his new lover, Dina, Stella refuses to recognize it as such, stating that Dina's pubic hair looks like "lichen," like "moss on a rock" (39). Stella's misrecognition of the photograph at once repeats and resists colonial and sexist language. Stella repeats that language when she conflates the landscape ("lichen...moss on a rock") with a woman's body (Dina's pubic hair), defining both as objects to be gazed at and objectified. Yet Stella resists that language when she refuses to recognize what David wants her to see, the photograph of the naked body of his new lover. David's response, "Don't be dumb, don't be cute. You can see her. See her legs" (39), denigrates and infantilizes Stella, as he does to other women. But it also defines her, in Mulvey's terms, as aligned with himself, the man who objectifies and sexualizes women. He invites her to look with him, to be at one with the male spectator and see another woman as the object of his desire. Stella ultimately succumbs to David's way of seeing: "'Well, I can see it now,' she says in a sensible voice" (39).

Stella's action of agreeing with David—not to mention Munro's tongue-in-cheek comment that she does so 'in a sensible voice'—demonstrates Barry's point that Munro's women are often trapped: they are either aligned with patriarchal ideologies, as Stella is here when she agrees with David, or they are degraded objects of those ideologies, as she is when David calls her "dumb" and "cute" (39).

Just as Munro "likens" Catherine to Stella, so too does she "liken" Catherine to Dina. "Catherine sits down suddenly, and spreads out her long legs in a tomboyish way, letting her dress drop between them" (43); in a similar manner, in the photograph of Dina that David shows Stella, Dina is naked and her legs are "spreading into the foreground" (39). One image resembles the other, though Catherine's stance is described as "tomboyish "(43), whereas Dina's is sexual. Therefore, Munro plays with gender fluidity and gendered perceptions. Those who look the same or occupy the same bodily position can be deemed masculine or feminine: an agent of action, as in the tomboyish photograph, or the object of that action, as in the sexualized one. Stella comments that Dina's pubic hair "looks like lichen" (39). Mark Levene observes Munro's play here on the homonyms "lichen" and "liken" (150). Munro once again intertwines language that references human bodies to natural landscapes, and in such a comparison, "women are placed on the natural side of the nature/culture divide" (Omhovère 92). Munro associates Dina—like she does with Stella and Catherine—with nature and the environment. The author juxtaposes youth and ageing bodies, implicating them all in natural cycles of environmental decay and renewal. The images of Catherine and Dina—descriptions or snapshots—are similar but can be read differently according to their framing and the contexts in which they are produced and consumed.

David attempts to dissociate himself from his lovers, positing himself as superior to them and using derogatory language toward them. David takes it as an "affront to the male sex" that Stella "has renounced the work of 'prettiness'" (Barry 2). He describes Stella as ugly when "Stella appears to him...as a 'short, fat...troll'" (Barry 20); he describes Catherine as ignorant and unaware—"she hasn't the remotest idea of what's going on in the world" (38); and he describes Dina as ridiculous and childlike, since on her dresser she has "a silly cigarette holder" and "toys" (44). However, Munro blurs imagery related to David with imagery related to his lovers, undermining his assumed superiority over them. The word

Time and Corporeality   77

"troll" (30), for example, which David uses to describe Stella, is equally applicable to Catherine and Dina. A troll is ugly but also has supernatural qualities, just as Catherine is "inclined to be fey" (38) and Dina is David's "little witch" (40). It is also applicable to David, since he too is a troll: he lures and "trolls" for women. Munro plays on that word, referring to it as both a noun and a verb. David cannot escape his own description of Stella as a troll, and he cannot escape the ageing process according to which he dismisses women: "Did you notice his hair?" Catherine says to Stella, "He's dying it!" (41). Munro collapses David's self into his Other, those women upon whom his identity depends. To put it in Butler's words, "The radical dependency of the masculine subject on the female 'Other' suddenly exposes his autonomy as illusory" (*Gender Trouble* vii). In this way, "Lichen" is a feminist story that contests patriarchal time, that which posits the masculine as superior to the feminine, ageless as opposed to ageing. Munro exposes David's progression through time, from one woman to the next, alongside his false belief that his masculine subject position is invincible.

"Lichen" breaks down the boundaries between human bodies and natural environments and challenges the patriarchal assumption that the masculine subject is unchanging. Munro's valuation of the body aligns with Kristeva's notion of women's time and supports the idea that time is cyclical and at one with natural rhythms. Women's time, like Kristeva's *chora*, pushes back against the teleology that seeks to contain and limit it. Moreover, Munro's association of women's identities and bodies with the natural environments of which they are a part contests not only patriarchal discourse, but also Western and capitalist discourse. Munro demonstrates that the landscapes that capitalistic forces seek to dominate continually slip beyond their grasp. The "clay bluffs" (30) are about to fall and the beach erodes, despite the "wire baskets" that attempt to hold them (37). Both women's bodies and the landscapes themselves refuse to conform to the patriarchal and Western values that attempt to define them. By so doing, Munro works toward the liberation of women and an acknowledgement of environmental movement and change. She articulates a new and evolving female identity that is independent and does not function as the Other against which the masculine subject position defines itself.

Munro challenges the boundaries between human bodies, natural environments, and written bodies of work such as documents and photographs. Munro's play on words demonstrates the material and dynamic dimensions of language. Just as Stella's summer house is "a copy of the old farmhouses nearby" (30), so too is the word "liken" a copy of "lichen"—and yet they are not exactly the same. If we apply Jacques Derrida's notion of *différance* here, we might deduce that "liken," as a homonym of "lichen," invokes a deferral of and differentiation from the materiality and meaning of the word "lichen."[1] There is, then, an association between repetitions and copies in nature and those in language. In her analysis of his writing on biological evolution, Grosz states that Darwin's work demonstrates "the play of repetition and pure difference" in his depiction of the dynamism of species over time: "he is perhaps the most original thinker of the link between difference and becoming, between matter and its elaboration as life, between the past and the future" (*Time Travels* 18). Both Derrida's notion of *différance* and Grosz's analysis of Darwin's work are relevant to Munro's story. Time "progresses" through repetition, difference, and "slight variation" (Grosz, *Time Travels* 18). Though there is "natural deterioration" (31), there is also "sprouting" (31). The summer house is a copy of those that precede it. Words copy yet vary over time to make meaning. David repeats and replaces his lovers with new ones: he seeks those who suit him, but is belied by their ongoing transformation and becoming.

Munro gestures towards the evolution of language of which Grosz speaks. Dina's name, for instance, has earlier origins. That "Her name is Dina. Dina without an 'h'" (39) suggests a deterioration, an erosion like the bluffs on which the house resides—the name drops its final letter. But the name also signals productive play, production, and development. As Micros asserts, "her name can also be read as Diana without the 'a'" (50). In Stella's viewing of the picture of Dina, David "reverses the result of Actaeon's viewing of Diana's nakedness" (50), as Munro rewrites and revises the figure of Diana in Roman mythology. She recasts the female nude as it has been represented in paintings through time, alluding to the sixteenth-century painting by Paolo Caliari of Actaeon watching Diana and her nymphs bathing. Time works on the materiality of environments and language, weathering and decaying until there is a transformation of what once was. That transformation, for Munro, is akin to what Del's mother, Ada, predicts in *Lives of Girls and Women*: "There is a change coming, in the lives of girls and women," she says (165). That change might entail a shift from object to subject, from the one who is sexualized and pacified by others to the one who is an active agent in her own right.

In "Lichen," the summer house and the photograph of Dina, like bodies and environments, are subject to change over time. The summer cottage ages like the people it houses: "[The house is] so nice," Catherine notes, "that lovely weather-beaten colour" (33). And when Stella later stumbles upon the photograph of Dina, like the characters in the story, it too has aged: "Lying in the sun had faded it, of course" (52). The focus on colour and artistic representation is relevant since the photograph alludes to the art historical legacy of female nudes, and since the house envelopes and defines the people who inhabit it. The painting or remaking of the house, which Stella's father suggests they do "every seven years" (33), is like the makeup that Catherine applies to her face: "Lately she has taken to wearing blue eye shadow and black mascara" (31). Though the house paint and Catherine's makeup are not directly equated in the story, Munro makes an implicit comparison between them. The movement toward change and erosion over time for Stella's house and Catherine's body is masked by paint and makeup. In a similar vein, Munro suggests that the phrase "lying in the sun" (52) and its effect of fading and ageing is equally applicable to people, paintings, and photographs. Even the reference to the dying of David's hair (41), Munro implies, is an example of artistic remaking or re-presentation to work against ageing and deterioration. The house is an object and the photograph is both an object and a text. Like people and the landscape, they are material bodies that are created and subject to erosion and weathering. That time-worn weathering, which the story celebrates, works against the constant attempt to recover and repaint; to hide, to dominant, and to restrict.

In her article "On Sitting Down to Read 'Lichen' Once Again," Magdalene Redekop makes the following statement: "'Lichen' is about the mystery of a process that literary critics describe with words such as representation, mimesis, imitation, and simulacrum—a version of an old Latin word meaning 'likeness'" (291). Munro invokes this process through documents—memoirs and histories—as she blurs the boundaries between those documents and what they represent. Stella, for example, writes her "memoirs" and a history of the lighthouse (33). Similar to the paint, the makeup, and the hair dye, these texts both hide the body that they reference and recreate it. Munro plays with the slippage between the signifiers—memoirs and histories—and their signifieds, the life that these documents describe. Stella jokes that she will stop writing her memoirs "for a cash payment" (33), implying that they contain secrets about David, which she exposes and creates through literary art. The lighthouse about which she writes a history is only visible from a corner of the window (33), though she will expose it and make it new with her writing. Both of her literary projects are historical: they preserve the past, and yet they are also new artistic creations in and of themselves. Moreover, in her invocation of the lighthouse, Munro alludes to Virginia Woolf's *To the Lighthouse*. Both Munro's story and Woolf's novel entertain temporal themes and artistic motifs. Thus, Munro reaches back to her literary ancestors to invoke the symbol of the lighthouse and the knowledge or "light" that it represents.

Besides memoirs and histories, Munro mentions a religious document that goes back to 800 AD, the Book of Kells. Known as an "illuminated manuscript," which associates it with other light imagery in the story such as the lighthouse, the book is an illustrated bible that was likely produced in a monastery in Ireland or Scotland. It is held at Trinity College Library, Dublin. Catherine finds "the Book of Kells on her trip to Ireland" (39). This discovery implies that she, much like Stella in her writing of her memoirs and the lighthouse history, will read about and build upon the past to enact her own creative art. Such a discovery, then, is undoubtedly an optimistic gesture toward the future, one in which Catherine might separate from David and remake her own self and identity. The "light" of the lighthouse and the illuminated manuscript of the Book of Kells represent glimpses of knowledge or spiritual awakening. It is as though the women in this story are on the edge of discovery, that the "change for women" (165) that Ada predicts is coming. Such discoveries are both outside these women and inside of them, as is implied by Stella's oscillation between her memoirs and the history of the lighthouse. They are both individual and collective discoveries: individual because it is Stella and Catherine who create and discover them, and collective because both the lighthouse and the Book of Kells have a long history that exceeds them. Lichen itself is an organism that lives in a symbiotic relationship with others, a composite of fungus and algae: two organisms functioning as a single, stable unit. Munro implies that artists also live in such a relationship with their predecessors, continually renewing and remaking them.

Time and Corporeality 81

Thus, in a postmodern moment of self-reflexivity, "Lichen" comments on the evolution of artistic discovery and creation. Munro invokes narrative time: she shows that language is in a complicated relationship with that which it represents. She implies that stories themselves go back through time, can be discovered anew, and are dynamic and ever-changing.

Stella's act of writing and Catherine's discovery of the Book of Kells suggest insight and light, unearthing that which is hidden. Similarly, tropes of blindness and sight in the story further signify insight and knowledge. Hercules, Stella's cat, has one "grayed-over eye" (30); Stella's father's blindness is "almost total now" (48); and Stella thinks that there is something "the matter" with Catherine's eyes (37). Such references to blindness or near blindness emphasize bodily deterioration and highlight what goes unseen. In this story, Munro's women seem to be on the verge of change: from being the object of the gaze to the gazer herself, from passive object to active agent. Thus blindness is juxtaposed with—and perhaps even transforms into—insight: Catherine discovers the Book of Kells; Stella unearths the history of the lighthouse; the house itself is "full of light (34); and Stella's "words...come true" (52).

At the end of the story, "a week or so" (52) after David and Catherine have left Stella's beach house and gone home, Stella rediscovers the photograph of Dina, which David has left at her house. Stella's description of the photograph highlights decay and transformation, yet it also hints at the materiality of texts and the power of analysis and interpretation. Time itself has altered the photograph. Faded and aged, it is itself a material body subject to decay, though like the house that is "full of light" and the "lighthouse," it has itself lightened; not only decayed but renewed. The author demonstrates its materiality and its status as a signifier that represents a signified, a sign that can make meaning. Although it once depicted a woman's body, it now means something else: "The outline of the breast has disappeared. You would never know that the legs were legs" (52). With the use of the word "pelt" (52) to describe Dina's pubic hair—which Stella compares "lichen" (52)—Munro signals to the exterior, the covering of the body. An animal's skin, the home's paint, David's hair dye, and Catherine's makeup all cover and produce the person with whom that covering is in a symbiotic relationship. Likewise, the text of the photograph itself, like language, signals meaning, yet that meaning shifts and changes over time. A "pelt" (52) is a skin, but as a verb rather than a noun, it also means to hit or to hurt, as David, at least emotionally, might have done to Stella, or as humans in general do to one another. On Mulvey's terms, the male gaze on a female sexualized subject is a kind of violence, and that violence is encapsulated in Munro's use of the word "pelt."[2] Therefore, Munro plays on this word as a noun and verb in the same way that she does with "lichen/liken" and "troll." As Mary Conde explains, "a major function of photographs in Munro's stories is to reveal an unsuspected truth, not in a straightforward way" (106). In this instance, the photograph embodies endlessly proliferating and slippery significations. Munro's story melds people with nature, the mind with the body, and the text with its referent. In so doing, the author contemplates the complexities of identity, time, and meaning.

"White Dump"

Howells argues that in *The Progress of Love*, the "emergence of story via digressions" is prominent. In these stories, she asserts, possible meanings "are unsettled at every stage in the process of its telling, so that every story in this collection is a series of disarrangements opening up spaces for new meanings" (*Alice Munro* 85). Howells posits that in the stories of *The Progress of Love*, "instability and irresolution characterize [Munro's] narratives of human behaviour alone and in relationships" (86). While Howells situates this instability in terms of place, explaining that stories such as "White Dump" are about "houses and what they enclose and the connections made there through narrative" (86), she also notes that the stories emphasize the shifting of time: they "make connections between experiences in the present and in the past...[and] depend on shifts from one point of time to another, from one point of view to another, covering and recovering the same ground from different angles" (87). "The endings of these stories," Howells asserts, "are not closures—but they give significance to what has gone before, allowing us to see what is outside—and inside—the story in a new way" (89–90). "White Dump" is an ending in and of itself, since it is the last story in Munro's collection. It is an ending worth considering, since, as Karen Houle explains, Munro leaves us with a hopeful conclusion that highlights the character Sophie as "a person living in her own skin...a whole person who happens to be a female person" (228). Furthermore, Thacker suggests that "White Dump" "is an equally powerful rendering [as 'The Progress of Love'] that includes autobiographical touches without explicit personal analogue" ("The Way the Skin" 26). "At one point in the making of *The Progress of Love*," Thacker notes, Munro "suggested 'White Dump' as the book's title" (26), emphasizing the importance of the piece to the collection.

The story begins with Denise's visit to her father Laurence and his current wife Magda's summer home, near Ottawa, Ontario. Denise has driven up from Toronto to see them, as she does a couple of times each summer. Laurence tells Magda that Denise took him up in a plane for his fortieth birthday, and then the story moves into Denise's memory of that day. It was the summer of 1969, the day of the moon shot. This was the day that Neil Armstrong—who was the first person to ever do so—stepped onto the moon. We find out that the day of the birthday plane ride is also the day that Isabel—who was Laurence's wife and is Denise's mother—first meets the pilot of the plane, with whom she later has an affair. We move from Denise's memory of that day to Isabel's, and finally to Sophie's (Denise's paternal grandmother). The story is told through third-person limited-omniscient narration, as it moves into these three different perspectives of the summer of 1969. Like "Lichen," the story takes place on a birthday: "Lichen" on Stella's father's ninety-third birthday, and "White Dump" on Denise's father's fortieth birthday. "White Dump," then, is also about ageing and change through time, layering the memories of three generations of women. Each of the women's perspectives add further memories and details to the tale.

Space and time are interconnected in "White Dump," as they are in "Lichen" and throughout *The Progress of Love*. The word "progress" in the title of the collection is related to time and can be read ironically. Throughout her many works, Munro mocks the idea of linear progression through time as she depicts the problems and complexities of love, both romantic and familial. In "White Dump," Munro continues her implicit critique of progress and emphasizes landscape, bodies, and corporeality. Much of the story is about the occupation of space and how people move through it in time, as Howells suggests. The story asks the following questions: To what extent do we stay in our place, that is, the place that society has deemed right for us? What happens when we move beyond our borders and boundaries, and when we venture outside of our homes? Does such movement encroach upon the spaces and identities of others, or does it create a productive upheaval and challenge societal assumptions and norms? Highlighting perspectives from three generations, "White Dump" addresses time and space while rejecting any singular time or authoritative narrative voice. The story considers the daughter, mother, and grandmother "as a way of examining the 'progress of love' through generations" (Thacker, "The Way the Skin" 24). New explains that land "[functions] not just as the revelation of the status quo, but also as the *space* or *place* or *site* of challenge to the accustomed borders of power" (7, emphasis in original). Such is the case in "White Dump," where both space and time have ambiguous and multifarious significations. Munro's writing, as Maria Löschnigg states, "is characterized...by multiplicity, polyphony, digression, and indeterminacy" (60).

That indeterminacy, including the shifting in time back and forth between the present and the past, is reflected in Munro's process of writing the story of "White Dump." It was first published by *The New Yorker* in 1986. *The New Yorker* had previously published "Miles City, Montana," and "The Progress of Love" (Thacker, *Alice Munro* 411), and the magazine editors and Munro's agent had raved about both. After these two stories were published, expectations for Munro's writing were high; however, when Munro submitted "four more stories and two revisions" (411), *The New Yorker* bought only one: "White Dump." *The New Yorker* published "five of eleven stories in *Progress* (411). The revisions Munro made to the story before its publication reflect the very notion of space and time shifts that she thematizes in the story itself. There are "multiple drafts and fragments" of this story in Munro's archival papers at the University of Calgary, whereby "the rearrangements and gradual emergence of the final version may be plainly seen" (Howells, *Alice Munro* 99).

There are various versions of Isabel's romantic affair with the pilot in the drafts of the story, and these versions play with the idea of determinism (Howells, *Alice Munro* 100)—as if Isabel's affair with the pilot is inevitable from the moment she considers it. Howells describes the evolution of the author's drafts as follows: "The drafts show Munro experimenting with different kinds of significance that events may assume when they are put together in different orders, as if events in themselves have undecidable meanings and can only be taken account of being fitted into a narrative framework constructed by the storytellers (who include, of course, Munro herself)" (100).

Time and Corporeality   85

That Munro continually revised the versions of Isabel's affair with the pilot suggests the centrality and importance of that scene to the story; it is its central moment. Isabel's affair and her subsequent divorce from Laurence result in the unravelling of the family itself. As Thacker puts it, Isabel's decision to act on her attraction to the pilot "has cataclysmic consequences for the family, subsequently sundered because of her act" ("The Way the Skin" 27). But it is important to note that in the final version of the story, the author emphasizes not the affair itself but the moment before it, when Isabel feels sexual attraction to the pilot. It is a moment of possibility, which is likened to the "glint" from the White Dump and the St. Elmo's fire that the pilot describes. Munro pieces together this so-called beginning with subsequent moments to make sense of them, to make them significant, and to create narrative flow. In this way, she shows that meaning is made by discovering and/or creating narrative. The act of stringing events together in sequence—of moving them through time—is necessary to comprehend and articulate their meaning.

Houle argues that the four women featured in this story—Magda, Denise, Isabel, and Sophie—each exemplify "possible trajectories of women in rural Ontario in the late twentieth century" (221). In other words, the story is an examination of the roles of women in a settler and patriarchal society, each of them "progressing" through society in a different way. Magda uses her style and good looks to attain her rich husband, Laurence (221), while Denise tries to distance herself from her capitalistic father by fighting for social justice. However, as Houle points out, by positioning Denise as the white daughter of a rich businessman, Munro backlights "the grotesque complicity between patriarchal capitalism and white feminist social justice, in Ontario, in the 80s" (224). Isabel aims to "progress" from a working-class background to a business class status by marrying Laurence; however, Denise likely senses "the precariousness of that [marital] bond," between her parents, and she knows "the special precariousness of the female body" (225). Munro highlights the trajectories of these women characters as she emphasizes both their desire to move forward and the futility or failure of that desire—particularly as they move through time, their bodies ageing "into something quite spectacularly human though not at all 'sexy'" (225).

86   ALICE MUNRO AND THE ART OF TIME

The character of Sophie swims naked in the lake at her home: "she had swum naked in the lake since she was a child and all this shore belonged to her father, down as far as Bryce's farm" (278). But when her terrycloth bathrobe is taken by someone on the beach, she has to come up to the house naked, and her family is there. Her ageing human body, as Munro describes it, is represented and celebrated in the image of Sophie naked "in full view of the family on the morning of Laurence's birthday" (Houle 225). It is an image of hope that offers the possibility of women's roles and identities outside of the boundaries that patriarchy ascribes them. That Sophie stands naked in full view seems inappropriate within the confines of a patriarchal society: "'Christ, Mother!' said Laurence" (290). That she has been "dispossessed of [her] bathrobe" (290) suggests that she sheds the expectations and roles of the patriarchy, and stands now, as she is, as her own person.

The title of the story refers to the silica quarry Denise and her father see during their plane ride. It also refers to the "quantities of vanilla icing" and candy that the "biscuit factory" regularly discarded when Isabel was a child (295). Discussion of the silica quarry reminds Isabel of the factory. "You know we used to have the White Dump," she explains, "at the school I went to—it was behind a biscuit factory, the playground backed on to the factory property" (295). On the one hand, the word "dump" suggests garbage, that which is removed from one's space or home because it is no longer needed. It also has implications for romantic love: one lover can be "dumped" for another. In this story, however, images associated with the word suggest both illusion, that which is on the surface rather than in the depths, and treasure, that which is valuable and worthy. For example, whereas the candy is discarded as trash by the factory, it is considered "the most wonderful and promising thing you could ever see" (296) by Isabel and the other schoolchildren. Isabel emphasizes the White Dump's promise rather than that promise's fulfillment. When Peter, Denise's brother, asks if they ate it, Isabel replies, "It wasn't that...It was something about the White Dump—that there was so much and it was so white and shiny" (296). Such "wonder" and "promise" are echoed in Isabel's description of her glance at the pilot before she has an affair with him: "the promise [of them meeting again] hit her like lightning" (295). As Thacker explains, Munro "[likens] the sweetness Isabel sees in the 'White Dump' to that her character feels in her attraction to the pilot" ("The Way the Skin" 27). Sophie is "dumped" by Laurence's father, who goes back to his family, his wife and children, which he believes is his rightful place. In response to Sophie's childhood story about how she moved some frogs who later went back to their home, he says, "Ah Sophie, you see?" (285), implying that he, too, must return. It is noteworthy here that Munro writes Sophie's childhood play metaphorically; the author draws attention to metaphorical language and invites the reader to read it in this way too. Isabel too is "dumped" by the pilot, since, according to him, she has replaced someone and is therefore replaceable by another: "she was to find out that he had been successful [with women] some times before, in very similar circumstances" (298). The "promise[s]" of both the sight of the candy and of the pilot are not fulfilled. The "glint" (286) of light from the candy and in the pilot's eyes offer new possibilities but are also only superficial, only illusions.

Denise and her mother first meet the "catering woman" (273) upon picking up a birthday cake for Laurence. Denise sees the pilot there who will take them up in the plane. Soon we find out that he is the woman's husband. Denise suddenly says, "Mom, that's the pilot!" and Isabel replies, "Damn it, Denise, don't scare me like that" (273). This moment is significant because it instigates Isabel's affair with the pilot, and Munro implies that Denise feels guilt for her parents' subsequent separation, since she arranged the plane ride (268). Isabel asks the caterer if the two young boys there are hers. "Are you kidding?" the caterer responds, "Those are my daughter's she dumped on me" (273). Munro here mobilizes the word "dump" from the title of the story to mean something unwanted, what is left behind or to someone else, and yet, with this reference, she also implies that the children represent potential, like the "white dump" of candy that is both waste and hope for the future. Houle notes that Isabel is likened to the caterer (226), since their husbands, Laurence and the pilot respectively, leave them. However, Isabel, Houle suggests, differs from the caterer too: "Both are hot, but Isabel is also very smart, and that combo initially launched her like a rocket out of the gravitational pull of the working class into the sort of life with inherited cottages at the lake" (226).

With the reference to Laurence and Denise's sighting of the silica quarry, which sparks Isabel's memory of the "White Dump" of candy, Munro suggests the notion of creation and becoming. Words the characters use to signify the silica quarry are not fixed but slip from one to the next. Laurence calls it a "silica quarry" and a "snowfield"; Sophie calls it "white marble"; and Isabel relates it to the "White Dump" of candy. Responding to Darwin's work on evolution, Grosz says that his "concept of life" is one of "dynamic, collective change" (*Time Travels* 36). Referencing Gilles Deleuze, she explains that "the creation of a new concept can be marked by a proper name, which serves to locate its 'origins' but does not limit its future use or value: a concept 'begins,' and may therefore be attributed a proper name...but its life consists in the uses to which it is put, the different concepts that develop out of or as it" (36). The concept of the "White Dump" evolves and changes as its meaning slips from the grasp of its creators and its signifiers. "White Dump" comes to life as an idea through collective collaboration and creation, since there are not one but three characters—Laurence, Sophie, and Isabel—who attempt to define it. It is "dynamized, put into interaction, made to move and interact with the forces that act and move it" (37).

Silica, or silicon dioxide, is a compound "of the two most abundant elements in Earth's crust. The mass of Earth's crust is 59 percent silica, the main constituent of more than 95 percent of...known rocks" (*Encyclopedia Britannica* "Silica"). Silica is fundamental to our place on Earth. The author's mention of silica is not the only reference to geology in this story. The other is a "glint lake," which the family sees from their plane ride along Rideau Lakes, which "straddles the geologic transition from the St. Lawrence Lowlands to the Canadian Shield" (Thacker, "The Way the Skin" 27). These geological references, which are associated with the earth, contrast with references to air and space. For example, there is the "moon shot" (268) that Laurence, Isabel, and Sophie watch on their television in July 1969, and the plane ride during which Sophie experiences a new and different perspective of her environment: both are experiences of being above or outside of Earth. Silica is, on the one hand, that which has "spoiled the park" (295), and on the other, essential to life. Just as Munro describes "lichen" as an organism that is dependent upon the rocks on which it grows, here she introduces silica as a compound that her characters (and people in general) need, since it is such a significant part of the earth. Munro metonymically links the concept of the "White Dump"—including the silica, which is to be both trashed and treasured—to images of sunlight, lightning, and whiteness throughout the story: the "sunlight" that Sophie "[swims] toward [at] the middle of the lake" (280); "the ball of lightning" that the Bryce children see "danc[ing] across the bedroom floor" (283); and the absence of colour in the house noted at the beginning of the story—"I don't really remember any colour in this house at all" (265).

The metonymic associations to which I've already referred—the white dump, the glint in the pilot's eye, the lightning strike at the Bryces'—apply here too. In this instance, Denise startles Isabel, just as the lightning strike that the pilot remembers hitting his plane gives him "a start" (277), and just as the plane "starts" its engine and shifts Isabel's and Denise's lives. Similarly, the catering woman says, "I was an early starter" (272), referring to her grandchildren and Isabel's assumption that they were her children. Munro plays with meanings of the word "start" and draws attention to the social expectation that motherhood begins at a particular age, at a certain moment in time. She invokes and critiques the notion of time socialization and expectations of motherhood and grandmotherhood relative to time.

That the concept of the "White Dump" is intertwined with the self is evident in the instance in which Denise sees herself in the glass, a "glint" (286) or "flash" (280) of her reflection: "the extension is all *glass*— walls and slanting roof, all *glass*. In the darkening *glass*, she sees herself" (278, emphasis added). It is also evident in the epiphany that Sophie experiences during the plane ride. She realizes her "exquisite smallness" (285), her bodily interconnectedness with the "glittering veins of ripples on the dark water" (285). The water flows in the "ripples" like blood through her own "veins" (285) and those of other people. The environment and the people who inhabit it are one. The repetition of the word "glass" in Denise's momentary sighting of herself, her own reflection, emphasizes its illusory nature. As in Lacan's mirror stage, the perceived wholeness of oneself in the mirror is an imaginary projection of a complete self. By contrast, the sense of "shrinking" (285) that Sophie feels gestures towards that which is true and genuine: interconnectedness rather than separation between oneself, others, and the environment. As Grosz explains, "If bodies are to be reconceived, not only must their *matter* and *form* be rethought, but so too must their environment and *spatio-temporal location*" (*Space* 84, emphasis in original). Here, Sophie's self is humbly rethought as small, "shrinking," and intertwined with her spatial surroundings of which she is a part.

Denise locates the "start" of the affair between her mother and the pilot at the moment she sees him at the caterer's house; by contrast, Isabel locates it later, moments after the plane ride ends and the pilot's "bold eyes [meet] hers" (296). In her statement that Isabel "was kindled" (277) for her affair with the pilot, Munro furthers the imagery associated with lightning, sunlight, sparks, and glints, and she suggests another "start"—the spark that is Isabel's affair with the pilot. Later, when Isabel discusses the affair with Denise, who is now grown up, she says that the "best part" of an affair is "right at the beginning," and then corrects herself—"perhaps even before the beginning...when it flashes on you what's possible" (297). Explaining the concept of "temporal framing," Huebener notes that "the frame of time is composed of conceptual borders that define the moments when the counting of time is initiated or terminated" (*Timing* 19). Munro plays with such "temporal framing," pushing the frame's boundaries and demonstrating that beginnings are not fixed but variable and dependent on subject position. What is thought to be the beginning is not quite right: it is "even before" (297). One "start" is deferred and displaced with another—not the moment Isabel first sees the pilot, but rather the one in which his eyes meet hers (296). In this way, Munro continually presents her readers with false beginnings. She challenges normative time by pushing the boundaries of temporal frameworks and depicting dislocations in both space and time.

Such dislocation occurs again when the pilot notes a time when his plane was hit by a lightning bolt: "Once, I looked out and I saw blue rings of fire around the propellers," the pilot said. "Round the propellers and the wing tips. Then I saw the same thing around the nose. I put my hand out to touch the glass—this here, the plexiglass—and just as I got within touching distance, flames came shooting out of my fingers. I don't know if I touched the glass or not. I didn't feel anything. Little blue flames. One time in a thunderstorm. That's what they call St. Elmo's fire" (277). Here, the pilot touches the plexiglass at the moment of St. Elmo's fire in the same way that Denise sees herself in the glass at her father's home. Both instances imply moments of sudden self-recognition: both the "start" that it gave the pilot (277) and the recognition of one's reflection in a mirror; wholeness and illusion. Isabel suggests that her attraction to the pilot "hit her like lightning," then corrects herself, "split her like lightning," and then corrects herself yet again, "but it isn't like lightning, it isn't a blow from the outside. We only pretend that it is" (295). These assertions demonstrate both illusion—that which is on the surface—and the true or the genuine—that which is within the self rather than outside of it. Isabel's use of the word "split" suggests a fragmentation, a tearing apart of the self, a movement back in time (to reference Lacan's mirror stage trajectory) to when one was fragmentary, not whole.

Furthermore, this imagery recalls Sophie's experience of witnessing her robe being taken and torn in two, another splitting of the self. While Sophie swims naked in the lake, two young men and a woman come down to the beach. One of the young men puts on Sophie's robe and does "a little shimmy," and Sophie notes that he "[imitates] a woman" (281). Here, Munro not only breaks the barriers of temporal frameworks and assumptions of time, but she also challenges gender roles. She shows how, in this case, the young man's playacting (281) is a performance of gender identity. Like Bobby Sheriff performing in a feminine way when he serves Del cake at the end of *Lives of Girls and Women*, here too, Munro invokes gender play and reversal.

Interestingly, this gender performance is also an infringement upon Sophie, an intrusion into her space. On the one hand, the space that the "marauders" (281) presently inhabit, the beach by the lake where Sophie swims, is geographical: the "entire east side of the lake" had once belonged to Sophie's family, the Vogelsangs (281). On the other hand, the young men and woman intrude upon Sophie's private space, since she swims in the nude. The young man clothes himself in her robe and rips it or "splits" (295) it in two, which suggests an intrusion and a breaking down of identity. That Sophie subsequently shows up at the cottage naked suggests that she is born anew, that she takes on an alternate, perhaps truer self. In another part of the story, Denise and Peter, when they are children, intrude upon their parents, who have just had sex, when they come into their bedroom to present Laurence with his birthday present (287). Like the "playactors" or "marauders" (281) who intrude upon Sophie at the lake, this is an invasion of domestic space and personal intimacy. In both cases, the encounter with or infringement upon another's space is both geographical and corporeal.

Sophie moves some frogs when she is a child, only to have them return to their original home (284), and Laurence's father and Isabel encroach upon others' spaces and homes when they have extramarital love affairs. In various ways in "White Dump," Munro entertains the idea of "moving into illicit territory (which would turn out to be shockingly like and unlike home)" (297). The author contemplates how invaders can claim foreign or domestic space as their own. Just as she questions and challenges Uncle Benny's ownership of the riverbank that he claims at the beginning of *Lives of Girls and Women*, she challenges the Vogelsangs' entitlement and history of land ownership near Aubreyville. To put it in Heble's words, this story "is engaged in a series of what might loosely be called colonizing (and decolonizing) moments" (159). Viewed another way, however, Munro presents the movement away from one's own space or domain not only as colonialist but also as productive and creative. Such movement can break traditional or historical gender roles. It can challenge spatial and temporal norms and produce new and dynamic subjectivities.

One of the ways in which Munro challenges such norms and gestures towards new subjectivities is with her references to history and the temporal setting of the story. The story moves back and forth between the present and the past. The past is marked by particular events: the moon shot (July 20, 1969), Bastille Day (July 14, 1789), and Laurence's fortieth birthday (July 18, 1969). The moon shot could be considered the epitome of moving outside of one's own space or home: for the first time, humans stepped onto the moon, crossing new frontiers and beyond planet Earth itself. Bastille Day could also be considered as such. Those who stormed the prison in France moved outside the territory deemed their place. They challenged the authority of King Louis XVI and sparked or "started" the French Revolution. Both historical instances signify encroachments on space and new beginnings in time: paradoxically, they both adhere to and upheave colonial and patriarchal orders. Laurence's birthday is itself a reference to time, age, and personal and corporeal history. That the story itself moves back and forth in time between the present and the past and shifts in narrative perspective between three different characters demonstrates how its form mirrors its thematic content.

Sophie's career as a linguist who can read Old Norse is particularly interesting. With the moon shot, Munro references recent history, but with Bastille Day and Old Norse, she gestures much further back in time. Old Norse was spoken from about 1150 to 1350 (*Encyclopedia*

Britannica, "Old Norse"). In a sense, Sophie is the matriarch of the historical Vogelsang family in "White Dump," yet we might also view her as a literary matriarch, one whose language reaches way back into history. Moreover, Laurence states that Sophie can read Old Norse, and also that "she *is* sort of an Old Norse" (270, emphasis in original). Jarrett argues that Sophie's naked white body, when she comes up from the lake, could be associated with the notion of the "white dump" (85). If this is the case, then her naked body is a text like the white pages of the story we read. Indeed, Isabel, from whose perspective this part of the story is told, reads and interprets her body: "the smoothness of the skin...the smallness of the breasts" (289). Likewise, the readers of "White Dump" both read and interpret the story itself. As in "Lichen," Munro foregrounds corporeality as central to self and depicts the body as a text that can be performed and written.

"Playactors" or "marauders" (281) encroach upon the space of others in "White Dump," and Sophie's naked appearance at Laurence's birthday party is no exception: she is unclothed and out of place. Likewise, the literary past erupts into the story's present, into Munro's narrative. The story ends with two lines in Old Norse. As Héliane Ventura explains, these lines are from "Lay of Atli," "part of the heroic poems of the *Codex Regius* dating back to the thirteenth century" ("The Female Bard" 168). "With this allusion," Ventura asserts, "Munro establishes intertextual links with Scandinavian oral poetry as well as the pagan antiquity of Germanic Europe, as she recasts her contemporary Canadian story against the life stories of Brynhildr, Gudrun, and Sigurdt in 'Lay of Atli'" (168). Munro "entrusts the reader with the responsibility of transferring meaning from one context to another and linking the stories of today with the stories of the past" (169). When read in relation to "Lichen" and its references to the Book of Kells, the inclusion of Old Norse in "White Dump" is even more interesting. The Book of Kells is thought to have been produced by monks of St. Columba's order of Iona, Scotland, though the exact origins of its production are disputed. It was likely moved from Iona to Kells, Ireland, to try protect it from Viking raids in the ninth century (Mark). It is significant that the language Sophie has mastered in "White Dump" is Old Norse—the Vikings' language. That Sophie is the only one in her family who knows the language suggests that she has a special knowledge—a truth—that others do not. That truth is much like the treasure that is the Book of Kells that Catherine finds in "Lichen." It is a spark that has the possibility to provide for the one who found it; it is a muse that instigates and helps one create and enact anew.

In addition to including such references to the ancient language of Old Norse, Munro also includes new creations of literature in her story. When Denise and Peter come into Laurence and Isabel's room on Laurence's birthday, they recite and perform a birthday poem that they wrote, and it becomes part of the text of "White Dump." Munro highlights the past erupting into the present and the creation of new and innovative literature. Such literature is notably dependent upon the language and literary conventions of the past: Denise and Peter's language employs historical words, such as "hail" (288). The author leaves open the extent to which such creations are "charades" (298)—a game the characters play at the end of the story—and the extent to which they are genuine and truthful. She forecloses further reading or interpretation with a reference to deferred time: "(It's too late to talk of this now: it has been decided)" (299). This final statement is paradoxically open ended, since she never locates or interprets the Old Norse for the reader. It is, Munro suggests, "too late" (299) for more.

In "Lichen" and "White Dump," Munro strategically brings together people and their environments, demonstrating that each is a part of the other. For instance, in "Lichen," eroding bluffs near Stella's cottage mirror both the characters' own bodily deterioration and that of representations and things, such as the fading photograph of Dina. In "White Dump," the author contests the Vogelsangs' claim to territorial space, invoking and yet disputing the notion that the family's occupation of the land was its so-called beginning. She contests the very idea of beginnings or "start[s]," showing that they are not fixed but subject to re-evaluation and revision (277). To this effect, Munro implies that what appears to be true is not always so, and she mobilizes imagery related to surfaces and depths, the illusory and the genuine. To a significant extent, as in her earlier works, she writes self-reflexively. For Munro, bodies, so-called natural environments, and texts themselves are a part of the past yet also make up the very fabric of the present. Her implicit challenge to the self as masculine, unified, and singular adheres to French feminist theories delineated by Julia Kristeva, Hélène Cixous, and Luce Irigaray; she returns to and revalues what is fragmentary and indeterminate. Stacy Alaimo and Susan Hekman's 2008 anthology,

Material Feminisms, aims to bring "the materiality of the human body and the natural world...into the forefront of feminist theory and practice" (1)—an aim that we might easily attribute to Munro's writing in *The Progress of Love*. The two stories, like the collection overall, demonstrate the multifaceted nature of Munro's work. The collection critiques the assumption that time progresses in an ever-bettering way; instead, Munro suggests, people, environments, and things undergo a continual process of fixing, correcting, and revising. Such repetition with slight variation through time enables imperfect yet productive creation and renewal.

4

Time and Narrative Framing

"Friend of My Youth" and "Meneseteung" in *Friend of My Youth*

IN *FRIEND OF MY YOUTH*, published in 1990, Munro continues some of the themes she develops in *The Progress of Love* such as corporeality, the coming together of bodies and their environments, and the complexities of passing time. Yet her work becomes, arguably, more experimental, fragmentary, and postmodern. One aspect of *Friend of My Youth* that distinguishes it from the author's previous work is its distinct layers of narrative framing. Munro always engages in careful and complex narrative perspectives, but in *Friend*, she escalates the complexities of narration, telling the story from various points in time and in layers, one story overlapping with another in time. In addition, she addresses spatiality and temporality together, demonstrating how each is a part of the other, and how both are intertwined with bodies that punctuate her stories and the socio-political landscape they inhabit. In this chapter, I discuss two stories in the collection that most explicitly demonstrate space and time: the title story, "Friend of My Youth," and a story that is frequently studied and anthologized, "Meneseteung." In "Friend of My Youth," Munro creates a narrator who ostensibly tries to understand her mother's friend Flora's story, but more truthfully, desires to know both her mother and herself. In "Meneseteung," Munro takes as her subject a fictional Victorian poet of Huron County, Ontario. The narrator, a researcher and archivist, discovers and creates her subject as she writes her anew, exploring the poet's literature, newspaper articles about her, and the environment itself. These stories are epistemological in that they probe what it is we can know, and what is left buried and

97

undiscovered. They involve a contemplation of time in relation to subjectivities, corporeality, and the environment.

After the publication of *Friend of My Youth*, Munro continued to receive recognition for her work not only in Canada, but also internationally. By the time *Friend of My Youth* "was published in spring 1990, eight of its ten stories [had] already been published in *The New Yorker*" (Thacker, *Alice Munro* 370). Thacker outlines how important *The New Yorker* was to Munro's career, noting that 1985 was the last year that Munro's stories went to a magazine other than *The New Yorker*. The two stories from the collection that were not published in that magazine were published in *The Atlantic Monthly* (370). Daniel Menaker,[1] who was the fiction editor at *The New Yorker*, described *Friend of My Youth* as "a very painful and disciplined examination of the self," and Thacker notes that this comment "captures just what Munro was still undertaking in that collection" (433). Thacker highlights the two stories that I discuss in this chapter, the title story and "Meneseteung," as those which "have drawn the greatest attention" and "for good reason" (433). These stories are metafiction because they emphasize storytelling and narrative time. As Philip Coleman explains, "Friend of My Youth," "perfectly placed as the opening story of the collection, is important, not just because it gives the collection its title, but also because it introduces some of the key themes explored in more detail throughout the other nine stories—especially the theme of the power of stories and storying in human relationships and the pursuit of self-knowledge through memory and recollection" (165).

Munro dedicates the collection to the memory of her mother, and indeed, versions of Munro's mother figure in both "Friend of My Youth" and "Meneseteung." As Thacker explains, Munro's memories of her mother influenced her work in this collection:

> Munro moves well beyond the transcription of facts recalled. The story is based on her mother, and presumably on her own dreams, yet there is much more there besides. Munro had Chamney relatives who divided their house in ways similar to Flora and to Robert and Ellie, but the information about the Cameronians she got from a friend, who had known some in this section of the Ottawa valley. Using this information, grafting it on to her own mother's story to

make "Friend of My Youth," the logic is the story's own. (*Alice Munro*, 434)

Likewise, Munro drew upon autobiographical details in her writing of "Meneseteung." While the character of Almeda Roth is "Munro's own creation" (434), she relied upon "historical prototypes for nineteenth-century small-town southwestern Ontario poets," such as those of Clara Mountcastle and Eloise A. Skimings. Munro "creates a first-person narrator analogous to herself as the author of Roth's story" (434). The self-reflexive, metanarrative ending spoken by the first-person narrator was cut from the publication of "Meneseteung" in *The New Yorker* in 1988, but then re-incorporated into the collection of stories in 1990. "I may have got it wrong," the narrator says of her story of Almeda Roth. "I don't know if she ever took laudanum. Many ladies did. I don't know if she ever made grape jelly" (73). That Munro re-incorporated those lines for the collection of stories shows that she placed importance on the narrative framing of her story and on the narrator's own voice, which can be likened to her own. The autobiographical details that Munro weaves into her stories and the overlay of Munro's own narrative voice as the researcher of the poet are part of the brilliance that she brings to these stories. The stories move through time—both the past and the present—and examine the histories of Munro's home and her own self. The narrator's statement near the end of the story highlights the precariousness of the details themselves, indicating the slipperiness between truth and fiction. This blurring of boundaries between the two is evident here and throughout Munro's work.

"Friend of My Youth"

"Friend of My Youth" is a contemplation of how the past occupies the present, a consideration of how we understand and create histories through memories, bits of information, and fragments of written and oral narratives. To construct the past, as Gayle Elliott explains, "pieces of missing story...must be called upon from a multiplicity of sources... hints, confessions, gossip, news accounts, primary and secondary letters, photographs" (80). Munro considers how the past resides within the present by writing a story within a story. On the one hand, "Friend of My Youth" is about the narrator's mother's friend, Flora, and her suitor, Robert, who marries Flora's sister, Ellie, and then Ellie's nurse, Audrey. On the other hand, the story is about the unnamed narrator and her mother: the narrator's mother tells her about Flora in an outer story that frames the inner one. These two narratives conflate at the end when the narrator confuses her thoughts about Flora with those about her mother: "of course it's my mother I'm thinking of" (26). Through this narrative structure, the narrator—and ultimately Munro herself—repeatedly and seemingly unsuccessfully attempt to recover the so-called truth of the past. Like the narrator's dream that opens the story, stories that already happened constantly change, intersect with other stories of the past, and slip beyond the narrator's—and the reader's—grasp. As David Crouse puts it, Munro "manipulate[s] time in a variety of ways, extending or expanding a series of events so that any one moment becomes less and less definitive" (52).

The story begins and ends with the narrator's dream about her mother. In the first sentence of the story, she locates her dream firmly in the past: "I *used* to dream about my mother" (3, emphasis added). Though over, the dream is not static but recurring and dynamic: "*Sometimes* I would find myself in our old kitchen...*But other times* I would run into her on the street" (3, emphasis added). In Howells's words, "'Friend of My Youth' is a daughter's story about the mother who will not go away but even after death seems to go on living and changing in the underworld of her daughter's dream life" (*Alice Munro* 102). The dream recreates and represents the narrator's mother, and yet its details do not reflect those of so-called real life. In the dream, she notes, "my mother was still alive," though in life, she indicates, "she died when I was in my early twenties and she in her early fifties" (3). Moreover, the dream contrasts not only her life experience, but also her own memory: "[My mother] would be looking so well...so much better than I remembered" (3). Though dreams are usually thought of as derivatives of life, here, this notion is reversed. The dream seems to reveal a truer, more personal, and unmasked version of her mother than the one she remembers. "I recovered then," the narrator says, "what in waking life I had lost—my mother's liveliness of face and voice before her throat muscles stiffened and a woeful, impersonal mask fastened itself over her features" (3-4). Indeed, at this moment, the narrator sees her mother anew, as though the present has rubbed up against the past, free from the narrator's emotions and biases, which have conglomerated over time. At the end of the story, she returns to this moment and describes it as one in which her mother moves "rather carelessly out of her own prison, showing options and powers" (26). That "prison" might be her mother's home, domestic demands, or disease; but significantly, it might also be the story of her mother itself—the narrator's own discursive frame. Her mother's escape from it is an epiphanic yet fleeting moment for the narrator, since the narrator's elation quickly changes to worry—"How relieved I was, and happy. But now I recall that I was disconcerted as well" (26). Her mother's release results in her happiness. Her own elision—that is, her receding power as the narrative voice that frames her mother—results in her agitation and unsettlement.

This agitation and unsettlement might come from the narrator's awareness, even if subconscious, that her understanding of her mother's past is slippery, that her articulation of that past does not necessarily match its "truth." Referring to the narrator's explanation of her mother's appearance in her dreams, Heble states that "the options and possibilities ascribed to the mother in this sequence are available only through the agency of dream, are only, in other words, part of the narrator's memorialization of her mother's life" (175). Munro "openly acknowledges that she is using the imaginative mode as a way of compensating for deficiencies in the past" (175). At the beginning of the story, the narrator clearly articulates the difference between her mother as she appears in her dream, and her mother as she remembers her. But soon, as Heble points out, that distinction becomes blurred, challenging the boundary between what is real and what is imagined: "the line of demarcation between these alternative modes of experience is somewhat obscured as the narrator refers to a moment in her dream as 'reality': 'How could I have forgotten this, I would think in the dream—the casual humour she had, not ironic but merry, the lightness and confidence?...I had kept a bugbear in my mind, instead of this reality'" (176). Right from the outset of the story, therefore, Munro "undermines that narrator's ability to keep separate the domain of imaginative inquiry and the realm of experience" (176).

Flora, like the narrator's mother, is also entrapped within the discursive framework that defines her. The narrator notes her mother's act of encasing Flora ("I could see what she would do with Flora. What she had already done" [19]), yet by attempting to free Flora from the "prison" (26) her mother has created for her, she situates her in another

Time and Narrative Framing   101

prison, that of the narrator's own discursive and ideological frame ("I had my own ideas about Flora's story...My Flora would be as black as hers was white" [20]). Interestingly, in a moment of self-awareness and self-reflexivity, the narrator recognizes that her narrative is as ideologically biased as her mother's: "The odd thing is that my mother's ideas were in line with some progressive notions of her times, and mine echoed the notions that were favoured in mine" (22-23). Thus, an attempt to undo Flora's narrative imprisonment is succeeded by yet another imprisonment, even as the narrator is conscious of her own act of confinement. Each attempt, moreover, is tethered to its contemporary context, the supposedly "progressive" (26) ideology of its time. Munro draws attention to the temporality of *progress*, the notion that the idea of progress changes depending on the generation and the era. She exposes its construction and undermines its dominant status. This problem of coming to know another is an epistemological one, since Munro's narrator cannot peel back the layers of so-called "truth" to get to the heart of the matter, to the essence of another.

Flora herself—the object of the narrator's and her mother's scrutiny—resists interpretation. The narrator tells the reader that in a written response to the narrator's mother's letter, Flora insists that "she did not know where my mother had been getting her information...[I]t seemed [my mother] had misunderstood, or listened to malicious people, or jumped to unjustified conclusions" (19). Similarly, when the narrator dreams of telling Flora that she knows her story, even though she has never met her, Flora "[listens]" but "shakes her head" and is "weary" of the narrator's "idea of her" (26). Such moments show that we cannot ultimately know Flora's truth, and that neither the narrator nor her mother reaches it. Glimpses of Flora, like those of the narrator's mother, are fleeting and incomplete. Flora's resistance to the narrator's mother's interpretation of her is not a catalyst for the narrator's mother to truly get to know her but rather an impediment: the "well written letter" from Flora "cut my mother," the narrator says (19), and "she and Flora stopped corresponding" (19). Likewise, in the narrator's dream, her glimpse of Flora's truth—the fact that she resists being written—is short lived, since her thought of Flora is displaced by her thought of her mother (36). In such instances, though we strive to hear the genuine "voice" (4) of the narrator's and her mother's subjects, that voice is quickly "mask[ed]" (26), and its "throat muscles stiffened" (4). In Mark Nunes's words, "'Flora' exists in two narratives, but Flora-as-fact overflows narrative containment" (20). In "Friend of My Youth," time folds in on itself: the mother's framing of Flora becomes the narrator's framing of Flora a generation later, and the narrator's construction of her mother and Flora promptly become one.

We have seen how the narrator, through the narrative itself, discursively confines and thus misrepresents her mother, and how her mother and the narrator, in turn, also confine and misrepresent Flora. The so-called real Flora, the ostensible subject of the story, Munro suggests, is not to be found. Just as the narrator interprets and narrates her mother, and just as her mother and the narrator narrate and interpret Flora, so too does Flora narrate others. Flora's position shifts from the person being narrated to the one doing the narrating: she becomes yet another storyteller. Flora reads stories to Ellie, while the narrator's mother listens (11–12). In these instances, Ellie is not a passive listener. She interjects to demonstrate her presence and determine how and to what extent Flora tells the story: "Sometimes Ellie said, 'I can't hear you.' Or if Flora paused for a little rest Ellie said, 'I'm not asleep yet'" (12). Ellie's act of speaking back to the stories told to her parallels the narrator's mother's act, in the narrator's dream, of speaking back to the narrator: "Oh well,' she said, 'better late than never. I was sure I'd see you someday'" (4). Likewise, it parallels Flora's act of "[shaking] her head" when the narrator, in another dream, tells Flora that she knows her (26). Though Ellie clearly comprehends the stories Flora reads to her, the narrator, the narrator's mother, and the reader do not. "The only title my mother could remember," the narrator exclaims, "was *Wee Macgregor*.[2] She could not follow the stories very well...because so much was in Scots dialect or read with that thick accent" (12). Time, in the form of memory, and language and culture, in the form of the Scots dialect, prevent the narrator's mother from understanding and reiterating what Flora reads. This disjunction suggests a miscommunication or missing of the mark between the present and the past. We might think of the narrator's and her mother's relationship to Flora's inaccessible stories as unsettling—the past that they attempt to confront is, to use a Freudian term, *unheimlich*, which, in its literal translation, means "not of the home." History is neither familiar nor assimilable. If, as Nunes suggests, Munro's narratives "negotiate between stability and moments of destabilization" (15), then this is a notable moment of such destabilization.

This destabilization manifests in place as well as time. Just as factual and definitive historical truth is not, Munro suggests, readily accessible, neither is place easily attainable, as it is manifested in history and through narration. This unstable notion of place is not only manifested in "Friend of My Youth"; it goes back as far as Munro's first collection of stories, *Dance of the Happy Shades*. Critics have analyzed Munro's depiction of place extensively, as I mention in the introduction to this book, and they generally agree that place, for Munro, is not definitive or static but slippery and dynamic. As Merilyn Simonds explains, "In the fictional world of Alice Munro, place is a shifty thing...In an Alice Munro story, there is almost always more than one version of a place" ("Where Do You" 34-35). In "Friend of My Youth," the narrator explains how her mother" empahsiz[ed] things about [the Ottawa Valley] that distinguished it from any other place on earth. Houses turn black, maple syrup has a taste no maple syrup produced elsewhere can equal, bears amble within sight of farmhouses" (4). Upon travelling to that place herself, however, the narrator is "disappointed" (4), since her experience of it does not match her mother's description. First, the narrator opposes the Ottawa Valley's name: "it was not a valley at all," she exclaims (5). Second, she articulates how it is not frameable, not definable; she notes that it is "a scrambled, disarranged sort of country with no easy harmony about it, not yielding to any description" (5). That its name does not adequately represent it suggests a disjunction between signifier and signified, between the attempt to speak or write meaning and the elusiveness of that meaning. That it is "disarranged" (5) implies that it cannot easily be limited, framed, or even fully understood. Like the narrator's mother and Flora herself, who "overflows narrative containment" (Nunes 20), so too does the landscape upon which she resides exceed the frameworks by which we might know it; it defies narrative and discursive closure. New points out that "Canadians...have long thought of themselves in connection with the land" (17). Yet, in "Friend of My Youth," that connection is complicated, since the narrator's mother's description does not line up with the narrator's own personal experience. The place itself—according to the narrator—does not lend itself to narrative description at all. Landscapes, like the people that occupy them, Munro suggests, cannot be fully known because they slip beyond their discursive or narrative definitions.

Moments of mismatch or destabilization run throughout "Friend of My Youth," and often occur as elements of surprise or moments in which expectations are unmet. For instance, when the narrator's mother arrives at the Greives's home where she will board, both the house and the people who reside within it do not match her expectations. The house was "divided in an *unexpected* way...in the *expectation* that Robert and Ellie would have a family...This hadn't happened" (6, emphasis added). The Grieves are Cameronians, a sect of Scottish Presbyterians who renounce worldly pleasures in favour of their service to God. Much to the narrator's mother's surprise, in Flora's part of the house there are games and entertainments (6). The townspeople too, the narrator speculates, also experience surprise, since they expect Robert and Flora to marry, although it turns out that Robert and her sister Ellie do: "some people, seeing the names in the paper, thought the editor must have got the sisters mixed up" (10). Later, after Ellie dies, Robert marries her nurse, Nurse Atkinson. "The surprises did not stop at the wedding" (17), since the nurse begins to "[fix] up" the house, adding electricity and a telephone (17). Even for the reader, the story does not match expectations. We assume that Flora is disadvantaged, since she resides "in the poorer part of the house," but that view is complicated when the narrator says that Flora prefers it (6). Thus, our assessment of circumstances cannot be trusted: we do not know the structure of time as it unfolds and events do not succeed or progress as we anticipate.

Crouse explains that "Munro uses framing, somewhat similar to stacking in that it involves radical time shifts, except that a sort of home base is established early in the narrative, a look-out post in the present where the protagonist can stand and look back at the past" (58). "Because of this framing technique," Crouse continues, "narrative is free to move between present and past, generating a kind of friction of not-quite-right juxtapositions" (58). This narrative framing is evident in "Friend of My Youth," where the narrator encloses Flora's story within the story of her relationship with her mother, and implicitly, within Munro's story of her relationship with her own mother. Layers of story within story provide the structure for "Friend" and produce juxtapositions and mismatches. These mismatches occur in time, since the present (the story of the narrator and her mother) is juxtaposed with the past (the story of Flora, Robert, and Ellie). Layers of mismatches also occur in terms of communication, or rather, miscommunication: the narrator tries but struggles to understand both her mother's and Flora's pasts, just as the narrator's mother remembers and attempts to understand *Wee Macgregor*. The strength of Munro's structure here is that when the narrator returns from the past of Flora's story to the present of her and her mother's, the present is infused with meaning. This structure, in other words, "adds layers of meaning to the present," so that "when the narrative 'returns,' the circle [is] complete, [the] present now resonating with the complications of the past" (Crouse 58).

Earlier, I discussed how the narrator's mother's "prison" (26) is both her role as a housewife—her domestic duties—and the narrative frame that encases her. Of course, what entraps her is also her disease, from which the narrator imaginatively frees her in her dreams. That Munro's own mother suffered from Parkinson's disease is important here, since it suggests a parallel between Munro's life and her narrator's. In *Alice Munro: Writing Her Lives*, Thacker explains that "Munro has repeatedly seen her mother's circumstances, once she had fallen ill and was in decline, as her default material, her central subject" (536). While Thacker names earlier stories such as "The Peace of Utrecht," "The Ottawa Valley," and "Soon" as examples, this observation is equally applicable to "Friend of My Youth." Just as the narrator's domesticity and disease entraps her, so too Flora's house entraps her. Yet Flora's house signifies both entrapment and freedom, and it is a metaphor for narrative framing. The house is divided between Flora, on the one hand, and Ellie and Robert, on the other. While the narrator's mother implies that Ellie and Robert occupied the more desirable part of the house, "the parlour and the dining room, the front bedrooms and staircase, the winter kitchen" (6), she describes Flora's part of the house as more free with words such as "open" and "uncovered": "Flora had the summer kitchen, with its open rafters and uncovered brick walls" (6). Likewise, the narrator's mother emphasizes Flora's martyrdom, making it sound as though Flora gave up niceties for Ellie, and yet the narrator subtly shows Flora's advantage. For Flora, "it was not even true that all amusements were forbidden. She had a crokinole board—she taught my mother to play" (6). Flora's home seems to shape her and emphasizes either her selflessness or advantage, and yet that reading depends upon how the narrator's mother, the narrator, and the reader might interpret her in relation to her surroundings. The "open rafters and uncovered brick walls" (6) signify either poverty or freedom. Flora's dividing up of the house is an act of a "saint" (8) or one who pursues amusements and pleasures.

As the narrator conflates Flora with her mother at the end of the story (26), so too are Flora and Ellie a part of each other: they can be seen as one. The narrator notes that not only are Flora and Ellie "wonderfully fond of each other," but also that "Ellie...[is] like a copy of Flora" (9). In another interpretation, one might say that Flora represents the ego, while Ellie represents the id. According to Freud, "Normally, there is nothing of which we are more certain than the feeling of our self, or own ego. The ego appears to us as something autonomous and unitary, marked off distinctly from everything else" ("Civilization" 724). Yet he also notes that such as distinction is "deceptive," and that the ego "continue[s] inwards, without any sharp delimitation, into an unconscious mental entity which we designate as the id" (724). Ellie, the id to Flora's ego, is continually described as wild: "Ellie was then a wild tease...a girl full of lolling energy" (9). She is a "horse" or "colt" who evidently needs to be tamed (9). Flora, the ego to Ellie's id, is seen as the one to subdue her: "Nobody but Flora could control her" (9).

Such taming can be interpreted as another discursive framing or narrative enclosure. Once again, Munro suggests that we cannot fully understand or communicate the complexities of personhood in words. Each attempt is a misrepresentation and an imprisonment. Yet that limitation might also be seen as freedom, newness, or creation. For example, Munro suggests new sexual identities when she hints at relations between the three characters Flora, Ellie, and Robert: when "Robert laid claim to Flora, or Flora to him—nobody knew how it was—Ellie had to be included" (9). Ellie, the narrator suggests, "sneak[s] up behind" Robert and Flora to "blow on their necks" (9). Ellie upsets the accepted order of things—a clear marriage between Robert and Flora—by "putting thistles in Robert's bed," "sett[ing] his place at the table with the knife and fork the wrong way around," and "switch[ing] the milk pails to give him the old one with the hole in it" (9). Therefore, she is not only ostensibly "deranged" herself, but she also "derange[s]" (10) others. If we deduce that Flora, Ellie, and Robert have sexual relations together, then we might argue that the "amusements" in Flora's domain of the house go beyond "crokinole" (6).

Ellie's act of blowing on the necks of Flora and Robert is not in and of itself evidence for sexual relations between the three of them, though it does indicate a sexual innuendo. However, taken alongside the other hints that Munro provides for us, we might interpret their relations as such. In her examination of "Friend of My Youth," Lynn Blin draws attention to the linguistic construction of Munro's sentences, analyzing the polyphonic narrative voices in the story and showing how Munro engages in sexual suggestions through the piece. As an example, Blin points to the following passage, spoken by the narrator: "by the way everyone spoke, my mother expected the Grieves sisters to be middle aged at least, but Ellie the younger sister was only in her thirties and Flora seven or eight years older. Robert Deal might be in between" (quoted in Blin para. 69). On the one hand, this declaration indicates that Robert's age is in between Ellie's and Flora's ages; on the other hand, however, it might also indicate that Robert is "in between" Ellie and Flora. To put it in Blin's words, "it is perhaps pushing it a little to conclude that we are to interpret this as a tongue-in-cheek insinuation that these three were into unorthodox practices, but it is in these gaps that Munro not only enables us to play our role of active readers by inviting us to fill them in, it is in these gaps she constructs the space in the text to enable various narrative voices to be heard" (para. 71).

Thus, if we agree that Munro hints at sexual relations between Flora, Ellie, and Robert, then the narrator's mother's notion that Flora can be "trusted fully...in her own purity" (10) is tinged with irony. After Flora and Ellie's father dies, Flora does not move the wedding date between Robert and herself closer but rather further away in time (9-10). The narrator says that "No one knew how to speak to Flora about this being scandalous or looking scandalous. Flora would just ask why" (10). On the narrator's mother's interpretation, Flora does not understand why because of her ignorance, innocence, or "purity" (10), but in the narrator's interpretation, Flora's question is a confrontation. Why, in other words, should she be disgraced by her sexual encounters, however unconventional? Kathleen Wall argues that "the bodies depicted in the stories of...Munro are not traditionally the object of the male gaze" (75). I would take this interpretation a step further: Munro resists conventional depictions of women's bodies and the sexual behaviours expected of them. In such instances, then, Munro's writing is feminist. It highlights sexuality and corporeality, and it suggests that both exceed the confines of limiting and conventional patriarchal discourse. Munro seems to be aligned with women's time, that which pushes back against the attempt to exert power over the body. She suggests a woman-centred sexuality. Note that when the narrator hints at Ellie's inclusion in Flora and Robert's courtship, she says that "nobody knew how it was" (9). In the same way that some of the characters and the readers themselves do not have access to the content of the literature that Flora reads to Ellie, we do not have access to the details of Flora's private life.

Referring to Munro's autobiographical writing and the connections and disjunctions between her life and work, Morra explains that "intimate disclosures are at times offered and at others denied the reader," and that Munro considers "the right to access the private details of a life—any life" ("'Don't Take'" 258). Thus, Munro addresses ethical questions about personal lives, the past, and about knowledge itself. Flora's letter to the narrator's mother indicates her belief that her private life is indeed just that: her own. What happened in her own life, Flora exclaims in her letter, "was nobody's business, and certainly nobody needed to feel sorry for her or angry on her behalf" (19). When Flora reads books to Ellie, there are three witnesses to that act: the narrator's mother, who sits beside Flora as she reads; the narrator, who hears about it from her mother; and the reader. None of these witnesses knows the content of the stories, only Ellie herself, who does not just listen but receives the story. Likewise, the letter Flora writes is meant for the narrator's mother, but the reader too is witness to it. In it, Flora rejects the narrator's mother's knowledge of her life, while, at the same time, Munro rejects the reader's. Ultimately, Munro emphasizes "not only the ambiguity between fact and fiction, but also the necessary *distance* between the autobiographical text and the reader or witness to that text" (Morra, "'Don't Take'" 258, emphasis in original).

The letter from Flora to the narrator's mother is one of many letters in the story. This one is sent but not well received, since the narrator's mother is offended by the letter and stops corresponding with Flora. Other letters in the story, like the story itself, are "unsettling," because they "[leave] so many things out" (24), or they are unfinished or not sent at all; the narrator "find[s] them lying around the house" (24). Löschnigg explains that "Munro's stories abound with letters," noting that "of her 148 collected stories, twenty-two contain letters, and there are a dozen more where letters or notes play an important role" ("Carried" 97). She argues that in these letters, "intradiegetic correspondents build up realized imaginary worlds that often radically contrast with the reality they inhabit" (99). Thus, Munro uses the epistolary form to highlight the disjunction between signifier and signified, the literary and the material, the past and the present. In the story's only reference to its title, the narrator states that one of her mother's letters was addressed, "Friend of My Youth," then notes that she does not know specifically who that friend could be (24). That salutation refers to the narrator's mother's friend and to the readers of the story themselves. The narrator and Munro address their readers in a move that implicates readers: they want to know more than they should. As Morra puts it, Munro "situates human curiosity within larger existential questions about why knowing is important and what ends it will serve" ("'Don't Take'" 265).

That the letters the narrator's mother writes are not sent demonstrates unfulfilled desire for communication. That desire, moreover, is repeated in the references to sexual desire in the story—including the fact that the narrator's mother prepares her "trousseau" (12)—and to the desire—on the narrator's, the mother's, and the reader's part—to know more about their subjects. The narrator's subject is both her mother and Flora; her mother's subject is Flora; and the reader's subject is the narrator, the narrator's mother, Flora, and even Munro herself. However, that the letters are not sent also shows arrested communication, incomplete creation, or writing-in-progress. Ellie becomes pregnant time and time again, yet each life stops before it begins: "Ellie had one miscarriage after another, then another stillbirth and more miscarriages" (11). In a similar vein, the narrator's mother writes letter after letter and addresses them to her "dear friends," though, as mentioned, they do not get finished or sent. Rather, the narrator must piece together their relevance after the fact as the reader must do with Munro's story. Writing, a material and bodily act, like unconventional sexual acts or the continual attempt to give birth to life, can be both limiting—even, as in Ellie's case, deadly—or the beginning of an identity or paradigm, something new. In "Friend of My Youth," the so-called truth that is repeatedly sought is ultimately slippery and elusive. Munro paradoxically both laments and celebrates that deferral and elusion. She marks and repeats continual disjunctures, misrepresentations, and revisions.

"Meneseteung"

"Meneseteung" is one of Munro's most well-known and anthologized stories. As Tracy Ware explains, "None of Alice Munro's stories has been more quickly canonized than 'Meneseteung,' the first harvest of an interest in the nineteenth-century history of southwestern Ontario that culminates in *The View from Castle Rock*" (67). The story is told by a narrator who examines the life and work of a fictional local and historical poet of the nineteenth century, Almeda Roth. When the story begins, the narrator examines Almeda's writing and finds out about her life through old issues of a Huron County newspaper, *The Vidette*. The narrator is on a quest to discover more about Almeda, and at the end of the story, she discovers where her body rests. She finds the "stone" that is marked with her name under the "grass" and the "dirt" of the gravesite (202). Almeda, we find out, was a single woman who was courted by Jarvis Poulter, a businessman who owned salt mines and farms in the area.[3] The story begins with their courtship, but before long, Almeda rejects him and seems to descend into insanity, at least according to the records of the time and the narrator's retelling of them. The story centres around an instance in which Almeda is awakened one morning by the sounds of a woman in pain outside her window. When she looks out, she discovers what she believes is a woman's dead body. She calls Jarvis over, and they find that the woman is not dead but badly beaten. Jarvis treats the woman condescendingly, compounding the abuse she has suffered. This event is quickly followed by a series of subsequent ones: Jarvis acknowledges to himself his desire to marry Almeda; Almeda feels ill and has her period; and she rejects Jarvis. The story ends not only with the narrator's discovery of Almeda's gravesite, but also with her questioning of the details of the story she has just told. "Meneseteung" is a layered story that engages literary history and complex narrative devices.

Wall notes that in "Meneseteung," Almeda Roth "is mediated by several framing devices, almost amounting to frames within frames, areas of differing degrees of narratorial authority or omniscience" (82). In a comment that relates to such narrative framing, Nunes suggests that the question "How do our narrative arrangements bring a state of affairs into being?" is central to Munro's *Friend of My Youth* (11). Or, as Heble puts it, "recovery of the past in Munro's writing is complicated by the fact of language" (195). Munro skilfully enacts narrative framing devices to demonstrate how the past and its people are not fully or accurately recoverable through language and story; yet she also shows that an attempt at such recovery is crucial to create anew. The present, she implies, hinges upon the past. "Meneseteung," like "Friend of My Youth," is narrated by a researcher who confronts history. The narrator reads the poet Almeda Roth's history primarily through written texts, whereas in "Friend of My Youth," the narrator is a daughter who attempts to interpret her mother's oral stories about her and her friend's histories. The narrators of both works are storytellers, and through them Munro explores "not only memory but the processes by which people account for and make sense of experience" (Elliott 77).

Thacker explains that Munro grounds "Meneseteung" in touch points related to her own place and life. For example, "Joynt" was the name of one of one of the schoolteachers in her hometown; *The Vidette*, which is the newspaper in "Meneseteung," was one of the predecessors to Wingham's *Advance-Times*; and Munro situates the poet in her own hometown of Wingham (*Alice Munro* 434). Thacker and other critics have commented on the blurring of boundaries between the narrator and the author of the story: "there is little difference between the author and the narrator" (Ware 75). The fictional river that gives the story its title is based on the Maitland River that runs through Munro's Wingham (Stich 107), yet another way that the author connects the story with her own self and home. As in Munro's other writing, details about her own self and surroundings abound in "Meneseteung."

Apart from considering Munro's biographical details and their relation to "Meneseteung," critics have interpreted the story variously. Klaus P. Stich addresses literary allusions in the story and focuses on its references to mythological figures. He argues that the story "thrives in intimations of Dionysis and Medusa. Their presences surface here, unexpectedly perhaps, as part of the historical transformation of a mid-nineteenth-century Ontario settlement into a thriving small town on a river" (107). Drawing upon Mikhail Bahktin's notion of dialogism, Elizabeth Reimer states that Munro's style in "Meneseteung" "innovatively suggests the interrogative nature of biographical inquiry," and that she "attempts to unsettle conventional biographical narrative arcs," which allow readers to "rethink what Sara Ahmed refers to as the 'relation between identification and desire' in biography's 'affective economies'" (200). This desire to know another is evident in both "Friend of My Youth," where the narrator attempts to remember her mother's story of her friend Flora, and "Meneseteung," where the narrator attempts to understand the poet, Almeda Roth. Reimer's reading of the story highlights Munro's narrative framing, the narrator's own story in relation to her biographical subject, and asks ethical and epistemological questions regarding the desire to understand another person, whether in the past or the present. Kim Jernigan examines the coming together of theme and form in "Meneseteung," stating that "theme and form conjoin in particularly complex and interesting ways in many of Alice Munro's stories because narrative so often *is* her theme" (44, emphasis in original). Jernigan observes that "Munro frequently sets up a tension between our very human desire to find life meaningful (to tell a story) and our suspicion that every story is a version, constructed in accordance with one set of purposes or interests, perceived and interpreted in accordance with some other set of purposes or interests" (45). This is precisely what Munro does in both "Friend of My Youth" and "Meneseteung."

In "Too Little Geography; Too Much History: Writing the Balance in 'Meneseteung,'" Dennis Duffy states that by "mapping the Munro Tract,"[4] the author "transmutes geography and history into an alloy giving them both their due" (198). Thus, Munro brings together place and time, as her "development of her Tract piles up greater depth and density over the period of her imaginative explanations" (199). As in *The View from Castle Rock*, Duffy explains, the narrator voice in "Meneseteung" is that of a storyteller: "That voice intrudes upon the supposedly fictional narrative, throwing in what are at times facts, at times suppositions that appear part of an ongoing mediation about the tangled relationship between historical *fact* and historical *understanding*" (199, emphasis in original). Duffy argues that the genre of the historical novel offers "the surest guide to what Munro is up to in 'Meneseteung,'" since, when successful, that genre evokes "something greater than antiquarianism, or a nostalgia-driven curiosity about how those who came before us lived their lives" (201). Yet, as Duffy further articulates, "Munro's historical fiction is not fully congruent with classical historical fiction" (201). It involves "a preoccupation not with being but with being in time" (201).

Her historical work is aligned with Marcel Proust's vision of the imagination: "the dizzying prospect that comes from understanding that we are one with and yet at the same time alien from those preceding us" (201). This notion is indeed what Munro conveys in both *The View from Castle Rock* and "Meneseteung."

Drawing upon the work of theorists Roman Jakobson, Jacques Lacan, and Jane Gallop, Pam Houston—who wrote the first article on "Meneseteung" (Ware 67)—analyzes the story in terms of metonymy. She identifies that Munro's writing engages in metonymic associations rather than metaphoric substitutions to make meaning. "Desire and lack run through 'Meneseteung,'" Houston notes, "as deeply as the river from which it gets its name, and in 'Meneseteung,' as in life, all desire is unlimited and insatiable" (85). Summarizing a point Gallop makes in "Metaphor and Metonymy," the fifth chapter of *Reading Lacan*, Houston explains that "while a metaphoric relationship is often construed as complete in itself, as independent from any context, a metonymic relationship is always context bound…any metaphor we make is shifting, metonymically, even as it is written, and as each word is written after it, it shifts again and again. Meaning can only be derived metonymically because the context is at every moment changing" (83). She suggests that Munro's writing is more metonymic than it is metaphoric, and that the metonymic associations in "Meneseteung" create layers of meaning.

If, as Houston argues, metonymy is coupled with the feminine—as it is associative, horizontally oriented, and non-linear—and metaphor is associated with the masculine—since it is non-associative, vertically oriented, and linear—then Munro's writing might be defined as feminine, though she certainly uses both metaphor and metonymy in her writing. In "Meneseteung," Munro engages in sophisticated metonymic associations. The grape jelly that Almeda Roth makes, for instance, is metonymically associated with Almeda's menstrual blood, since they are similar in colour and texture. Her menstrual blood is further associated with the river that gives the story its title, since they both flow: one internally, one externally; one through the body, the other through the land. These metonymies provide connections between the woman's body and her environment, as though the two are one. That metonymic associations are non-linear, moreover, suggests that they cannot be understood in terms of forward, progressive movement through time. Thus, Munro works against masculine conceptions of time and linearity by using metonymy to put women's bodies and their environments at the fore. As Jarret explains, "it is women's bodies, above all, which...register the capricious, unforeseeable leaps of time which are the basis of all of Munro's plots" (88).

Munro's foregrounding of women's corporeality is often, but not always, a foregrounding of motherhood. Redekop says that Munro asks "how to affirm the *lives* of our mothers and daughters when the only means available to do so return us to the fact of artifice" (*Mothers* 217). Ware notes that this question is central to "Meneseteung," noting that "Munro does not think like other writers, especially when she thinks of mothers. Her sense of resistance of the past to the needs of the present is the mark of her ethical rigour" (68). Indeed, the narrator's contemplation of the fictional poet Almeda Roth is the contemplation of a mother. Unlike the narrator of "Friend of My Youth," who contemplates her own relationship with her mother as she explores Flora's story, the narrator in "Meneseteung" examines not a biological mother but a literary one. In this way, Munro returns to a trope that she introduced in earlier works such as *Lives of Girls and Women.* This is the idea that writers, and in Munro's case, women writers, build upon and simultaneously depart from their literary ancestors—a concept that became familiar to readers due to works such as Virginia Woolf's *A Room of One's Own*, published in 1929, and Alice Walker's "In Search of Our Mother's Gardens," published in 1972. Yet, as Ware explains, Munro's perception of mothers, related to Munro's own experience, is neither simple nor straightforward. Rather, she unearths the tensions between mothers and daughters as well as the inability to fully know another, especially when one works to uncover a past "truth." This notion of literary daughters building upon their literary mothers is clearly evident in "Meneseteung." As Houston puts it, Almeda's poem "is written through her by the unnamed narrator, and she is written yet again through Alice Munro. These women give birth to one another, and their lives are inextricably meshed into some sort of life dance that feels 'generational,' in all of its slipping meanings. A story, a poem, a history, a life, a river: 'Meneseteung' becomes all things female, all things generative, all things that can never be absolute" (91).

In the first paragraph of "Meneseteung," the narrator examines the nineteenth-century poet's work, beginning with the cover of Almeda's book and noting the author's name, her photograph, and the date (50).

She also immediately explains that the local newspaper, *The Vidette*, describes Almeda as "our poetess" (50). The newspaper, it would seem, claims ownership to the poet as the narrator herself does, since throughout the story the narrator relays but also embellishes what she knows about her. The narrator's approach to Almeda's book, moreover, mirrors Munro's: Munro, like her narrator, researches and retells Almeda's story. The narrator's and Munro's reading of works by Almeda Roth mirror our reading of "Meneseteung." We may notice the date of this story, look at its author's photograph, or examine newspaper articles about Munro just as the narrator and Munro do for Almeda. Almeda's book's title, *Offerings* (50), reflects both what the book offers to the narrator, a fragment of Almeda's past, and what the story "Meneseteung" offers to its readers, a part, arguably, of Munro's past. Therefore, Munro begins "Meneseteung" with a *mise en abyme* in which one story mirrors and folds into the next: the newspaper's story of Almeda becomes the narrator's story of her, which becomes Munro's story of her and her narrator, and then the reader's story of Almeda, the narrator, and Munro. Each story about Almeda becomes more complex because it includes another teller. Munro retells Almeda's story as she demonstrates how we get increasingly further away from it through time. By invoking the repetition, mirroring, and distancing implicit in *mise en abyme*, Munro contests linear, progressive time in favour of the cyclical and the repetitive. Her challenge to linear teleology is a strategy of resistance that is enacted through her storytelling form.

As the narrator moves beyond the cover of Almeda's book to read the poems within it, she relays to the reader only fragments of what she reads: "Titles of *some* of the poems" (52, emphasis added), and her own synopsis of each. Just as "some things must be disregarded" in the narrator's attempt to see the countryside as Almeda has described it (61), so too must certain details of Almeda's book be left out. Likewise, though the narrator attempts to list the "opportunities and dangers" (55) that *The Vidette* reports, she can neither include them all nor relate their full stories. The narrator's admission at the end of the story that she may not have gotten Almeda's story right has elicited scholarly interpretations, especially since that admission does not appear in the original publication of the story in *The New Yorker*. As Thacker explains, the editor at *The New Yorker* took the original ending out, but Munro put it back in for her book (*Alice Munro* 434-35). Ware states that the ending

116   ALICE MUNRO AND THE ART OF TIME

of this story in the book signals a break in the "link between Almeda and the narrator," which he argues is "extraordinary even for Munro" (73). Dermot McCarthy writes that this ending has "unwritten all that has come before it" (13). Analyzing various critical interpretations of this ending, Ware states that while Houston is pleased with the ambiguous ending, McCarthy and Deborah Heller "want affirmation, not resistance" (74). "[T]heir sense that 'Meneseteung' is a feminist recovery of a literary ancestor," Ware argues, "would be more compelling if Munro had not revised the ending" (74).

My own interpretation of the ending aligns more with Houston than it does with McCarthy and Heller. The narrator's admission that she may have not got Almeda's story right, to my mind, leaves readers with an ambiguity and uncertainly that is humble, laudable, and consistent with Munro's other writing. Munro often emphasizes the gaps between signifier and signified and highlights the tensions between the desire to know and the inability to fulfill that desire. In so doing, she pushes back against linearity, progress, and singular time. Rather, she celebrates both the desire to know and the mysteries of the unknown. The notion of missing the mark, of not getting things quite right that she implies by stating that she "may have got it wrong" (73) not only occurs in Munro's other writing, but elsewhere in this story: *The Vidette*'s "surmise" about the "courting" between Almeda Roth and Jarvis Poulter (58) is not quite correct, and the calls of the witnesses to the woman's beating, Almeda notes, involve "a clumsy sort of parody, an exaggeration, a missed connection" (63-64). As the narrator relates such mistakes throughout "Meneseteung," the readers also come to realize that we cannot rely on any definitive interpretation or any solidified notion of Almeda or the narrator's story about her. Her story, like Flora's in "Friend of My Youth," slips beyond our grasp. Those "mistakes," though, are not to be lamented. Rather, Munro seems to suggest that the mismatch between one story and the next, between an error and its correction, is where the "treasure" lies. It is the "glint" from "White Dump" that allows for recreation and renewal; the "great sea" that once lay beneath Huron County, where Jarvis extracts salt; Almeda's grave that the narrator discovers and upon which she builds at the end of "Meneseteung."

Both Almeda's poems and the newspaper reports include gothic elements. In this way, Munro extends gothic themes that she introduced in previous works such as *Lives of Girls and Women*. Through these gothic elements, those who are represented exceed the confines that attempt to contain them. In one of Almeda's poems that the narrator contemplates, the poet's siblings have been taken by gypsies, though she hears their "ghostly" voices calling her: *"Come over, cover over, let Meda come over"* (52). In another, the poet visits her family's tombstones in the cemetery, a "one-sided conversation," the narrator says (52). Even the poem titled "Angels in the Snow" is gothic, referring both to the snow angels Almeda makes with her brother and sister and the "angels" of the bodies in the tombstones referenced in the poem that begins section two of the story (53). The titles of the poems and their contents are significant beyond their gothic implications. The voices that call to Almeda, for instance, could be either her siblings or the narrator or author; a researcher and writer calling her forth from the dead to be part of "Meneseteung." The "one-sided conversation" is, on the one hand, Almeda herself visiting the tombstones of her family members, and, on the other, the narrator "find[ing] things out" (73) about Almeda, who has been dead for about one hundred years. Almeda's brother's act of making a snow angel and then "jump[ing] up carelessly, leaving an angel with a crippled wing" (52) is like the narrator's act of writing. She imprints Almeda's character on paper as her brother imprints his own on the snow. Yet he is not careful enough to represent himself accurately: he leaves "a crippled wing" (52), and likewise, the narrator "may have got [Almeda's story] wrong" (73). Her discussion of Almeda's poems and *The Vidette*'s representations of the poet and her town are already both limited and exceeded: limited by the narrator's discursive framework and exceeded by the gothic—the subjects' acts of "escaping" (71) the bodily confines that attempt to contain them. In "Meneseteung," Munro mobilizes gothic imagery to suggest the power of written work to misjudge or recreate.

Early in the story, Almeda connects the act of writing with "crochet work" (51), a historically female endeavour. She explains that since she was "too clumsy" for embroidery (51), she "offers...these rude posies, these ballads, couplets, reflections" (52). Later, she realizes that "crocheted roses could float away" (71), and in one of her poems, she wonders whether the "roses" on tombstones in the graveyard "rest below" or "in God's wonder, fly" (53). On one reading, since the crocheted roses and the ones on the tombstone are metonymically linked, the roses in the poem stand for the dead bodies beneath the tombstones—Almeda's question is therefore a religious and epistemological one. In another reading, since the poet, through the narrator, has already likened embroidery to writing and described "crocheted roses" (73), we might deduce that the roses could be her own words, the "posies" or "reflections" (52) she creates. In this interpretation, her work, embodied in her writing, does not "rest below" (53) but is released: it "fl[ies]" (53) or "float[s] away" (71)—the narrator has revived it. That the "crocheted roses could float away" suggests not only that they look like they are separate from the tablecloth onto which they are sewn, but also that they float as if they are in a river, the very river that gives the story its title. The river is the poem and the poem is the river. The words or signifiers can become detached from what they signify, floating away as if taking on a life of their own.

In Almeda's story, which the narrator recounts, Almeda finds a woman's body by her back fence and believes she is dead, but when Jarvis Poulter arrives, he discovers that she is beaten and inebriated, but not deceased. As she walks away, he says to Almeda, "There goes your dead body" (67). Just as Almeda imagines Jarvis himself as a "[tombstone]" who, with others, "[marches] down the street on [his] little booted feet" (69), so too the woman's body—which Jarvis, notably, has likened to Almeda's own—walks away. Metaphorically, the "dead body" that walks away is that of Almeda Roth, the poet who the narrator and Munro have revived, and who comes alive to readers of "Meneseteung." She, like Jarvis, are historical figures from the past who we read about now, in the present. The narrator, who uncovers Almeda's own "stone" at the end of the story, while "pulling grass and scrabbling in the dirt with her [bare] hands" (73), at once discovers and creates the poet's life and work. On the one hand, such an act of uncovering is exploitative, a misunderstanding and misjudgement, like the extracting of salt from the earth for one's own profit. On the other hand, it releases the poet from her "rest below," and enables her, like a ghost, to "float away" (71). Heller suggests that the narrator's act of digging at Almeda's grave indicates "a closeness to the animal life that she has imagined Almeda recognizing in herself on seeing the woman by the fence. Thus, the narrator's identification with Almeda is completed by her own final bodily identification with this other, unnamed woman" (quoted in Ware 71).

It is noteworthy that the title of Almeda Roth's book of poems, *Offerings*, denotes money one gives to the church, or a sense of devotion, yet it could also mean intellectual or artistic offerings, which are the poems themselves. On the one hand, the title can be read straight: the poems are treasures, gifts from God, like the treasure of salt that Jarvis finds in the earth, and like the treasure of "Almeda's" gravestone that the narrator finds at the end of the story. On the other hand, however, the title is ironic, hinting at economics and exploitation, what is not offered but taken. Jarvis, through his salt mining business, extracts salt from the earth for his own profit; Samuel de Champlain, referenced in the story, explores and claims Canada West, despite the Indigenous Peoples there; and the men of the town, the narrator implies, exploit the woman that Almeda finds at her fence and other so-called "tramps" (55). In these instances, Munro invokes imperial time and aligns Jarvis with it. Imperial time is always moving forward with linear momentum; it seeks to gain power and to control through economic and exploitative means. Poulter's salt mining business is a domination of the landscape and the environment. Like the silica quarry in "White Dump," it invokes monumental time in opposition to the linear time of so-called progress. As Jarvis exploits the earth, extracting salt from the ancient sea that provides it, he also exploits the beaten woman, treating her violently and condescendingly.

If Munro plays with the boundaries between the living and the dead, what "rests below" or "flies" (53), then she also plays with other kinds of boundaries—namely, those of place and time. Munro specifically cited both place and time as important when she was interviewed about writing "Meneseteung": "I knew for years that I wanted to write a story about one of the Victorian lady writers, one of the authoresses of this area [Clinton, Ontario]" (McCulloch and Simpson quoted in MacKendrick, "Giving" 72). In the story, Almeda's home faces Dufferin Street, a street, according to the narrator, "of considerable respectability," yet it backs onto Pearl Street, where "the poorest people, the unrespectable and undeserving poor" live (55). Just as the poet's residence teeters on the boundaries between the rich and the poor, the respectable and the so-called unworthy, so too does Almeda herself. She is well-to-do: her father was a "harness-maker by trade" but also a "cultivated man who could quote by heart from the Bible, Shakespeare, and the writings of Edmund Burke" (51), and she has "never walked past the row housing" on Pearl Street, since "no decent woman ever would" (56). Yet she is also associated with the indecent: as Jernigan explains,

Almeda feels an "anguished sense of connection with the beaten woman" (52) whom she finds at her back gate, near Pearl Street. Significantly, as Jernigan also points out, Almeda and the beaten woman are connected by their "stifling of voice": while "the woman's mouth 'seems choked with blood,'" for instance, "Almeda subsequently feels a parallel sensation of 'bile at the back of her throat'" (52). Munro therefore associates Almeda and the woman with agency and voice, or the lack thereof. In other words, as Stich has observed, "Almeda, the respectable spinster lady, [meets] her opposite or shadow self in the sexually and alcoholically loosened woman" (110). Furthermore, not only are the boundaries between so-called decent and indecent women blurred—Almeda occupying the role of both—but so are those between sex and violence, pleasure and pain. The sounds of the woman and man arguing and fighting in the street "devolve into something like the sounds of a sexual coupling, not only 'self-abasement' but 'self-abandonment'" (Jernigan 52). Thus, Munro contests Victorian and contemporary ideologies by complicating the binaries between rich and poor, decent and indecent, "angel" and "whore."

The sounds Almeda hears of the man and woman in the street are paradoxically both bodily and disembodied. The narrator describes the fight as physical. There is "a steady throbbing," as the narrator recognizes that the woman "is being beaten" (63). Yet she also describes the sounds as "theatrical," like an opera in which "two voices gradually distinguish themselves" (63). The "throbbing" could be of body or sound. Almeda cannot fully identify the sounds she hears. She does not know who the people are, nor can she easily deduce which sounds come from which person. In addition, there are witnesses to this brawl, those who call "Stop it!" or "Kill her!...as if at the theatre or a sporting match or a prizefight" (63). The separation of sounds from their origins and the presence of witnesses are significant, as the beating at once occupies the realm of experience and representation, violence, and show. Such is also the case when the "wheelbarrow" that the townspeople use to carry the tramp, "Queen Aggie," "all over town" (54), creating a spectacle of her, is later associated with a body. The word becomes disconnected from that which it originally represents: "Down against her fence there is a pale lump pressed—a body. *Wheelbarrow*" (64, emphasis in original). Here, the word, "wheelbarrow" (64), like the "crocheted roses," "float[s] away" (71). The narrator's uncovering of Almeda Roth's "stone"

(73), likewise, leads to her rewriting of her person in words. The tragic and parodic resurrection of the woman's body and Poulter's tombstone, respectively, stand for dead signifiers that become repurposed, revived, and recreated.

In "Meneseteung," Munro invokes what psychoanalytic theorists call the "abject"—"that which falls away from bodies in order for them to enter a social and ordered world" (Grosz, *Volatile Bodies* 92). As I have noted elsewhere, "feminist theorists such as Julia Kristeva and Elizabeth Grosz have associated the abject with feminine bodily fluids such as menstrual blood" (Davis 41). Near the end of Munro's story, Almeda begins her menstrual "flow" (68), which is associated metonymically with the flow of the Meneseteung River, the "deep...river of [Almeda's] mind" (70), and the "great sea" (59) that historically may have occupied the Ontario region where Almeda, the narrator, and Munro reside. Almeda identifies with the woman's debased body and her own bodily fluids. She becomes so enmeshed in them that she "walks through the pool of grape juice" (199), a metaphor for the woman's beaten body and her own menstrual blood. Critics differ in their interpretations of this scene. Ildikó de Papp Carrington points out that Almeda's vision of a great poem unrealized, her menstrual blood, and the grape juice that spills on the floor all symbolize waste. "Almeda's wasted artistic potentiality is ironically emphasized by the mode of her death. She does not drown in love, but she slowly drowns in the river of her mind" (215). By contrast, as Ware points out, Houston reads this scene differently. She calls it "a scene in which meaning [is?] constructed and derived metonymically, a scene which recognizes and celebrates the feminine metonymic abyss" (85). I again lean towards Houston's interpretation of the text rather than Carrington's, but I also think that it is worth keeping these two interpretations in mind, noting the tensions between them. That the scene may be interpreted in these two contrasting ways indicates the fine line between the creation and celebration of feminine agency, and the very precocity of that agency. The friction between these two is precisely what the story manifests.

As Almeda becomes abject through her menstruation and her experience of Poulter's mistreatment of the beaten woman, she dissociates from the *I* that keeps her from "hysteria"—a word that is historically and etymologically associated with the womb. Abjection is that which is opposed to the *I*: "for 'I' deposits it to the father's account" (Kristeva, *Powers* 2). It is that which is neither the ego nor the superego. Instead, "it lies outside, beyond the set, and does not seem to agree to the latter's rules of the game" (2). The *I* from which Almeda dissociates herself is aligned with patriarchy and Jarvis: she rejects him. However, Almeda's abjection does not deem her passive. On the contrary, Kristeva emphasizes the abject's power of opposition: "there looms, within abjection, one of those violent, dark revolts of being" (2). The "repulsion" in abjection, she notes, "places the one haunted by it literally beside himself" (1). Thus, Munro's abject subject, Almeda herself, has the power to resist the patriarchal discourses that frame her. In this way, Munro aligns Almeda with women's time, that fragmentation that exists prior to the teleological self that rejects it.

Katrine Raymond argues that "'Meneseteung' suggests a compelling thesis about hysteria" (101). Considering Almeda as a nineteenth-century hysteric, she argues that in "Meneseteung," "hysteria occurs when boundaries between bodies become openly porous and thus confused" (101). Such is the case, certainly, for Almeda and the narrator, neither of them separating Almeda's body from the beaten woman's, or her flow from the grape juice she makes (70). In a *mise en abyme*, readers take Munro and her story as their subject; Munro takes the narrator as her subject; and in turn, the narrator takes Almeda as her subject. Each collapses into the other as Almeda herself collapses into her environment: the Pearl Street bog in which she dies, the "great sea" that is at once that bog, her *chora*, and her unconscious. Munro's story "illustrates the porosity between humans and their environments," and hysteria "represents a rupture of that [patriarchal] system of control" (Raymond 108, 110). Almeda revels in this rupture and the indistinguishability between herself and her body and environment, as she "walks through the pool of grape juice...leaving purple footprints and smelling her escaping blood and the sweat of her body" (71). If the narrator revives or resurrects Almeda in part through a contemplation of her book of poetry, then the poet is paradoxically both caught up in the physical object of the book and freed by it, brought back to life once again. In the same way, through her menstrual flow and her implicit connection with the beaten woman and the environment she inhabits—including the river and "the great sea" (59) of the past—she is caught up in and yet freed by the language that defines her, called forth by the narrator, like the "ghostly voices of her brother and sister...*Come over, come over, let Meda come over*" (52).

In *The Nick of Time*, Grosz argues that "we need to understand [the body's] open-ended connections with space and time, its place in dynamic and natural and cultural systems, and its mutating, self-changing relations within natural and social networks" (3). Munro's "Meneseteung" ends explicitly with the female body and a depiction of Almeda's menses. It considers her body in relation to—and not apart from—her environment but also "cultural systems" and "social networks" (Grosz, *Nick* 3): the courting of Jarvis Poulter, the teetering on the boundaries of acceptable and unacceptable places and social norms. While the author contests the female body's socio-cultural place, she also gestures toward vast, ecological time. When Jarvis states that there is "salt everywhere under this land," Almeda responds, "Does this not mean...that there was once a great sea?" and Jarvis says, "very likely" (58). By referring to what is known as the Champlain Sea, Munro references geographical and glacial history that goes back over ten thousand years. The "great sea" (58) that is also associated with the bog behind Almeda's house at Pearl Street and Almeda's own mind might also be likened to Kristeva's notion of the *chora*. Kristeva explains *chora* as an "energy" that is "formed by the drives" and that which, paradoxically, "precedes...spatiality and temporality" ("Revolution" 93-94). Munro not only takes up vast, ecological, geographical, and developmental time, but also historical time. We readers experience the text in the present moment, taking as our subject the story that was first published in 1988; and the narrator, ostensibly writing the story in the late 1980s, contemplates a fictional writer of the Huron County region of Ontario, who was writing in the 1870s. Thus, we are confronted with layers of time as the reader, Munro, the narrator, and Almeda Roth attempt to make sense of history and experience. Ultimately, as Almeda collapses into the bog and her own self, so too do the layers of time, conglomerating and coalescing in "Meneseteung."

"Friend of My Youth" and "Meneseteung" are exemplary pieces that contemplate time and epistemology. "Friend" considers oral storytelling and memory: the narrator grapples with the stories her mother has told her. "Meneseteung," by contrast, addresses written literature and history, represented by Almeda's book of poems, *Offerings*, and the local newspaper *The Vidette*'s written accounts. As William Butt points out, however, "Meneseteung" also engages with the notion of oral history if we consider the fact that the title of the story is "the Aboriginal name for what today is called 'Maitland River,'" which flows "from Southwestern Ontario west into Lake Huron and the town of Goderich" (15). The story, therefore, contests geographical time, developmental time, and the march of progress. Indeed, commenting on one of Almeda's poems, "Champlain at the Mouth of the Meneseteung," the narrator states that "this poem celebrates the popular, *untrue* belief that the explorer sailed down the eastern shore of Lake Huron and landed at the mouth of the major river" (52, emphasis added). "Friend of My Youth," more explicitly than "Meneseteung" perhaps, addresses memory and communication or the lack thereof, since the narrator contemplates letters between her mother and her friend, many of which go unanswered, and since the title of the story refers to one of the letter's salutations, which could refer either to a friend of the narrator's mother, or to the readers of the story themselves. Underlying both of these stories is a sense of the author herself, implicated in the layers of storytelling since she—like her narrators and their subjects—is a writer too. As Morra notes, Munro "does little...to dissuade critics from seeing the autobiographical possibilities in her work" and "instead...nourishes this fascination" ("'Don't Take'" 256).

Time and Narrative Framing   125

5

Memory and Retrospect

"Fiction" and "Child's Play" in *Too Much Happiness*

IN *TOO MUCH HAPPINESS*, published in 2009, Munro continues to challenge and complicate notions of time. More so than her early works, such as *Lives of Girls and Women* and *Who Do You Think You Are?*, this collection focuses on retrospective aspects of time. Munro's characters look back upon their pasts, about which they have complicated feelings such as guilt or regret. Quoting Dorrit Cohn's *Transparent Minds*, Carrington notes that Munro's narrators are often older versions of themselves who "elucidate [their] mental confusion of earlier days... and know what happened to [them] next, and [are] free to slide up and down the time axis that connects [their] two selves" (7). "This temporal sliding," Carrington suggests, "is...one of the techniques that create the split selves of [Munro's] characters" (7). Munro's employment of older protagonists who look back upon their younger selves necessitates a large time span in each story, which, as Carrington puts it, "gives many of her short stories the breadth of perspective expressed only in novellas and novels" (7). In *Too Much Happiness*, "Fiction" and "Child's Play" contemplate memory in relation to ethical responsibilities for both younger and older selves. Munro's "split selves" in these stories demonstrate the movement back and forth between the present and the past, the current self and the remembered one. They challenge progressive time to consider the ethics of living a good life.

Between *Friend of My Youth* (1990), and *Too Much Happiness* (2009), Munro published five significant collections of short stories: *Open Secrets* (1994), *The Love of a Good Woman* (1998), *Hateship, Friendship, Courtship,*

127

Loveship, Marriage (2001), *Runaway* (2004), and *The View from Castle Rock* (2006). As Thacker notes, the Munro stories that Daniel Menaker was editing at *The New Yorker*, "especially those that were gathered in *Open Secrets*, had qualities that displayed Munro's further movement away from the linear and the realistic" (*Alice Munro* 449). Having established herself as a significant Canadian writer by the 1990s, critics such as George Woodcock, among others, began to assume a familiarity with her work (456). Between the publishing of *Open Secrets* and *The Love of a Good Woman*, there were many changes at *The New Yorker*. Menaker, for instance, left the magazine to take a job as senior editor at Random House (474). *The New Yorker* published "The Love of a Good Woman," even though it was seventy pages long—more of a novella than a story. The story was successful and received the O. Henry Prize (475). Thacker notes that the stories Munro published during the 1990s were "at once risky, strange, and familiarly rooted in Huron Country" (491).

"*Hateship, Friendship, Courtship, Loveship, Marriage* went into production in early 2001,"[1] and "by mid-October the book was atop the *Globe and Mail's* bestseller list" (Thacker, *Alice Munro* 500). Another book by Munro, *No Love Lost*, was published before *Runaway* (2004). It was published in Canada only and was aimed at school adoptions (513). Yet perhaps the most interesting book that Munro published during this time was *The View from Castle Rock*, published in 2006. In that book, Munro writes about her ancestors, recalling earlier autobiographical writings such as "Home" (1974) and "Working for a Living" (1981), among others (528). Thus, she circles back in time and turns inward toward herself and her ancestral past in these later writings. As Thacker notes, even apart from "Home" and "Working for a Living, "Munro has long tended toward the genealogical" (538), so in that sense the content of *The View from Castle Rock* is not a surprise. In *Castle Rock*, the author draws upon letters and other archival materials while also incorporating imaginative elements, demonstrating the tension between truth and fiction as she mines her own histories. As reviewer Karl Miller puts it, *Castle Rock* "is a rare and fascinating work, in which the past makes sense of the present and the present makes sense of the past, and the two are both a continuum and a divorce. It is very much a memoir, as well as a set of fictions. But then the whole corpus of Munro's stories is a memoir, the novel of her life" (para. 12). *Castle Rock* seems to be a coming together of contemplations and writing that Munro had been working on for some time, and it is also representative, in many ways, of the personal and autobiographical nature of her work.

Too Much Happiness includes ten stories, most of which appeared in *The New Yorker* prior to their appearance in the collection. The publication history around the story "Wood" is unusual in that it had been published early on in *The New Yorker*, in 1980 (Thacker, *Alice Munro* 559), but had not made it into a collection of Munro's stories until 2009. "Wenlock Edge" and "Dimensions" were published in *The New Yorker* before *The View from Castle Rock* (559), demonstrating some overlap in the timing of Munro's publications. The title story of the collection has perhaps received the most critical attention. Taking as her subject the historical figure of Sophia Kovalevsky, a 19th-century Russian mathematician and novelist, Munro uses a narrative method like the one she used in *Castle Rock*, a point that Leah Hager Cohen makes in her review of the book in *The New York Times*. The narrator's curiosity about a historical figure leads to an imaginative recreation of that figure. Just as she does in "Meneseteung," here Munro creates and demonstrates tension between research and imagination. "Too Much Happiness," is also the subject of Duffy's article, "Alice Munro's Narrative Historicism." While Duffy acknowledges the narrative similarities between "The Wilds of Morris Township," a story in *The View from Castle Rock*, "Meneseteung," and "Too Much Happiness," he focuses on how the latter story differs from the former ones: "if ['Meneseteung'] relies upon the author's imaginative grasp of the life and setting of its subject, ['Too Much Happiness'] largely confines itself to historical fact, as the acknowledgement section makes evident" 198-99). In other words, "when Sophia Kovalevsky (1850-1891) sprang into Munro's consciousness, her earlier reliance upon a more overtly fictional framework disappeared" (199).

Besides the title story, "Wenlock Edge" has received some critical attention, including in Joanna Luft's "Boxed In: Alice Munro's 'Wenlock Edge' and *Sir Gawain and the Green Knight*," an article that highlights Munro's "elaborate intertextual engagement with the Middle English Arthurian romance" (103) in the version of the story that was published in *The New Yorker* in 2005. The two stories that I analyze in this chapter, "Fiction" and "Child's Play," have received little critical attention or mentions in reviews, despite their fascinating approaches to time and memory, their autobiographical implications, and their emphasis on meta-narration. Both stories deal with the notion of a split self: two

Memory and Retrospect 129

sides of the self that are seemingly mismatched, or do not coincide. Both address the idea of an older person looking back on their younger self and address the very *oneness* of that self. "Fiction" and "Child's Play" suggest Munro's continuing focus on the self and selves, her emphasis on the present's engagement with the past, and her dynamic demonstration of the tension between truth and fiction, the autobiographical and the imaginative.

"Fiction"

"Fiction" begins with a depiction of the protagonist's early married life. Joyce is a cellist and a music teacher at a public school, and her husband Jon is a carpenter. They live in a small town on the west coast of Canada, in a home near a forest, where the townspeople consider the two of them to be hippies, though they do not seem to see themselves that way. Edie, a young apprentice and single mother, comes to work for Jon, and they soon fall in love. Jon and Joyce split up, and Joyce leaves the house while Jon, Edie, and Edie's daughter, Christine, live there. Joyce moves into an apartment in town and continues to teach music at the school—Christine is one of her students. The story then time jumps to much later in Joyce's life. She has remarried a professor of neuropsychology, Matt, and she is now a professional cellist and lives in North Vancouver. When Joyce sees a book displayed at a bookstore by Christie O'Dell, a friend of one of Matt's grown children, she buys the book—a collection of short stories—and begins to read it. Soon she realizes that Christie O'Dell is Christine, Edie's child, and Joyce, who was her teacher, is featured as a character in one of the stories. The latter parts of "Fiction" are a recount of Christie O'Dell's story and Joyce's reading and interpretation of it. "Fiction" is highly metafictional, and we, the readers, are invited to contemplate the boundaries between "truth" and "fiction," as well as between the elusive Christie O'Dell and Munro herself. Joyce contemplates her past and realizes that her memories both overlap with and differ from those of Christie O'Dell's.

The protagonist's realization that Christie is Christine is significant in that it demonstrates the notion that the adult self is both separate from and at one with its childhood counterpart, a concept that reappears in "Child's Play." It also relates to Munro's impetus to address, if subtly, the slippage between truth and lies, autobiography and fiction. Certainly, the title of the story "Fiction" itself begs the question of whether there is "truth" within it. Munro is like Christie insofar as she is a successful writer that might be recognized by others. "Fiction" is metafictional in that it gestures toward the alignment and misalignment not only between the adult and the child, but also between the writer and her characters. McGill notes that in Munro's stories, "the narrator's unreliability reminds readers that narratives are always subjective and therefore partial, and that audiences should not take any one account— whether fictional or nonfictional—as telling them the whole story and equipping them adequately for ethical judgements for the people involved" ("Daringly" 888). Munro keeps the fictional and the nonfictional in constant tension in this story.

In "Fiction," Munro foregrounds ethics, or rather perceptions about whether a person appears to be respectable or morally responsible. On the one hand, when the story begins and Edie first comes to Joyce and Jon's home, Edie presents herself to the couple as morally responsible. She makes a point of telling the couple that she does not drink, since she is an alcoholic who is a member of AA (31), and she explains that she is taking the job as Jon's woodworking apprentice so that she can provide for her and her child (31). On the other hand, however, Joyce suggests that Edie might have been a prostitute ("I think... she'd been on the streets"), and she compares her to Mary Magdalene (34), an ambivalent figure who is both a saint and a prostitute in the Bible and in literature. Edie's presentation of herself therefore contrasts Joyce's depiction of her. Edie is innocent: Joyce says she is "like a child" (30) but she is also wily, at least in Joyce's eyes. When Edie talks, Joyce says, "it is forceful" (30), and Edie subtly starts to occupy Joyce's spaces, such as her kitchen and her home. When Edie asks Jon and Joyce not to leave open wine bottles in the kitchen, Joyce says, "I really don't see what business—" (32). Jon explains that "sometimes she comes in and makes a couple of sandwiches for us—" (32), and Joyce says, "So? It's my kitchen. Ours" (32), trying to the reclaim the place of which she is losing hold. This conversation is significant when we consider that at the beginning of the story, Joyce and her new husband, Matt, hold a party in Matt's childhood home. Matt maintains his place in the home while Joyce—who leaves her house as Edie moves into it—is pushed out.

It is noteworthy that Joyce describes Edie's identity as an artistic creation, like Munro's writing of the character herself. When Joyce first meets Edie, and Edie shows her and Jon the tattoos that cover her skin,

Joyce exclaims, "It was as if her skin had become a garment, or perhaps a comic book of faces both leering and tender...too intricate or maybe too horrid to be comprehended" (31). Not only is Edie the writer's creation, this quotation implies, but she is also a character who is multifaceted, who must be interpreted. Reading her skin, we might interpret that she has experienced the "intricacies," of life, both wonderful and "horrid" (31). By drawing our attention to Edie's tattoos, Munro highlights the notion of body as text. She emphasizes corporeality, bringing the concept of the body to the fore. She again challenges the Cartesian notion that the mind dominates the body and takes precedence over it;[2] she suggests that the subject is inscribed and inscribes herself in and through the body. One might argue that women have adhered to the patriarchal order in part through their compliance to fashion trends, in this case by inscribing the body with tattoos, which are like "garments" (31). But in *Volatile Bodies*, Grosz explains the agency of one who might opt for such bodily inscription: "The line between compliance and subversion is always a fine one, difficult to draw with any certainty. All of us, men as much as women, are caught up in modes of self-production and self-observation; these modes may entwine us in various networks of power, but never do they render us merely passive or compliant" (144).

Munro privileges the body and specifically the skin as text. She implies not only that Edie is a character that the author inscribes, but also that Edie has the agency to inscribe herself. Her "skin" is a "comic book" (31), a joke but also an image that Edie has written, and that Joyce reads. Joyce's reading of Edie's skin as text parallels her later reading of Christie's story. The text on Edie's skin tells an ambiguous story of a woman who is both "leering" and "tender" (31); likewise, Christie's story describes Joyce as both predator and caregiver. In both cases, the figures can be read and interpreted but not in an easy or determinate way. Grosz notes that "every body is marked by the history and specificity of its existence" (*Volatile Bodies* 142), but in a "system of corporeal production" (144) one is not just passive and compliant but also active and subversive. The body is dynamic. As such, the body continually inscribes and creates itself in relation to the socio-historical specificity out of which it came. In "Fiction," Edie is not only Munro's creation, but a character who seemingly inscribes and creates herself. Moreover, she is reinterpreted yet again by the reader. Likewise, Christie O'Dell creates her truth in her story, a truth that does not fully align with Joyce's. Corporeal and written subjects push back against domination, telos, and linearity, pushing back against how they are written.

Munro hints at Edie's sexuality—and foreshadows Edie and Jon's affair—while simultaneously demonstrating that the movement from person to character, from what is real to what is created, is a reconstruction; a metamorphosis. About Edie's tattoos, for instance, Joyce states, "The first thing you had to wonder...was whether her whole body had been transformed in the same way" (31). Just as Jon is a carpenter who shapes wood into furniture, so too is the tattoo artist a creator who shapes bodies into artwork, and Munro is a writer who shapes people into characters. In this case, Munro rewrites the biblical story of Jesus the carpenter and Mary Magdalene the saint or prostitute into the fictional characters of Jon and Edie. The mill town where they all live has "fallen on evil days" (38)—like Adam and Eve falling in the Garden of Eden. Employment at the mill has been lost and the town has transformed; Joyce and Jon's marriage has disintegrated and changed into another pairing, that between her husband and his lover. Munro creates a *mise en abyme* as she portrays one artistic creation inside of another in a continual layering of bodies of people and bodies of artistic work that move through time.

Yet there is more to say about Munro's invocation of Mary Magdalene and the Bible in this story. Edie is Jon's apprentice as Mary Magdalene was Jesus's disciple. As historian James Carroll explains, "from texts of the early Christian era, it seems that [Mary Magdalene's] status as an 'apostle,' in the years after Jesus' death, rivalled even that of Peter" (para. 2). Moreover, Edie presents herself to Joyce and Jon as a repentant sinner when she says that she is in AA (31); likewise, in various texts Mary Magdalene is portrayed as repentant: "for many ventures the most obsessively revered of saints, this woman became the embodiment of Christian devotion, which was defined as *repentance* (Carroll para 1, emphasis added). If Munro compares the character of Edie to Mary Magdalene in "Fiction," then she also compares her to the other Mary—the mother of Jesus—even if only momentarily. Edie says that her nine-year-old daughter "was born without a father" (31). On the one hand, we can interpret that to mean that Edie is a single mother, and that the father of her child is not present in their lives. On the other hand, however, Edie's statement reminds us of the Virgin Mary and the

Memory and Retrospect   133

immaculate conception; indeed, this allusion is made evident when Joyce sarcastically and judgementally comments, "I daren't inquire about the virgin birth" (31).

The figure of Mary Magdalene is one who has been represented variously throughout the ages, throughout time. Who she is and what she represents depends on the politics and history of the moment in Western civilization. Carroll explains that "confusions attached to Mary Magdalene's character were compounded across time as her image was conscripted into one power struggle after another, and twisted accordingly" (para. 3). In the Bible, there are various other women in the story of Jesus: Mary the mother of Jesus, "three unnamed women who are expressly identified as sexual sinners" (para. 4), and others. Carroll notes that "the first thing to do in unravelling the tapestry of Mary Magdalene is to tease out the threads that properly belong to these other women" (para. 4). It is interesting, considering Edie's tattoos, that Mary Magdalene has been imaged not only in narrative, but also in visual art, in "Renaissance and Baroque painterly occupation," but also "through the Middle Ages and the Counter-Reformation, into the Modern period and the Enlightenment" (para. 35). Men of the Catholic church such as Gregory the Great set out to recast the powerful saint, and Magdalene became not a powerful woman but "nothing less than holy pornography, guaranteeing the ever-lustful harlot—if lustful now for the ecstasy of holiness—a permanent place in the Catholic imagination" (para. 35). By alluding to the figure of Mary Magdalene with the character of Edie, Munro gestures towards the complexity of that figure in the present and the past. There is no easily definable Edie just as there is no easily definable Mary Magdalene. Her image is one that changes and morphs through time and history shaped by herself, others, and a society that, to a large extent, determines women's roles and places.

The performance of Edie's self as a work of art written on her body is repeated in Joyce's own performance as director of the children's recital at the school where she teaches. Joyce imagines Jon and Edie's performance—their declaration of themselves as a couple to the town—when she anticipates their attendance at the recital. She plays up her performance for them and wears "a black silk skirt that shone with silver as she moved," with "silver bangles and glitter in her loose hair" (37). Yet, while her display is received at the recital—"some whistles mingled with the applause" (37)—ironically, Jon and Edie are not there (37), and so they do not see her bodily and musical performance. Munro seems to suggest that the coming-to-life of characters and stories depend on their readers. Those readers and the stories' outcomes can be anticipated, but they can never fully be determined. Joyce anticipates the arrival of Jon and Edie but ultimately performs for a different audience. Despite Christie O'Dell's and Alice Munro's guesswork about who their readers are and how they might read their work, it is the readers themselves who interpret the characters and the stories, creating and inscribing them. Thus, Munro resists clear and predictable endings and linear teleology, suggesting that created works of art are open ended. Finality is resisted and cannot be fully known.

Later in the story, Munro time jumps to a much older Joyce, celebrating her husband Matt's sixty-fifth birthday. Matt's two previous wives are at the party, the first of whom has suffered memory loss due to a car accident, and the second of whom is with her new younger wife and their baby (37-38). Joyce notes that the party is "positively a life story" (37), a microcosm of time, with representatives that include Matt's wives and his children from years past. The party takes place at Matt and Joyce's residence, Matt's childhood home in North Vancouver. That the house was Matt's childhood home suggests a connection between the present, Matt's adult self, and the past, his childhood one. The house sits at the edge of Grouse Mountain, on what used to be a forest. Joyce's statement that "houses keep climbing above it, most of them castle affairs, with massive garages" (39) suggests that the houses metaphorically represent the characters' relationships in the story, each wife attempting to "climb above" or outdo the previous. It does so by juxtaposing comments about the Matt's past wives with those about the past houses. In this interpretation, Matt's statement that "one of these days this place will go," and "a couple of hideosities will replace it" (39), anticipates Joyce's replacement by another. His exclamation that "the taxes are monstrous" (39) problematically suggests that each wife increasingly becomes a burden to own and maintain. Just as Edie notes that those in AA drink coffee, "changing one bad habit for another" (31), so too do the characters in this story continually change romantic partners. That the language of this replacement is couched in gothic terms such as "monstrous" suggests an ugliness that opposes the happiness of the collection's title. This pattern of continual replacement begs "the question of time and its relentless movement into the future" (Grosz, *Time Travels* 2). It also engages and critiques the meaning of time under capital. Invoking Paul Virilio, Burges and Elias note that "modernity overseen and defined by capital depends upon speed of communication, speed of consumption, and speed of obsolescence and innovation" (14). This speed is precisely what occurs when wives are consumed and replaced like houses, and when objects and people are defined solely in terms of capital—"the taxes are monstrous" (39).

Joyce's statement that the party is "positively a life story" is ironic when we consider that it is there that she meets Christie O'Dell, and through her comes to return in memory to an earlier part of her life, when she was married to Jon. Upon first seeing Christie at the party, Joyce describes her like a ghost, invoking the gothic mode for which Munro is known. Christie has "wispy pale hair," an "evasive pale face," and "invisible eyebrows" (40). Elusive, she leaves as soon as Joyce approaches: when Joyce "skirts a group of young people" at the party, Christie gets up and walks away to smoke a cigarette (40). Joyce's instant dislike for Christie and her feeling of discomfort around her (40-41) suggest that she experiences an uncanny moment: it is as though Christie represents a dark or unfavourable part of her past. Seeing Christie, she is confronted with what is both familiar and unfamiliar; she feels both at home and "unhomely," disjunct from the home; and she paradoxically experiences both recognition and dis-ease. According to Bhabha, "In the stirrings of the unhomely, another world becomes visible" (445). Here, for Joyce, the ghostly Christie appears and becomes part of her world. Joyce will soon come to the shocking realization that Christie is of Joyce's home, both literally and figuratively: she lived in her home when she was a child and is a part of her past.

When Joyce sees Christie's face on a poster at a bookstore advertising her new book, she recognizes her: "Where had Joyce seen her before? At the party, of course. But even then, in the midst of her probably unwarranted dislike, she felt that she had seen that face before" (43). After Joyce buys the book by Christie and begins to read it, she realizes that she is Edie's daughter, Christine—"translated easily into Christie" (46)— who took violin lessons from Joyce and performed in her school recital. When Joyce reads in the biography on the book cover that the author "lived with her mother...in a house between the mountains and the sea," she suddenly "feels too uncomfortable to keep reading" (44), since the scene invokes her memory of her life with Jon and his affair with Edie. Joyce has suddenly recognized that Christie is Christine, and that the place and time Christie O'Dell writes about is Joyce's too. Reading the book, Joyce is confronted with her own past. The past will not stay put and erupts into the present.

Joyce's reading of Christie's stories is both an interpretation and a creation of her own past. In Joyce's reading or imagining Edie's conversation with her daughter, for instance, she says, "How do you like Jon's house? Wouldn't it be nice to go and live in Jon's house?" (47), but then notes, "That was all wrong. Edie would never spout such blather. Give her some credit" (47). If we read these questions as part of Christie's story, then Joyce's command, "Give her some credit" (47), is directed at the author, but if we read them as though they are in Joyce's mind, not Christie's story, then Joyce embellishes Christie's fiction with her own, and Joyce's command is directed at herself. Munro conflates Christie's stories and Joyce's interpretations of them, leaving the reader to wonder what Christie has written and what Joyce has imagined: they become one. Joyce's replacement in her house by Edie and her daughter mirrors the replacement of one house for another, one lover for another.

Joyce's reading of Christie's book initiates both a struggle to bring forth her memories and an unexpected triggering of them. For instance, she cannot, at first, remember Edie's daughter's name: "She searches her mind for the name of Edie's child. Surely not Christie" (46). Yet her act of reading the story also invokes seemingly forgotten memories. Contemplating what she reads, she notes, "some of it was true, certainly. She does remember things she had forgotten" (49). Joyce reads her own past and discovers it anew, just as she notes the "life story" in the collection of people at her and Matt's party (37). Joyce reads and imagines herself in Christie's book, *How We Are to Live?*, as Munro reads and imagines herself in "Fiction." Munro writes short stories, as does Christie (43). Writing in this genre, in Joyce's estimation, results in Christie's position as an outsider in authorial circles. Likewise, Munro looks in as an outsider on this story. Christie, Joyce states, is "hanging on the gates of Literature, rather than safely settled inside" (43). She is, like Munro herself in "Fiction," as elusive as a ghost, passing by with her "wispy pale hair" (40). Joyce herself, of course, is also looking in from the outside. She is situated outside of Christie's story, as she was previously outside of Edie's new life with Jon, even as she peers in unnoticed.

Memory and Retrospect 137

The readers of "Fiction" are aligned with Munro, who artistically creates it, and Joyce, who reads and interprets *How We Are to Live?*—a title, we might note, that echoes the titles of Munro's early books, *Lives of Girls and Women* and *Who Do You Think You Are?* Whereas the so-called fictional character in Christie's story is Joyce's doppelgänger, the elusive Christie O'Dell is Munro's. Christie haunts the story, simultaneously "skirt[ing]" (40) it on the outside and integral to it, much like the author of "Fiction" herself. Thus, Munro generates another *mise en abyme* in which the reader and the writer are implicated in both the production and the consumption of literary representation.

After Joyce reads Christie's book, she goes to the bookstore to have her book signed by the author, and there, her subject position mimics the one represented in the book and earlier in her life. When Christine is a child, Joyce offers her candy, which can be read either as an act of kindness or as leering and witch-like. Now, she offers Christie candy again and is viewed in the same ambivalent way. Joyce brings Christie chocolate lilies, yet the saleswoman takes them away and "is not smiling now but taking a hard look at her" (53). Most significantly, Christie does not remember Joyce as her former teacher, the one who is supposedly represented in her fiction: "there is not a scrap of recognition in the girl's face" (53), and Joyce seems hurt by that oversight. Thus, this story is about the human need for connection with others, both past and present, and the failure to make that connection. Joyce works as a teacher and performs as the director of the recital so that Jon and Edie can see her, and yet they do not attend. Edie's child, Christine, vies for her teacher Joyce's attention, to no avail: she finds instead that her teacher attends to her because she is jealous of her mother and Jon's new relationship. Matt notes that his childhood home "will have to go" as one "hideosity" replaces another, just like the wives and lovers in the room at his and Joyce's party. Christie not only fails to recognize her former teacher, but also acts, in Joyce's estimation, as though the story she wrote about her "was disposed of long before" (53). In each case, one desires human communication and understanding, but such connection is not attained, resulting in a continual pattern of deferral and displacement; love and its dispensation; hope and resulting loneliness.

Munro employs both self-reflexivity and intertextuality. As we have seen, she invokes and alludes to the biblical story of Mary Magdalene and Jesus Christ. She also alludes to the fairy tale, "Hansel and Gretel."

In both cases, she suggests an ambivalent subject positioning. While Edie is Mary Magdalene, both saint and whore, Joyce is both a caring teacher and the evil witch of the fairy tale in relation to Christine. Like the evil witch, Joyce comes from a house in the woods: "Some of the other teachers had perfume on, but she never did. She smelled of wood or stone or trees" (46). Joyce comes to an awareness of her own morally ambivalent position as she reads Christie's book. Her own perspective is challenged by that of Christie's, and she is prompted to see her past anew. While Joyce believes that Christine's move from her own house into Jon's will be disruptive, even traumatic, she finds that in Christie's story it is "hardly mentioned," and that instead, "everything is hinged on the child's love for the teacher" (47). On the one hand, in Christie's story, the teacher, who Joyce interprets as herself, seems to care for the child, who Joyce interprets as Christine. On the other hand, however, the teacher verges on being a child-seducer, the witch in the fairy tale. In the tale, the witch offers the children candy but later eats them. In *How Are We To Live*, the teacher offers the child candy—"she reaches for the bowl of Smarties" (47)—but not to "encourage" (47) Christine, as she first believes, but to inquire, out of jealousy, about the relationship between her mother and Jon. The interpretation of teacher-as-predator is clear not only through the offer of candy, but also with her presence in the child's life as a way to pry or inquire about the status of Edie's relationship with Jon. Just as the protagonist in Christie's story gradually comes to an awareness that the teacher only attends to her to find out about her mother and Jon, so too does Joyce gradually come to an awareness of her own morally ambivalent position—as represented in the story—as both kind hearted and mean spirited.

The intertextuality of the "Hansel and Gretel" fairy tale is threaded throughout the story. In the Brothers Grimm version, the children's father is a woodcutter, which is similar to Jon's job as a carpenter. The wife of the woodcutter is the stepmother of the children, just as Joyce acts as Christine's mother in "Fiction": she takes Christine out for ice cream after school and drives her home, for instance (48), and she tends to her wounds when she trips at the playground (47). The focus on place and home is emphasized both in the fairy tale and in Munro's story. In the fairy tale, the children hear their parents' plan to leave them in the woods, so they use stones to mark their path so that they can find their way home. In the woods, they find another home, the candy one, but it is a lure into the wicked witch's trap. In "Fiction," homes are foregrounded even at the beginning of the story, when Joyce and Matt discuss the new homes in West Vancouver. The notion of home is emphasized again when Joyce is forced out of hers, replaced by Edie and Christine. Joyce imagines or reads in Christie's book what Edie might have said to her daughter, Christine, when Edie decided to move in with Jon: "Mommy and Jon like each other very much and when people like each other very much they want to live in the same house... Mommy and Jon are going to live in Jon's house and your music teacher is going to go and live in an apartment" (47). Joyce's construction or understanding of what Edie might have said to Christine here ironically aligns Joyce with the children of the fairy tale—they are forced out of their own home. The way Joyce imagines Edie telling Christine this news posits Edie, rather than Joyce, as the wicked witch who has forced a family member out. Yet Joyce questions the validity of what she has imagined (47).

In "Hansel and Gretel," the parents leave the children in the forest to starve; in "Fiction," Joyce suggests to Christine that the forest is not dangerous. In this instance, aligned with the wicked witch, Joyce ostensibly lures Christine there. Moreover, when Joyce describes the forest to Christine, she does so in terms of sweets, echoing the "Hansel and Gretel" fairy tale. She states the names of the wildflowers in the forest and notes that one kind is "chocolate lilies" (49): "I think there is another proper name for them, but I like to call them chocolate lilies. It sounds so delicious" (49). In another interpretation, however, with Joyce's depiction of the forest as enticing, Munro challenges the notion that forests and stepmothers are inherently dangerous or evil: "The teacher says it is a pity to be scared of the woods all the time" (49). Thus, Munro alludes to "Hansel and Gretel" as she probes the negative historical associations around stepmothers. The intertextuality that Munro incorporates in "Fiction" both draws upon and challenges historical associations around female figures such as Mary Magdalene and the wicked witch in "Hansel and Gretel." Both allusions are to works that have been rewritten and reimagined over hundreds of years. Munro reimagines them once again as she works against the disempowerment and denigration of women in her representations of them. She invokes and contests existing representations of female figures while she simultaneously suggests that the notion of time—of time immemorial—is embedded into the very fabric of the literary and visual works we engage with today.

In "Fiction," the past pushes into the present, as its protagonist, Joyce, moves back and forth between her life with her first husband, Jon, and her second husband, Matt. While doing so, Munro mobilizes biblical and literary allusions, including the invocation of Mary Magdalene and fairy tale characters such as Hansel and Gretel, playing with the boundaries between "truth" an "fiction," so-called real people and those who come from books. Significantly, Joyce's engagement with literature necessitates her confrontation with her own history. Her act of reading Christie O'Dell's story causes her to re-evaluate her past and see it in an entirely new light: it challenges and upsets the paradigm that determines her own identity, what she has told herself about herself, and her own lived and constructed "life story" (37). Moreover, Joyce is forced to acknowledge her own morally ambivalent actions and see herself as not simply "good" or "bad," but somewhere in between, dynamic and vacillating.

On the one hand, the story is about missed opportunities for love and human connection, demonstrated, for instance, in the replacement of one lover for another. On the other hand, however, it shows that very love and human connection through Joyce's reading of Christie's stories. That Christie does not recognize Joyce at the book reading is not the point, nor is it a tragedy. After all, as Joyce ironically and self-reflexively notes at the end of "Fiction"—in way that aligns her rather than Christie with Munro—"she might even turn this into a funny story some day" (53). What matters is that, through the act of reading, Joyce herself has seen her past through another's eyes, and that perception has enabled a new, more complex understanding of herself and her relationships with others, past and present. Thus, "Fiction" demonstrates the power and importance of literature itself, the need for us to engage in reading and interpretation to understand ourselves, others, and the complex and dynamic worlds in which we live. The "surprise ending" (53), by which, perhaps, we are "not surprised" (53), is the human connection that Joyce longs for and has found after all. That connection—though it is attained through others, through Christie's written story—is ultimately with herself.

"Child's Play"

The narrator of "Child's Play," Marlene, is an adult who looks back upon her childhood, contemplating a past that continues to haunt her. Like Joyce in "Fiction," Marlene takes her former self as the subject of her analysis. Joyce re-evaluates her past by reading Christie's story and begins to understand herself in a new way. Marlene, by contrast, reconsiders her past by confessing her childhood actions to her reader—a confession that is narrated but never fully enacted in the story. In other words, the story itself is Marlene's confession to the reader, but in the story, she tries but is ultimately unable to confess her sin to the priest.[3] In "Fiction," Joyce finds that her former music student, Christie, now a writer, does not recognize her when she comes to her book signing. It is as though the two are not one, as though Joyce's present life cannot be reconciled with her past—a seeming "fiction." Similarly, in "Child's Play," Marlene says that "every year, when you're a child, you become a different person" (164), and she does not recognize her camp friend, Charlene, when she visits her decades later (186). In both cases, time is central to the stories, and in both, the present does not grow naturally out of the past but is rather disjunct from it: the past does not make sense in relation to the present; the "self" is different from the one before. As Katherine G. Sutherland notes, a "complexity of Munro's adult/child narrators...is that the analyst and analysand are one and the same, a narrative singularity that is split into multiple temporalities of perspectives" (161). "The child and adult perspectives fold into and over one another" (161). In this story, the past is not over but "[sprouts] up fresh...wanting attention" (Munro, *Too Much* 164). It is ever new and dynamic.

In the story, the protagonist Marlene goes to summer camp as a nine- or ten-year-old child, and meets a friend, Charlene. The two revel in their rhyming names and matching hats, seeing themselves as twins or mirror images of one another. When a group of disabled children arrive at the camp, Verna is with them. Marlene has told Charlene about Verna, a girl who, with her grandmother, rented rooms in the same house as Marlene and her family. Marlene is repelled by Verna's mental disability and does not want to be associated with her. At the end of the week-long camp, Marlene and Charlene drown Verna while everyone is swimming. No one sees them do it, and they are picked up and brought home by their parents directly afterward. We, the readers, do not find out about the girls' crime until the very end of "Child's Play." The story time jumps between the young girls at camp and a time much later in their lives, when Charlene is on her deathbed with cancer. Marlene and Charlene do not keep in contact with one another much as adults, but when Charlene is dying, Marlene receives a letter from Charlene's husband to come see her, and then gets a note from Charlene—the note asks her to see a priest. Charlene's request for Marlene to see the priest, we can deduce, is to urge her to confess what they had done as children. The note indicates that Charlene has confessed. Marlene then goes to see the priest but does not confess to him. The story moves between the girls' childhood and adulthood to show how the act of murder they committed so long ago haunts them throughout their lives. For Marlene and Charlene, the past becomes part of the present.

With the title and the first few sentences of "Child's Play," Munro already confuses our conceptions of the child and the progression through time from childhood innocence to adulthood experience. She works both within and against notions of childhood innocence—innocence both as *purity* and as *ignorance.* The title is highly ironic. On the one hand, it invokes virtue, the so-called natural "play" of the child; on the other hand, however, it invokes malevolence, since the "play" to which the title refers is murder. Marlene's parents' reactions to Verna's death also demonstrate Munro's invocation and debunking of the child as pure. They find out about Verna's death by drowning shortly after the event, but they never know that it was at the hands of their daughter and her friend. Marlene's father's comment, "There should have been supervision," exposes his belief that children are either ignorant and unaware, or mischievous and not to be trusted. Marlene notes that her mother "had a habit of hanging on to—even treasuring—the foibles of [her] distant infantile state" (164), which suggests her mother views children as quaintly imperfect and inexperienced. The story, however, turns Marlene's parents' perceptions on their head. The children are not virtuous but rather capable of murder, and it is not them but their parents—the adults—who remain ignorant of that deed. Munro reinforces the idea that the adults rather than the children are ignorant when Marlene makes the comment that "only adults would be so stupid as to believe [Verna] had no power" (174). Thus, Munro invokes the

Western notion that the child moves from innocence to experience but she reverses it, throwing into question our assumptions about individual development and progression through time.

That Munro engages adult perspectives of that past event—both the perspective of Marlene the adult-narrator and her parents—suggests their responsibility for Verna's death. Are the children solely responsible for the murder, Munro seems to ask, or is it parents and the supervisory adults who should bear the blame? To answer that question, we might look to how Munro treats social responsibility in "Child's Play." The concept comes into the story right from its beginning. The camp tries to teach the children morals that align with the United Church that sponsors it. The morning "Chat" at the summer camp, for instance, is "relatively free of references to God or Jesus and [is] more about honesty and loving-kindness and clean thoughts" (167). The idea of "loving-kindness" flies in the face of the act of murder that Marlene and Charlene commit, and the notion of "clean thoughts" directly contrasts their thoughts of disgust about Verna that led to the murder. The camp's teachings, then, are ineffectual and highly ironic. Yet "loving-kindness" also stands in opposition to the actions of the adults themselves in the socio-historical context of the story. As Marlene notes, "It was wartime," and sometimes "a boy from our town or our street would be killed" (166). A camp counsellor wears what Marlene believes is a watch from her fiancé who died at war (167), and the children sing imperial war songs such as "There'll Always Be an England" at their evening camp-fires (166).

Clearly, Marlene, who attends the camp during World War II, lives in a time and place in which adults preach kindness while they simultaneously pose imperial superiority and kill others at war. The war songs that the girls sing at camp are markers of imperial time. As we can see from the title of the song mentioned, such tunes celebrate England's imperial power and proclaim its eternal presence. Imperialism is present at the camp in both senses of the word: it is present in *place* and *time*. The songs are geographically present at the camp in Canada, well beyond the country of England. England, the song indicates, will "always be" (166), suggesting that the country's imperial influence will be present throughout time. Munro thus depicts the insidious and ongoing influence of settler-colonialism, which posits the girls as colonial agents, even as they reside in a liminal space between the colonizer and its commonwealth, girlhood and womanhood, and—as we will see—lesbianism and compulsory heterosexuality.[4]

If there is any doubt that Marlene adopts the problematic values and hypocrisy of the adults around her and the society in which she lives, then Munro makes it clear when Marlene describes the matching hats that Marlene and Charlene wear at camp. That the hats are called "Coolie hats" implies that the girls take on the racist demeaner that the hats pronounce. "It was possible at that time—I mean the time when Charlene and I were at camp—," Marlene explains, "to say *coolie*, without the thought of offence" (165, emphasis in original). The hats are metonymic for the language and attitudes the girls inherit, even if they are not entirely aware of what that inheritance entails. "We had those names, those hats," Marlene says (165). Moreover, they represent collective exclusivity, since they are initially what bring the girls together. "We must have noticed the hats," Marlene notes about how she met Charlene, "and approved of each other" (165). The hats, then, serve as a marker, a coded message or call to a twin club in which only Marlene and Charlene can belong. They also signal a dominant cultural narrative and align the girls with imperial time, that which homogenizes and excludes in the name of so-called progress. When Charlene first asks another camper if she can "please be next to [her] twin sister?"— twins because they wear the same hats and have rhyming names—she asks the question in a "special voice" (165). The word "special" foreshadows the arrival of the "Specials," the handicapped children at the camp, but it also denotes a definition meant exclusively for Marlene: they mark themselves as collectively superior to Others, and especially to the arriving "Specials." To wear the "Coolie hats" is to wear an identity that is implicitly racist and eugenicist. "Coolie hats," Marlene explains, "became familiar later in the century, from television shots of the war in Vietnam" (165). The women who wore them, she notes, would be "walking in the road against the background of a bombed village" (165). In a shift from metonym to metaphor, the hats now represent the girls' exterior ("the women walking in the road"), set against an interior that is deep and dark after they commit murder ("a bombed village") (165).

Marlene and Charlene compare and contrast the "peculiarities and history of [their] bodies" (166), noting the differences between them. "We both had brown hair but hers was darker," (166) Marlene explains. "Her eyes had more green in them, mine more blue" (166). Critic

Anca-Raluca Radu states that "the way [Marlene] relates to Charlene can be described in terms of Lacanian mirroring" (182). The girls examine each other as if looking at themselves. Though they have identical hats and rhyming names, Marlene notes their differences to demarcate her own identity. Lacan's mirror stage focuses on a moment of infant development, recognition of the self in the Other; Munro focuses on a moment of adolescent development, self-creation and recognition. Lacan explains that the image in which the child recognizes themself is always illusionary, an ideal to which the child continually aspires: "This form would have to be called the Ideal I...[It] situates the agency of the ego, before its social determination, in a fictional direction" (2). For Munro too, I would argue, Marlene-the-adolescent attempts to create and understand herself in relation to another, Charlene—an image that is the fictional ideal she desires.

That ideal self—represented for Marlene in her twinned image, Charlene—is both an aspiration to be *like* the illusory self-image and a sexual desire *for* her. As Lacan explains, the "beauty" of the ideal is "both formative and erotogenic" (3). In "Child's Play," Marlene suggests that she had sexual feelings for Charlene, though she does not name Charlene directly in her confession of sexual desire: "I've experienced [erotic intimacy]...before puberty...[T]here would be confidences, probably lies, maybe leading to games. A certain hot temporary excitement, with or without genital teasing. Followed by ill feeling, denial, disgust" (168). That Marlene experiences homosexual desire but then denies it in "disgust" (168) implies that she repudiates the Other, embodied in her own homosexual desires, to establish the self. In some ways, the queerness depicted in "Child's Play" between Marlene and Charlene is similar to that depicted in *Who Do You Think You Are?* between Rose and Cora. In *Who Do You Think You Are?*, however, the relationship signifies a disruption of time socialization, a resistance to the expectation that a girl should have a romantic relationship with a boy. In "Child's Play," by contrast, queerness is coupled with a sense of repugnance toward the body, and thus a rejection of it. It is an establishment of the self over the Other and a negation of desire in favour of dominant social structures. In both instances, the protagonists of the stories experience their sexuality as they come of age and negotiate their sexual and gender identities.

In *Bodies That Matter*, Butler states that "'sex' not only functions as a norm but is part of a regulatory practice that produces the bodies it governs, that is, whose regulatory force is made clear as a kind of productive power, the power to produce—demarcate, circulate, differentiate—the bodies it controls" (1). In Munro's story, Marlene engages in such demarcation and differentiation from Charlene to reproduce normative heterosexual and material bodies, and to reject that which is deemed Other to them. Marlene's mention of "ill feeling" and "disgust" at her homosexual thoughts parallels the feelings of "disgust" that she has toward Verna. Thus, Munro situates Marlene's process of forming her identity as a repudiation of racial, sexual, and disabled Otherness. By wearing the "Coolie hat," Marlene rejects those marked racially different from her. By feeling "disgust" at both her homosexual desires toward Charlene and Verna's disabled body, she also rejects those whose bodies and desires do not fit the regulatory norm. Marlene achieves the materialization of her heterosexual body and herself by a "forcible reiteration of...norms" (Butler, *Bodies* 2).

Munro leaves the readers in suspense about what it is that haunts Marlene throughout her life, and only explains the murder itself at the end of the story. On the last day of the camp, when Marlene and Charlene are swimming in the lake with the rest of the campers, boats go by and make waves in the water, creating turbulence and chaos for the swimmers. At the same moment, Verna swims toward Marlene and Charlene. What follows is a description of the murderous drowning in language that is both sexual and horrific. Marlene's and Charlene's eyes lock—"our eyes did meet" (193)—as though they are lovers; and Marlene explains that the two of them kept their eyes on one another "rather than looking down at what our hands were doing" (193). "What our hands were doing" (193) could refer either to the drowning of Verna, or to the sexual touching of one another, a reading that is corroborated by the fact that Marlene describes such touching earlier in the story.

Earlier, when Marlene describes the sexual encounters she has had with girls, she says that there is "hot temporary excitement, with or without genital teasing. Followed by ill feeling, denial, disgust" (168). This description could also apply to the drowning of Verna. The "hot temporary excitement" of the sexual experience is like Charlene's eyes during the murder, which are "wide and gleeful" (193). The "denial" and "disgust" (168) that Marlene feels after such sexual encounters mirrors the same feelings Marlene feels after Verna's murder, and for the rest of her life. While the girls committed the act "consciously" (193), Marlene explains that it was "as if we were doing just what was—amazingly— demanded of us, as if this was the absolute high point, the culmination, in our lives, of being ourselves" (194). The act of killing Verna is what is "demanded" (194) by the imperial and patriarchal culture in which Marlene and Charlene reside, a society that requires the repudiation of the Other for the self to emerge—in order, that is, for the girls to reach "the culmination, in [their] lives, of being [themselves]" (194). If we read their act as a sexual transgression of heteronormativity, however, then their "wickedness" (194) is their lesbian sex that culminates in their womanly identities, those which contest the patriarchal norm. Munro leaves the scene ambiguous, mixing pleasure with denial, glee with disgust, sex with murder.

Of the drowning, Marlene says, "The whole business probably took no more than two minutes" (194), yet she is haunted by the act for the rest of her life. When Marlene receives the letter from Charlene's husband, she travels to see her at Princess Margaret Hospital in Toronto. After so many decades, this meeting parallels and contrasts their meeting at camp years before, when they compared bodily and family histories. Even before Marlene gets to Charlene's hospital room, she fears she cannot bear to see her: "I went up the elevator still thinking that I might be able to turn away" (185). When she does see her, she "look[s] down at a bloated body and a sharp ruined face, a chicken's neck for which the hospital gown was a mile too wide. A frizz of hair... No sign of Charlene" (185-86). If Charlene is Marlene's doppelgänger, an image of the self, then she is herself now the monster she tried to repudiate when she and Charlene murdered Verna. And yet, the guilt that both Marlene and Charlene harbour shows that such monstrousness cannot be suppressed. It keeps "sprouting up fresh, wanting attention" (164), like the note from Charlene that Marlene thinks she destroyed but then finds in her pocket (187).

Charlene's sick and aged body is a metaphor for the haunting guilt that—unlike Verna herself—cannot be killed: Charlene is not dead, nor even unconscious, but "sleeps" (186). The near-dead Charlene is the abject, that which, according to Kristeva, falls away from the body and is not reducible to it ("System"). From that which is repudiated, "the proper body, the obedient, law-abiding, social body, emerges" (Grosz, *Volatile Bodies* 192). At summer camp, Verna is the abject body that Marlene repels; later in life, Charlene is that same abject body. Marlene does not want to see Charlene on her deathbed, but "could hardly say no" (185). When she does see her, she is repulsed: "The enlarged liver, I thought, and wished I had run while I could" (185). Like Verna, Charlene has power over Marlene. To put it in Kristeva's words, it is the "powers of horror," the abject body that "upsets...violently the one who confronts it" (*Powers* 3).

Marlene and Charlene are "twinned" in "Child's Play," as are Charlene and Verna and Marlene and Verna. It is this doubling, this similarity between herself and Verna, that Marlene finds repulsive and fears. Indeed, Marlene differentiates herself from Verna, but that differentiation is continually belied. In many ways, Marlene's descriptions of Verna are of herself. For example, Marlene says that Verna "was not communicative in the normal way" (169), and yet Marlene goes on to demonstrate her own unusual way of communicating. She says, "I hated her" (169) and then immediately follows that statement with a qualification: "children use that word 'hate' to mean various things. It may mean that they are frightened" (169). Thus, Marlene implies that she uses the word "hate" to mean something else entirely, which could be read as not communicating in the "normal way" (169). Marlene says that Verna's "voice was hoarse and unmodulated, her words oddly separated, as if there were chunks of language caught in her throat" (170). Shortly thereafter, when speaking about how she communicates with her mother, Marlene says that she might have said something differently if she "had been more skilled at arguing" (171); later in the story, she is unable to confess to the priest, as if she—like Verna earlier—cannot speak clearly. Marlene's demarcation from Verna fails, for it is not only Verna's communication that is impeded, but Marlene's. However, though Marlene's language often fails, perhaps suggesting a subject not quite realized, she sometimes has the words she needs to act: "We had those names and those hats" (165). That Marlene focuses on language to separate herself from Verna implies that metaphorically, Verna is a part of Marlene, that fragmented, unformed, and prior self that is not a yet a self, and which, according to psychoanalytic theory, must be repudiated to be whole. The subject creates and demarcates the self at the moment of linguistic acquisition. By suggesting that

Verna metaphorically represents Marlene, I do not mean to diminish Verna's status as a person or as a character in her own right in Munro's text. Rather, I mean to show that in "Child's Play," the "emergence of the ethical subject is marked by ambivalence and paralysis" (Ventura, "From Accident" 158). As Ventura explains, Munro's story "ambivalently represent[s] the process of subjectification through metaphors or metonyms which depersonalize the characters while simultaneously making them account for their deed" (158).

Marlene's attempt to differentiate herself from Verna in voice repeats in Marlene's attempt to distinguish herself from Verna in body. Marlene describes Verna's body parts as unusual. Charlene notes that Verna has "the longest fingers [she] has even seen," and Marlene agrees (178). Yet when Marlene and Charlene compare their own bodies to one another, they also note their "peculiarities" (166): "We did not grow tired of inspecting and tabulating even the moles or notable freckles on our backs, length of our second toes (mine longer than the first toe, hers shorter)" (166). Marlene refers to Verna's "drooping snaky head" (176), a description that foreshadows the scene of Verna's drowning. And yet it is Marlene herself who "duck[s] her head" (176), as she and Charlene, like snakes slithering, dodge in and out of the "Specials" (176). When they are engaged in this game of trying to hide from Verna, Marlene notes that Verna did not notice them, and says that it was "perhaps because she was rather dazed, as most of the Specials appeared to be, trying to figure out what they were doing here" (176). But Marlene implies that she herself was dazed when she returned to school after that summer: she left behind "the *muddle* and *lethargy* of the summer vacation" (164, emphasis added). Therefore, once again, Marlene tries to separate herself from Verna, but to no avail. Previously, Verna lived in the duplex that was Marlene's home—its other half—and her grandmother, who she lives with, is named "Mrs. Home" (171). Just as the home is residence for the self, so too the body is residence for the soul. Verna is a part of Marlene in body just as she is in voice.

Perhaps the most interesting "twinning" in the story is the one between the older, adult Marlene, and the younger, childhood one. At times, the narration collapses into itself, so that Marlene-the-adult and Marlene-the-child momentarily become one. For example, when Marlene explains the religious "Chat" to which the campers were required to listen each morning, she explains that they didn't mind it:

"It was pleasant to sit on the beach in the warming sun and a little too cold yet for us to long to jump into the water" (167). Here, she at once describes her feelings as a child and as an adult. As a child, she does not yet want to jump into the water because it is too cold—it will warm up with the sun later in the day. Yet she might also be saying that she was young enough that she did not want to "jump into the water" (167)— take her own life—as she might want to do now, after living a life of guilt.

Often, when Marlene relays her childhood feelings, she remains distant from them, and she generalizes her past experiences and actions, rather than owning them by employing the first person "I." For instance, early in the story, she switches from first- to second-person narration: "Every year, when *you're* a child, *you* become a different person" (164, emphasis added), and she does so again later, slipping from first-person to second-person narration: "*I* supposed *I* hated her as some people hate snakes or caterpillars or mice or slugs...Not for any certain harm she could do but for the way she could disturb *your* innards and make *you* sick of your life" (174, emphasis added). She admits that she had homosexual desires, but distances herself from them: she does not name Charlene or specify the incidents (168). Her "confession" to the reader, like her confession to the priest later in the story, does not reach fulfillment. She constantly pulls back her own confession to the reader, slipping from "I" to "you," from the particular to the general, so that the ownership of her story is only ever partial and not quite complete.

Indeed, Marlene never achieves salvation, though she glimpses its possibility. The letter that Charlene leaves for Marlene asks her to go to her Catholic church in Guelph, and to speak to Father Hofstrader. It implies that Charlene has confessed, and suggests that Marlene could receive forgiveness if she chose to do so too. Images of light in the church symbolize the salvation that Marlene cannot quite reach. For example, she tries to "get a look at the altar" (189) but cannot because "the chancel being in the western wall was too bright for me to look into" (189). She says that the inside of the church is "glowing, dazzling" (189). Yet the light imagery is ambiguous, since it seems to represent not only the possibility of salvation but also that which is fake, artifice: it is both that which transcends the human and that which is made by humans. The "flocks of angels" she sees in the church, for instance, are both "gauzy" and "pure" (189). Therefore, Munro gestures toward the possibility of redemption, while simultaneously suggesting that it is a human construction and is—at least for Marlene—out of reach.

Marlene comes close to confessing when she asks a patron where she can find the priest, and he points to a confessional. But neither the United Church she attended as a child nor the religious "Chats" at the camp have adequately prepared her, though she "recognize[s] the confessionals" (189). Even when she meets the priest, who is not Father Hofstrader, she cannot confess: "I knew what was necessary and possible, but it was beyond my strength, for the moment, to do it" (192). Like many of Munro's stories, this one ends ambiguously. Marlene can neither look into the light of the church nor "join the bright everlasting flow of cars toward Toronto" (192). Rather, she is stuck uneasily between the two. Munro provides us with a story of longing and regret, identity and memory, a story in which time is disrupted so that the past is forever in the present, maintaining a firm grip on it.

In his book *Imperfection*, scholar Patrick Grant writes,

> The sense we have of ourselves as individual moral agents is closely bound up with our ideals. That is, by aspiring to some (perfect) ideal and falling short, we become aware of our imperfections, which in turn might cause us to feel guilty and irresponsible. In this case, the stability of the self and its enduring identity over time is assumed: if a person is responsible for actions committed to the past, there must be some substantive, continuing identity between that person then and now. In short, the more strongly one feels guilt, the more sharply defined is the self as a bearer of responsibilities. (79)

In many ways, Grant's assertion depicts what is at the heart of both "Fiction" and "Child's Play." Unlike Munro's early work, which is future oriented, these two stories are retrospective, and in them, the protagonists analyze and evaluate the past and their own place within it. In "Fiction," Joyce's reading of Christie's book instigates an epiphany: she sees herself and her past in a new light, not only as a victim of her husband Jon's affair and eventual marriage to Edie, but also as a predator or stalker, the witch from "Hansel and Gretel" who offers candy to Christine. She is a complex being who is not always or necessarily benevolent and innocent. In "Child's Play," conversely, Marlene lives with the knowledge of her badness, her falling short of an ideal self who respects and honours human life. For both Joyce and Marlene, there is a gap between their ideal selves and the selves that they evaluate; for both, the failure to meet ethical responsibility results in strong feelings of guilt. In each story, the protagonist views the self when looking at another, as though through a mirror. Joyce's doppelgängers are her former self and Christie O'Dell, who can also be likened to Munro; Marlene's doppelgängers are Charlene, Verna, and her former self. In "Fiction," the mismatch between the present and past is most evident at the moment of misrecognition, the moment when Christie does not recognize Joyce. In "Child's Play," the mismatch also occurs at a moment of misrecognition, when Marlene views Charlene on her deathbed, and does not recognize her (186). If Christie is a metaphor for Joyce's former self, and Charlene is a metaphor for Marlene's, then the selves in the present and in the past are disjunct. Thus, Munro challenges the notion that there is a "continuing identity between that person then and now" (Grant 79), even as both of her protagonists assume "the stability of the self and its enduring identity over time" (79). The fragmentary, non-linear, and imaginative nature of memory—each protagonist struggles to remember her past as she simultaneously recreates it—belies our assumptions and upsets our perceptions of both identity and time.

6

Time and Life Writing

"Corrie," "The Eye," and "Dear Life" in *Dear Life*

IN THE PREVIOUS CHAPTER, I examined two stories from Munro's *Too Much Happiness*, noting how that collection looks at lives retrospectively, and how "Fiction" and "Child's Play" negotiate the self in relation to the Other. In *Dear Life*, published in 2012, Munro also looks back, as the title of the collection implies, and she continues to address the disjunction between past and present identities; the mismatch between present and remembered selves. I address three stories in the collection, "Corrie," "The Eye," and "Dear Life," to demonstrate how Munro depicts the progression of time as both linear and cyclical. In "Corrie," I reveal that Munro depicts linear and normative time to show how repetition is stagnant: the protagonist remains trapped within societal systems. "The Eye" and "Dear Life" are autobiographical. I examine how Munro turns toward the self to contest singularity and embrace communal and shared identities. In all three stories, Munro suggests that there is the possibility for both stagnancy and newness. The potential for a paradigm shift emerges as we contest linear narratives. In "The Eye" and "Dear Life," Munro looks back upon her own life to examine how she has received gifts that she necessarily passes on to others, including her readers, in an offer of hope and in an attempt to make identities and creations anew.

In "States of Perception and Personal Agency in Alice Munro's *Dear Life*," critic Claire Marrone explains that "prominent in the collection are issues of being and consciousness, crucial to ontology and phenomenology respectively, as well as questions of selfhood explored in autobiographical theory" (85). Since stories such as "In Sight of the Lake," "evoke the life span," Marrone argues, "they anticipate the autobiographical segments that constitute the finale—the four stories that close *Dear Life*" (85). Analyzing the stories "Gravel," "In Sight of the Lake," and "Dear Life," Marrone concludes that these pieces "invite readers to discern multiple forms of insight and to ponder the deliberate ambiguity of Munro's autobiographical project" (86). Munro had said that *Dear Life* would be her last book, and indeed, in the note that prefaces that last four stories of the collection, she indicates that the stories will be the last "things I have to say about my own life" (255). In his article, "This Is Not a Story, Only Life," Thacker notes that after completing her collection *Runaway*, which was published in 2004, Munro "turned her attentions back in time" (31). He points to *The View from Castle Rock* as an example of a collection in which Munro included stories that she had written earlier in her life but had not yet included in a collection, such as "Home," "Working for a Living," and "Hired Girl" (31). Munro was starting to look back to her genealogical and literary ancestors, Thacker explains, but was also looking back in time to earlier stories and written materials (31). "*Dear Life* recreates Munro's early times as context for character, although with 'Corrie' and 'In Sight of the Lake,' she works toward mysteries and a reversal" (32). Thacker identifies the writing and publishing of *Dear Life* as one of three important moments in Munro's career. In the moment in which *Dear Life* was written, Munro considers earlier work and revises it. Taking the story "Train" as an example, Thacker explains that Munro worked on a story through the 1960s and 70s in which a soldier "returns from war and gets off a train too soon in another town"—much like the story that appears in *Dear Life* (31).

Even the stories in *Dear Life* that are not marked as autobiographical include autobiographical elements. "The columnist whom the poet-narrator meets at the Vancouver literary party in 'To Reach Japan' is based on the first professional writer Munro ever knew," for example (Thacker, "This Is Not" 31). Yet the final four stories of the collection, which constitute the "Finale," are notable since they are the only stories—other than the ones in *The View from Castle Rock*—that Munro has explicitly said are autobiographical. As such, it is worth quoting the note in full:

FINALE

The final four works in this book are not quite stories.
They form a separate unit, one that is autobiographical
in feeling, though not, sometimes, entirely so in fact.
I believe they are the first and last—and the closest—
things I have to say about my own life. (255, emphasis in original)

Indeed, this is an extraordinary preface to the concluding stories in Munro's last collection. The title, written in capital letters, announces the final stories of the collection but also the final stories that Munro will write in her sixty-year career. In terms of time, this note adheres to a linear progression of time, marking with both its title and its content the end of Munro's public writing since her first publication in "the University of Western Ontario's literary magazine, *Folio*, in the spring of 1950" (Thacker, "This Is Not" 20). Yet, the tone of the note is tentative, as the author acknowledges the slippages between fact and fiction, and the dynamic and unreliable nature of memory. She understands that written language, her tool, can only come close to representing her "own life."

As Sidonie Smith and Julia Watson put it in their seminal book on autobiography, "the boundary between the autobiographical and the novelistic is...exceedingly hard to fix "(12). Unlike novelistic writers, they contend that "autobiographical narrators are expected to remain faithful to their personal memory archives" (12). Smith and Watson explain that autobiographical narrators perform "several rhetorical acts: justifying their own perceptions, upholding their reputations, disputing the accounts of others, settling scores, conveying cultural information, and inventing desirable futures, among others" (14). Munro's engagement with the intricacies and problems of autobiographical discourse is not new, since she had been enmeshed with them throughout her career. She had long written about her father in her fiction, for example. Her father's death in August of 1976 "allowed her the freedom to write 'Royal Beatings,' since its central beating was based on those he had administered; but it also led to 'Moons of Jupiter,' an elegy for him and a tribute to his spirit, his inquisitive humour, and to his life of hard physical work" (Thacker, "This Is Not" 23). Munro noted the unfairness in the way her father was portrayed by writers on her work, for example in a

Time and Life Writing   157

biographical note about her in anthology by which her father was represented poorly. Munro wrote to her agent to protest the depiction of him, and she stated that it was "appalling...snide and cruel and untrue" (36).

Munro, a fiction writer who implicitly incorporated autobiographical elements into her stories, was acutely aware of these complexities of autobiographical writing, as the preface to final four stories in *Dear Life* makes clear. Even so, she decided to mark the last four stories of her career as autobiographical, and in so doing, sets up a different set of expectations for her reader—expectations of some sort of "truth" about her own life. Munro tempers this expectation with her statement that the stories are only autobiographical in "feeling" and not in "fact." Her note, however, still invokes fundamental questions that readers ask of autobiography: "What is the truth status of autobiographical disclosure? How do we know whether and when a narrator is telling the truth or lying? And what difference would that make?" (Smith and Watson 15). The stories in *Dear Life* taunt the reader as they play with these questions but never fully answer them. Munro blurs the boundaries between autobiographical and fictional discourse in the stories that precede and follow the note that prefaces the "FINALE," knowing that she can only approximate the "truth" that readers expect.

The extraordinary fact of the finale in *Dear Life* is, in part, why I have chosen to write about *Dear Life* rather than *The View from Castle Rock* in this book. Whereas *View* considers the legacy of the author's ancestors and their relevance to her own life, juxtaposing collective and personal histories, *Dear Life* focuses more explicitly on Munro herself, and on individuals and their dilemmas. In addition to the content of the stories, the title of the collection makes this clear: Munro addresses her own life, looking back on it endearingly, even as the title suggests a kind of survival mode, evoking the phrase "hold on for dear life." By juxtaposing a reading of "Corrie" with readings of two autobiographical stories, I aim to show how Munro teases the reader with her life stories as she addresses time within them. The final story in the collection, which is the title story, is fascinating and worth considering for its placement at the end of the author's final collection of her career, and for its retrospective and metafictional elements.

"Corrie"

In his chapter "Obsolescence/Innovation" in *Time: A Vocabulary of the Present*, Burges explains that in the 1940s and 1950s, the notion "of investing in obsolescence, of making the most out of the temporariness of the mechanical arts" became prevalent (85). This period, he notes, "is characterized by redundant overproduction in which innovation and obsolescence assume key economic and technological roles in advanced capitalist economies" (82). Interestingly, Burges argues that this planned cycle—technological innovation that leads to obsolesce and then more innovation—functions as a "rhythmic experience of historical time" (83). In other words, we understand and remember the past according to the technological innovations that become obsolete: for example, the television replacing the radio, or the second generation of Apple computers replacing the first. Significantly, Munro's "Corrie" takes place during this period in the 1950s, marked by the story's reference to Tommy Douglas, who was the premier of Saskatchewan for seventeen years, beginning in 1944, and Howard Ritchie's comment that "this was the mid-fifties" (155). Crucially, the story implicitly addresses this time of obsolescence in its subject matter, which involved the plight of a factory owner whose factory has been shut down. Corrie's father owns a factory that sells shoes and boots in their town, and its closure essentially shrinks the town. This, of course, was and still is a common phenomenon in small Canadian towns in which the central industry goes bust. Munro, it seems, is interested in such circumstances and what ensues: how the old is commemorated—Corrie creates a museum—and how the town struggles but survives, despite the factory's closure. In this way, "Corrie" exemplifies Burges's idea of historical time that distinguishes this period. The old, in the story, is continually displaced, and the story's protagonist, Corrie, perpetually lags behind the present moment. She navigates her disjunct position in time and place as she experiences both downfall and awakening. Corrie's awakening near the end of the story, however, does not necessarily suggest freedom from her entrapment in patriarchal and linear time, since the story's conclusion—whether *The New Yorker* version or the *Dear Life* one—seems to suggest that while her awakening leads to emotional and intellectual change, it does not necessarily lead to change in action.

The story begins with Corrie, her father—a wealthy businessman who owns the town factory—and a houseguest, Howard Ritchie, who is about twenty-six years old, like Corrie. The three of them have dinner at Corrie and her father's house, and Corrie's father, Mr. Carleton, jokes about how his daughter is not yet married, but should be. Howard is already married, though soon it becomes clear that he wants to court Corrie. When Mr. Carleton passes away, Corrie becomes Howard's mistress, and he leaves his wife and family to visit her every so often. His wife and family, of course, do not know about his secret affair with Corrie. One day, Corrie dismisses her housecleaner, Lillian Wolfe, because she no longer wants someone to clean her house, and provides her with some funds to take a typing course. Later, Howard tells Corrie that Lillian was a server in someone's home where he and his wife had dinner. Shortly thereafter, Howard received a letter from Lillian, telling him that she would tell his wife about his affair with Corrie if he did not pay her twice per year. He tells Corrie and she agrees to pay Lillian by giving Howard the money to send to her, so that they can continue their affair without Howard's wife knowing about it. By the end of the story, after Lillian dies and Corrie attends her funeral, we—along with Corrie—discover that Howard lied; he did not receive a letter from Lillian. It was Howard who blackmailed Corrie, and she inadvertently paid him for years. The story addresses themes related to economics and class, but also gender roles and power dynamics. By the end of the story, Corrie shifts her perspective. In some ways, she stays the same, but she also embraces a new community of women and a new way of thinking.

The first reference to time occurs right at the beginning of the story, when Corrie's father comments that she may be too old for marriage, at twenty-five. "You missed a year," Corrie corrects him, "twenty-six" (154). Already, Corrie's father is outdated. Not only has he misjudged time by forgetting that she has had her twenty-sixth birthday, but he is also behind the times, since he understands her age as too old for marriage. Mr. Carleton seems to believe in social time, which his daughter has defied, having not met the expectations of what she is supposed accomplish by a particular age. As Isla Duncan explains in her article, "'A Cavity Everywhere': The Postponement of Knowing in 'Corrie,'" this opening scene in the story presents Corrie as the object of the male gaze, much like Stella is presented as the object of David's gaze at the beginning of the story "Lichen," in *The Process of Love* (para. 1). At the beginning of "Corrie," both Corrie's father and Howard judge her: in the first instance, her father judges her with his comment that his daughter is too old for marriage; in the second, Howard's internal dialogue reveals that he judges her as "not a soft woman...not much meat on the bone" (quoted in Duncan, "A Cavity" para. 3). Howard notes the outdatedness of their home: "Everything looked as if it had been in place before the turn of the century" (155). Time at the story's beginning is intertwined with anxiety around money. Mr. Carleton reveals such anxiety in the first sentence of the story, when he expresses his trepidation about having his only daughter as the sole inheritor to his fortune. "It isn't a good thing to have all the money concentrated in the one family," he notes (154). Mr. Carleton's anxiety is both about Corrie's age and her impending inherited wealth. Munro's reference to wealth in Mr. Carleton's guest's name, "Ritchie," foreshadows his role in the story and hints that he will be the "creepy fortune hunter" (157) that Howard Ritchie ostensibly disdains. That Mr. Carleton draws attention to Corrie's unmarried status and impeding wealth causes Howard to pursue her and reveals Mr. Carleton's outdated values. He believes, that is, that Corrie must marry even though she will be independently wealthy, while simultaneously remaining anxious about her inheritance of his wealth. Munro mobilizes the concepts of time and money in the first pages of "Corrie," suggesting both temporal disjunction and economic angst.

Time is not only intertwined with economics in "Corrie" but also with religion and patriarchy. Mr. Carleton refers to Howard as a "church architect," since he is "restoring the tower of the town's Anglican Church" (155). "The tower is on the verge of toppling," which implies that it is old, even outdated. Mr. Carleton, who has the money to fund its repair, and Howard, who will fix it, are the ones to "rescue" it (155). Thus, we might interpret it as a phallic symbol: it will be propped up by the two men in an attempt to retain the patriarchal order. Munro highlights the intertwinement of religious belief and patriarchal values when Corrie says that she does not have time for God because "her father was enough to cope with" (159), as if her father and God are one. As a Methodist, Mr. Carleton himself does not identify with the religion that the tower represents, placing himself above the Anglicans in class, nationality, and belief: "they were a poor class of Irish Protestants" (155). The Methodist church is a newer offshoot of the Anglican one, suggesting, in Burges's terms, that Mr. Carleton believes that the old religion is obsolete, while the newer, Methodist one is innovative—and yet he still invests in the old ways. The story, however, undermines Mr. Carleton's views. For instance, he disparagingly says that the Anglicans would prefer a "carpenter"—the profession of Jesus Christ—over an "architect." This statement reveals both Carlton's class elitism and his religious misjudgement: he values a profession over a trade and dismisses the carpenter's Christian symbolism. Thus, we question Mr. Carleton's faith and sincerity just as we question Howard's when he exclaims that "he still believed in God, *to some extent*" (159, emphasis added). Paradoxically, Mr. Carleton and Howard uphold old ways in religion and patriarchy even as they ostensibly disassociate from them. They are both part of and apart from the religion and patriarchy for which the church tower metonymically stands.

When Corrie and Howard first meet at Corrie and her father's house, Corrie tells him that she will be travelling to Egypt the following week (157). Howard interprets her question to him, "do you think that would be fun?" (157), as an invitation for him to come with her, and responds with "I have to earn a living" (157). This is their first flirtatious interchange, and the next week, when Corrie is in Egypt, she continues this flirtatiousness by sending him strange postcards, to which he responds. In the postcards, she seems to play jokes on him, making him wonder whether she is in Egypt or elsewhere: "one [postcard] showed the Rock of Gibraltar with a note that called it a pyramid in collapse" (157). The threat of the "toppling" (155) of the church tower that Howard is hired to fix in Corrie's town is echoed in the "pyramid in collapse" (157) that Corrie refers to in her postcard. That "toppling" is repeated yet again in the closure of Corrie's father's shoe and boot factory. Each instance hints at the impending collapse of the economy, of patriarchy, and of the old ways; each instance metonymically stands in for the old passing into obsolescence and the new entering into innovation. Mr. Carleton's and Howard's attempts to uphold the old religious and patriarchal values seem to fail. Near the end of the story, Corrie notes that "the United Church and the Presbyterian Church were just hanging on: the Anglican Church had closed ages ago" (170). Despite their efforts, they have been deemed obsolescent and replaced by "freak religions," including "the Church of the Lord's Anointed," where Lillian Wolfe's funeral is held (168).

In a letter to Howard, Corrie comments on the steeple of the new church: "I never thought before what a giveaway those upside-down ice-cream-cone steeples are. The loss of faith is right there, isn't it?" (172). The image of the upright Anglican steeple is now reversed in the image of this new church's steeple—the phallus inverted. Here, Corrie criticizes the new steeple and aligns with the old ways, though her statement that the new steeple proclaims a "loss of faith" (172) fore-shadows her own—a point I will return to later. The movement of the people from the church with the upright steeple to the church with the upturned one symbolizes the failure of the old patriarchal and religious ways.

As those ways become obsolete, so too do Corrie's father's shoe and boot factory and the economic system it represents, despite Corrie's attempts to uphold them. Corrie indicates that after her father's death, his "shoe factory had been taken over by a large firm that had prom-ised—or so she believed—to keep it running. Within a year, however, the building was empty...nothing left, except a few outmoded tools that had once had to do with making boots and shoes" (163). With a view to retaining the past, Corrie turns the shoe and boot factory into a museum, but she is forced to abandon that endeavour by "strangers" who "tear the building down" (164). "The contract she thought she had to use the building," as it turns out, "did not allow her to display or appropriate any objects found within the building" (164). In this instance, the move-ment from the old factory to the new museum, itself an homage to the past, does not promise betterment or salvation but results in repetition and stagnancy. Corrie is prevented from creating and maintaining a museum out of the factory. The new order, of which the strangers at the boot factory are a part, is no different than the old. Neoliberalism replaces the old economic order. Both systems oust Corrie from places like the boot factory that she is unable to claim as her own.

Corrie occupies a subject position that both plays into and resists economic, religious, and patriarchal systems. For example, the limited-omniscient narrator of the story—who is mostly in Corrie's mind, but sometimes in Howard's—depicts Corrie as both a victim of the "strangers" (164) at the museum, but also shows how others view her as a criminal rather than a victim. She is depicted as a victim because she was unaware of what the contract regarding the factory entailed: as the daughter of the factory owner, she should have the right to it, but does not. She is depicted as a criminal, since she does not have permission to turn the factory into a museum, and is therefore—according to the contract and

Time and Life Writing   163

the law—trespassing on the factory grounds. The patriarchal system within which she resides delineates her as a criminal who does not adhere to its laws. That she is ignorant about the contract demonstrates her exclusion from the male-dominated economy of the time: she laments that Howard, as a man, could have taken care of the matter of the contract if he were available (164). That she is perceived by the contractors and lawmakers as a trespasser on what should be her own property further demonstrates how she is excluded from a patriarchal legal system that does not recognize her rights: "she was fortunate not to be hauled up in court now that the company...had known what she was up to" (164). With her brilliant style, Munro creates a narrative voice that goes back and forth between one that perceives Corrie as innocent and victimized, and one that perceives her—on neoliberal and legal terms—as manipulative and criminal.

Corrie's connection to the economic, religious, and patriarchal systems from which she is simultaneously excluded is demonstrated by her disability, the fact that she is "lame in one leg" (156). Metonymically, her disability ties her to the factory and the museum, and thus the past, in its connection with shoes and boots. Similarly, the people who move away from the town are still connected to it, since their families request their burial there (167). It is noteworthy that both Corrie's connection to the factory through her disabled leg and the people's connection to the town are metonymic and corporeal: "it was interesting how many people showed up here—*or their bodies did*—with this last request and bother for their relatives" (167, emphasis added). Corrie haunts the boot factory with her leg as the dead town members haunt the town with their bodies. Munro foregrounds corporeality and emphasizes women's time, which highlights and values the body as much as the mind. Corrie's disability is an example of Derrida's notion of trace, that which is left behind as we move from one moment in time to the next. It serves as a reminder that the museum was once a boot factory. The citizens' bodies are also a trace from the past—part of them returns and does not go away. Derrida's concept of *différance* is also relevant here, since the present repeats the past with both a *difference* and a *deferral*. In the perpetual movement of signs—from the boot factory to the museum, from male inheritance to unregulated competition—there is repetition with a difference that leaves a "trace" of the old in the new: Corrie's leg, the bodies of the citizens. Munro disrupts the logocentrism

164   ALICE MUNRO AND THE ART OF TIME

of the phallus to demonstrate how values in economic, religious, and patriarchal systems both *differ* and *defer*, leaving a trace of the old through the progression of time.

In "Alice Munro's Dramatic Fictions: Challenging (Dis)Ability by Playing with *Oedipus the King* and Embracing the Queer Art of Failure," Marlene Goldman traces the links between disability and identity in Munro's stories. In "Corrie," we first hear about Corrie's disability through the perspective of Howard: "he was able to see what he hadn't been sure of before. She had a lame leg" (156). He is attracted to her because of rather than in spite of her disability: "He hadn't been sure how he would react to the foot, in bed. But in some way it seemed more appealing, more unique, than the rest of her" (158). Like her father, he treats her as a "damsel in distress" who needs to be rescued or helped: "Isn't it a steep climb back up?" he asks as they walk back to her house from the river. Yet it is noteworthy that Corrie resists that interpretation of her: "I'm not an invalid," she responds (156). Goldman says that, "By circling back to shamed bodies that stagger, tremble, and limp, Munro's stories remind us that they serve as profound sources of insight regarding the ebb and flow of human power and our innate fallibility" ("Alice Munro's" 82). Redekop, like Goldman, has "interpreted Munro's fascination with performance and shame as a challenge to reified notions of femininity" (82). Drawing upon Dolezal's work on theories of disability, Goldman suggests that Munro does not portray disability as innate. Rather, her narratives "align disability with performances that fall short of social depictions of the 'normal,' the 'ideal,' or the socially accepted body" (83). The performative aspect of Corrie's disability—the fact that she cannot hide her disability as its manifests in her body—draws attention to corporeal identification. Corrie's "lame leg" is tied to how she is perceived by her father and Howard as a "damsel in distress" or a "wounded maiden," just as it is tied to her familial identity as the daughter of the boot factory owner. Yet, as Goldman points out, Sophocles's Oedipus "must learn to read the meaning of his own body's imperfection to glean crucial information about his true origins" (83). So too must Corrie, to come to her awakening about the truth of her relationship with Howard. As such, "Corrie" is one of Munro's texts that, as Goldman puts it, "offers insight into the revivifying, idiosyncratic and embodied origins of creativity that always remain tethered to shame, failure, imperfection, and death" (83).

Corrie is at once a part of and apart from the places she inhabits: her body, the factory-museum, her house, and the library. "Strangers" exclude Corrie from her inherited right to her father's factory and what is in it, even though "there was no question of these ancient bits of hardware belonging to her" (164). She continually attempts to be a part of her father's economy, but is pushed out, first from the factory and then from the museum, both of which become obsolete. Corrie exempts herself from her father's house, occupying the library instead: "she was sick of her big and empty house—she wanted to get out, and she set her sights on the public library down the street" (164). Yet the library, like the factory-museum, is old and outdated, and resides not in the present but the past. Corrie "dusted off the shelves" and "phoned people who were shown by the records to have had books out for years" (165). Her claim that books are "library property" is moot, since she belatedly occupies the library space, ironically staying there to keep it open while everyone else in the town is at Lillian's funeral (168), which she does not attend until later. Her occupation of the library, like her occupation of the factory-museum, her father's old house, and even her own body—indicated by the awkwardness of her leg—is off-time, deferred. Museums and libraries are places where written records are stories, yet in "Corrie," they are thwarted. Through them, the protagonist continually and unsuccessfully attempts to reassert her agency. She is impeded by the economic and neoliberal systems she occupies.

At the crux of the story, of course, is the suggestion that Corrie is duped by her lover, Howard. Corrie's recognition of Howard's lie is belated, since she has discovered it only after years of paying a biannual sum to Howard, not Lillian. Her realization occurs too late, after she has established a long-term affair with Howard. We should be careful, though, not to judge Corrie too quickly as Howard's victim. Indeed, she warns us against such a view of her when she says, "I'm not an invalid" (156), which can be a statement meant as much for the reader as it is for Howard. Moreover, the paradigm shift that Corrie and the reader experience in the realization that Lillian has not blackmailed Corrie after all offers us an opportunity to view Lillian differently. Munro puns on Lillian's surname, Wolfe, and implicitly suggests that Lillian might prey upon Howard's wife as a wolf hunts a fox: Howard says that Lillian referred to his wife in the "big *silver-fox* collar on her coat" (161, emphasis added). Lillian is portrayed as the predator, and Howard, his wife, and

Corrie are her victims. However, Munro does not endorse those identities but critiques them, highlighting the prominent and problematic categories of women as either sinful or virtuous; predator or victim.

In this regard, my interpretation of "Corrie" differs from Duncan's. She argues that Corrie is definitively Howard's victim, but I wonder if there is another way to view the story. Before Corrie and Howard begin their affair, Corrie tells him that she will be taking a trip to Egypt next week, and asks him, "Do you think it would be fun?" (157). Howard replies, "I have to earn a living" (157), and then is immediately embarrassed by what he has said, since it implies his assumption that she was asking him to go with her. Yet if we read his statement as a continuation of his musing on Corrie's wealth, then he might in fact be speaking to himself, suggesting that he needs to make a living by prostituting himself to her. In one interpretation, then, Corrie gives Howard money to give to Lillian, so that Lillian will not tell his wife about their affair. In another interpretation, however, Corrie gives Howard money to pay him to have sex with her, thus providing him with "a living" (157). The latter interpretation is corroborated when one considers the other ways in which Howard works for Corrie. For instance, he takes over Lillian's housekeeping duties: "Howard took over [from Lillian] when he came. He looked after the fires and saw to various things around the house and was even taken to visit Corrie's father, if the old man was able" (158). Caring for the house and Corrie's father might be deemed women's duties. Therefore, Munro reverses gender roles: Corrie plays a man who pays his prostitute for services, while Howard plays the prostitute and the housekeeper who works for a living. From one perspective, Corrie is Howard's victim: duped by him, since he has lied about Lillian blackmailing them, and used for sex. Corrie thus occupies the identity of the "invalid" that she actively resists. From another perspective, however, Corrie is the wealthy and even powerful one in the relationship. In either view, Corrie is trapped within the economic, religious, and patriarchal systems that the story critiques. She is either a perpetrator or its victim; a predator, or its prey.

As a result, Corrie is tied to the patriarchal and economic systems she resists. Such is the case when she laughs at her father's comment that she is too old for marriage, an act that can be viewed either as agreement or defiance. Corrie implicitly plays into and resists the idea that women should not be too educated. When Corrie no longer needs

Lillian to do her housework for her, she provides her with funds to take typing lessons and tells her that she is "too smart to mess around doing housework" (159)—an ironic statement, since Howard ostensibly outsmarts Corrie. Later, when Howard tells Corrie that Lillian has blackmailed them, Corrie says to him, "She's learned things, then...I always thought she was sly" (160), and further notes, "Already we've contributed to Lillian's education—she wasn't this smart before" (162). At this point, Corrie seems to regret providing Lillian funds that contribute to her knowledge. Howard's reply to Corrie, "We don't want her getting any smarter" (162), from his perspective, applies as much to Corrie as it does to Lillian: Corrie's knowledge of his lie could mean the end of their relationship.

At the end of the story, the steeple metaphorically topples, symbolizing Corrie's "loss of faith" (174), and she is born anew. Her movement from the library, where she volunteers, to the new church, where Lillian's funeral is being held, is a movement through space and time, from a phallocentric world to a woman-centred one. Corrie has been stuck in the old library as everyone else has already moved on to the new church: "Was this where everybody had gone?" (170). Significantly, all of the people Corrie meets at the funeral are women: "A woman called to her" (169); "Another woman brought her a slice of spice cake" (169); "A woman who used to be Corrie's hairdresser said" (170); "'It was a lovely service,' another woman said" (170). Corrie experiences a paradigm shift as she witnesses the women's departure from a phallocentric perspective. They do not view women such as Lillian, for instance, as either sly and cunning or feeble and ignorant, but rather with respect and admiration: "Lillian worked for us ever since she came to Kitchener," one woman says. "The children adored her. Then the grandchildren." (170). Even the church minister is a woman: "At that moment, a stout, smiling young woman came up and introduced herself as the minister" (171). Notably, the discourse among the women is free and amiable. The women embrace communal acceptance and exchange and seemingly break down barriers between the self and Other. The views that the women express about Lillian are kindly, contrasting the previous conceptions of her set forth by Howard—namely that she is sly and manipulative. Ironically, Corrie disparages the church and mocks its upturned steeple, yet it becomes the very place of her "liveliness"

(168). In a place and time associated with death, a funeral, Corrie is awakened.

Corrie's belated arrival at the church for Lillian's funeral parallels her belated awareness that Howard has not given the money to Lillian but kept it for himself. In both cases, Corrie has been the victim of the patriarchal and capitalist society in which she lives but becomes the agent of her own awakening. Just as she is welcomed into and occupies the space of the new church, so too she begins to occupy the space of her home and claim it as her own: "she gets up quickly and dresses and walks through every room in the house, introducing the walls and the furniture to this new idea" (173). The reclaiming of her home at this moment of awakening is also a reclaiming of her body: "a cavity everywhere, most notably in her chest" (173). The "cavity" that is her departure from the old ways will be filled with new ways, a new life. The old economic, patriarchal, and religious systems which were part of Corrie have—at least for the moment—left her, creating in her an openness, a roomy home, and a "cavity" (173) to be filled. They have exited her residence and her body as she works to reclaim herself. The final sentences of the story, typical of Munro, are complex and ambiguous: "So that's the way they're going to leave it. Too late to do another thing. When there could have been worse, much worse" (174). The reader is left wondering, does Corrie continue her relationship with Howard, and if so, on what terms? I would argue that the answer to that question is less important than the reader's knowledge that Corrie has experienced a paradigm shift. This shift is marked first by the understanding that Howard has lied and then by her experience of a women-centred way of being at the church.

The ending of "Corrie" is noteworthy because there are three published versions of it. Munro commonly revised her stories, particularly their endings. "Corrie" was first published in 2010 in *The New Yorker*, but she changed the ending before publishing it in the *Pen/O. Henry Awards Anthology* in 2012, and then again for the story's inclusion in *Dear Life* in 2012. Notably, the name of Corrie's housekeeper in the story is Sadie in *The New Yorker* but "Lillian" in *Dear Life*. Sadie is the name of Alice Munro's babysitter in her autobiographical story, "The Eye," in *Dear Life*, which I discuss later in this chapter. It is likely that Munro changed the name from Sadie to Lillian in "Corrie" so as not to repeat the name across two stories in the collection. On the one hand, the Sadie in *The New Yorker* version of the story might have been inspired by the Sadie in Munro's life. On the other hand, the name could have been inspired by other literature, such as the Sadie in W. Somerset Maugham's story, "Rain," a suggestion that Atwood makes in her reading of "Corrie" with fiction editor Deborah Treisman in *The New Yorker*. In "Rain," Sadie is a prostitute who brings down the fortune of a missionary. As a scheming woman, that character could certainly have been a model for Munro's, even as Munro contests the notion of the scheming women with the ways in which the women at Sadie's/ Lillian's funeral kindly describe her. Page proofs of "Corrie" at *The New Yorker* indicate that the character's full name was originally "Sadie Fox," before Munro changed it to "Sadie Wolfe" for publication (Treisman). It may be that Munro made this change because of the importance of "silver-fox collar" that Howard's wife wears in the story. When Howard tells Corrie that Sadie/ Lillian has blackmailed him, he asserts that she said, "I would hate to have to break the heart of such a nice lady with a big silver-fox collar on her coat" (160), and Corrie's response foreshadows Howard's lie: "'How would Lillian know a silver-fox collar from a hole in the ground?,' Corrie said...'Are you sure that's what she said?'" (160). That Lillian wears a silver-fox collar is itself interesting, since Howard says she is left-wing and has mixed feelings wearing it—it demonstrates both wealth and animal cruelty. That Lillian's surname is initially Fox and then Wolfe is also intriguing, since both suggest a predatory nature. Finally, the reference to a fox fur might also be Munro's "wink to herself," as Treisman suggests, since Munro's father raised foxes for fur collars and coats.

Clearly, deception is a key trope in the story, since we find out at its end that Howard has deceived Corrie all along. The three different endings push this trope of deception even further. They contrast in Corrie's deliberation about whether to deceive Howard about her knowledge of Sadie/Lillian's death and the fact that her payments were going to him, not Sadie/Lillian. In the *Dear Life* version of the story, Corrie writes a letter to Howard to tell him that Lillian has died, but the readers are not told of the contents of the letter. She decides not to send the letter and writes a very short note instead: "The briefest note. The letter tossed. 'Lillian is dead. Buried yesterday'" (173). Then she waits, knowing that she may or may not hear from Howard again. "She turns off the phone, so as not to suffer waiting. The silence. She may never hear again" (174).

However, while Corrie has been honest about Lillian's death, she has not told Howard that she knows of his deception. She is herself deceptive, or "sly"(160): she keeps her knowledge of his deception to herself. In Howard's reply, a letter, "hardly more to it than there was to hers," he seems to suggest that their affair will continue, even though it is clear that Corrie will no longer pay: "All well now," he says in the letter. "Be glad. Soon" (174). But we, the readers, do not know if he will follow up on his suggestion that they will see one another "soon." If we believe Howard that he intends to continue his affair with Corrie, then the story is satisfactory: Corrie will continue her affair with Howard but will not continue to pay.

In *The New Yorker* version of "Corrie," Corrie does not tell Howard about Lillian's death, knowing that if she tells him their affair might end. In this way, she is able to keep their affair going by deceiving him, as he has deceived her: "If he doesn't know that Sadie is dead he will just expect things to go on as usual. And how would he know, unless his is told? And who would he be told by, unless by Corrie herself? She could say something that would destroy them, but she does not have to" ("Corrie," *The New Yorker*). This ending is satisfactory in that the power lies with Corrie, and she recognizes that she has the agency to determine the course of their affair. Yet it may also be somewhat dissatisfactory in that nothing changes. Corrie maintains her affair and companionship with Howard and thus fends off loneliness, yet she also remains within a system that keeps her as his mistress. The old religions and economic ways are on the brink of disaster, about to topple, but they do not; her place within the old ways of patriarchy remains. She is, once again, too late. Munro's practice of revising her stories is in itself interesting in relation to time. Munro's characters are dynamic. She carefully considers their choices, and they seem to remain alive, in her mind, as she returns to them, even after publication, to offer them another chance, another choice. Munro's stories are not stagnant, but dynamic, changing as she publishes them in each successive venue.

The movement through time from the boot factory to the museum to the library repeats economic stagnancy. Likewise, Corrie's movement from her father's influence to Howard's repeats her entrapment in patriarchal systems. Finally, Corrie's choice to tell Howard about Lillian's death, in the *Dear Life* version, and not to tell him, in the earlier *New Yorker* version, both ultimately situate her still within economic and patriarchal time and place. However, the temporal moment in which Corrie moves from the library to the church, from her ignorance about Howard's lie to her awareness of it, are not merely a repetition of the old masked as the new. Rather, it is the *différance* in the deferral from one moment to the next—the movement from one ground of value to the next—that causes her awaking. This moment, when she introduces herself to her new rooms and body, is precisely where the hope and potential for newness lie. But it is also fleeting, only momentary. We are left, after the moment passes, with the ambiguity of Corrie's present situation. And we do not definitively know, at the end of either version, whether her affair with Howard will continue. "Corrie" ends on a note of hope, as the protagonist is changed in her new awareness, even if that hope is tenuous. She negotiates the old ways in relation to the newly emerging ones, the past and its legacies in relation to her newly emerging world.

"The Eye"

In "Corrie," Munro demonstrates a resistance to teleological time and a movement, near the end of the story, toward a more woman-centred paradigm—one that resists linear progress implicit in capitalistic notions of time. The author continues with such resistance in "The Eye," albeit differently, since this story is one of four that she identifies as autobiographical and which form the "finale" of her final collection of short stories, *Dear Life*. Munro's preface to the finale suggests neither a commitment to nor a rejection of autobiographical discourse: "autobiographical in feeling, though not, sometimes, entirely so in fact" (255). If they are the "closest" Munro gets to her own life, then they still do not quite represent it. They are an approximation, a gesture towards truth but ultimately an unsuccessful attempt at it. Yet, as Morra suggests, such approximation is "not just about the 'estimate' of how close the representation is to the life being represented, but also about 'proximity,' to call upon the root of the word, between the reader and the narrative" ("'Don't Take'" 259). In other words, Munro explores levels of intimacy between the author, the narrator, and the reader. She meditates not only on the inability of language to accurately represent her life, but also on her willingness to represent it; she muses on the ethics of intimacy and on the extent to which we have a right to know about others'

172   ALICE MUNRO AND THE ART OF TIME

private lives. Her pushback is at once against traditional autobiographical discourse and the time socialization embedded within it.

As Julie Rak points out, referencing Smith and Watson, "the term 'autobiography' literally means 'self-life-writing' in Greek, and has been in use in English since the eighteenth century" (16). Early theorists of autobiography such as Georges Gusdorf and James Olney tie autobiography to individualism and consciousness. They argue that an autobiography is essentially a story of the individual differentiated from their environment and community: the self as distinct from the Other. In "The Eye," Munro works within and against this individualism. On the one hand, the word "eye" recalls its homonym, "I," and so Munro draws attention to the idea of the self; on the other hand, the same word invokes the notion of the gaze—the reader is the "eye" who watches Munro while having the privilege of remaining anonymous. Here, Munro repeats the trope from *Lives of Girls and Women*, where, in "Heirs of the Living Body," Del simultaneously contemplates the cow's "eye" and her own "I." With a play on words, the author draws attention to the singularity of the self while already undermining that singularity: the "Eye/I" of the title gestures towards the relations between writer and reader. Moreover, just as Munro summons the "I" of autobiographical discourse, so too does she begin her story in a traditionally autobiographical way, with the birth of an individual. As she undermines the singularity of the "I," however, she also undermines the notion of an autobiographical story beginning with the author's birth: it is not her own birth that opens her story but her brother's. Autobiographies that begin with an individual's birth and follow a life trajectory are a form of time socialization. They are stories that indoctrinate readers "into the shared forms of social time that shape the functioning of society and that serve as measurements of individual productivity, success, and belonging" (Huebener, *Timing* 20). Munro's "The Eye" calls upon storytelling traditions that rely on the "I" and the story of a life that begins with birth; the story simultaneously upsets such traditions, playfully questioning their validity and throwing them into disarray.

To understand the time trajectory of the "I," we might once again turn to Lacan. As I have mentioned in earlier chapters, Lacan argues that infants see themselves as separate from their environment when they first perceive themselves in a literal or figurative mirror. Yet that perception of the self as separate from the world is imaginary, a fiction that is sustained in the ego. For Lacan, the moment of such self-recognition is also a moment of separation from the mother, an understanding that the mother is distinct from the self. In *Reading Alice Munro with Jacques Lacan*, Murray argues that Munro's stories "embrace the whole of human experience in its different stages: from childhood to late adulthood" (5). Munro's characters, she asserts, "confront the enigmas of desire, of love, and of the lacking self" (5). In Nancy Chodorow's groundbreaking book, *The Reproduction of Mothering*, the author revises Lacan's trajectory of child development, arguing that a daughter, unlike a son, does not fully separate their identity from their mother. Therefore, there is a likeness between mother and daughter—hence the reproduction of mothering, its continuation from mother to daughter. In "The Eye," Munro plays with this idea of the self's formation: her own identification with and potential separation from her mother. Mothers, daughters, and their complex relationships are common in Munro's stories. She said in interviews that this is because of her own troubled relationship with her mother, the fact that her mother had Parkinson's disease, and Munro's role growing up as her mother's caregiver. "The Eye," however, differs from her other stories about mothers and daughters because it is directly autobiographical. Alice,[1] the story's narrator, is the eldest child. When she was five years old, she explains, her brother was born, and a year later, her sister. The first moment of separation from her mother occurs after her brother's birth: "Up until the time of the first baby I had not been aware of ever feeling different from the way my mother said I felt" (257). The moment of her brother's birth, then, is ironically the moment of her own, since it marks her awareness that she is not the same as her mother.

When Alice's brother is born, her mother hires a babysitter to look after Alice, so that she can have time for the baby. Alice begins to admire and look up to her babysitter, Sadie, who sings and plays her guitar on the local radio show. Sadie is Alice's friend and mentor, but also someone who models the life of an independent young woman. The townspeople, however, judge Sadie as somewhat suspect or immoral, since she is so self-sufficient; she goes to dances by herself, without being courted by a boy. Later in the story, Sadie is hit by a car between the parking lot and the road at one of the dances, and she dies. The rest of the story depicts Alice's attempt to understand both Sadie's death and her parents' and the townspeople' perspective on it. Alice attends Sadie's funeral and experiences an epiphany when sees her body in the open coffin, seemingly seeing herself as well as Sadie. The story negotiates the boundaries between self and Other as it depicts Alice's trajectory of coming to know herself through another; coming to know life through death.

At the beginning of "The Eye," Alice rejects identifications of herself in art and literature, metaphorical mirrors. Referring to the picture in Alice's room of children coming to Jesus, her mother says that Alice is the girl "half hiding around the corner," the girl who "wanted to come to Jesus but was too shy" (258), however Alice resists that idea—"I rather wished it wasn't so" (258). Here, Munro rejects not only Lacan's teleology, but also, ostensibly, Christianity and traditional autobiographical discourse. Munro hides from the reader just as Alice hides from Jesus; true to the note with which she prefaces the finale, she does not fully reveal herself, peeking around the corner, ever aware of the reader's— and Jesus's—watchful "eye."

Just as Alice rejects her identification with the girl in the picture, so too does she reject an identification with Alice from *Alice in Wonderland*. The connection between the two is implicit because they share a name. While she appears to delight in the story's character, that outward appearance is a lie, a fiction that she produces to please her mother: "I laughed because my mother seemed delighted" (258). To the reader she notes that she "felt miserable" because Alice was "huge and trapped in the rabbit hole" (258). In this instance she hides from her mother but reveals herself to the reader, creating an intimacy between writer, narrator, and reader. Just like Alice from *Alice in Wonderland*, Alice the narrator is "huge" in that there is more to her—to anyone—than meets the eye. Complex and multifaceted, like all individuals, she is too big to fit into the "hole," exceeding the language that represents and contains her. Such representation is evident in the picture of Jesus in her bedroom, the story of *Alice and Wonderland*, and "The Eye" itself—Alice's own story in which she is the subject. In each work of art or literature, Alice—like Munro—is there "in feeling, though not, sometimes, entirely so in fact" (256).

While the young Alice separates herself from her mother and denies identification with the images her mother presents to her in art and literature, she embraces an identification with her babysitter, Sadie, much to her mother's dismay. Her mother's worry about Alice looking up to Sadie is part of a larger concern that she will not follow proper time socialization. Sadie eschews dating and does not wish to get married (261), whereas Munro's mother believes that courting and then marriage represent the proper time trajectory for a young woman. Yet, just as the protagonist of *Alice in Wonderland* is too big for that "hole," Munro implies, so too is Alice in "The Eye." She does not want to follow the expected order of things. Notably, Sadie is "a celebrity" (259), at least in the eyes of the young Alice. Her voice, which is "strong and sad and she sang about loneliness and grief" (259), seems to hold an authenticity—a closeness to "truth"—that Alice craves. Alice does not yet exemplify such authenticity herself, first unable to separate herself from her mother, then laughing at Alice in *Alice in Wonderland* because her mother expects her to do so.

Sadie's authenticity is also evident in the fact that she sings for her own people, those on the surrounding farms, rather than residents of large cities who live afar: "the more sophisticated people in town tended to joke about her songs and about the whole station which was said to be the smallest one in Canada. Those people listened to a Toronto station that broadcast popular songs of the day" (259). Sadie is a doppelgänger[2] for Munro in "The Eye." Sadie's celebrity voice is like Munro's, though Sadie's is communicated through song, and Munro's through story; Sadie sings and Munro writes of small towns and farms, rather than of more glamorous places. Even as Sadie's songs seem to have the air of authenticity, she too sings what the townsfolk wanted to hear. Munro explains that "you could look out from almost any farmhouse and see another farmhouse only a few fields away," but that "the songs the farmers wanted were all about lone cowhands, the lure and disappointment of far-off places" (259). Even the songs Sadie sings, then, do not precisely represent the reality of the town. Munro highlights the inability for language and art to adequately articulate life, the desire for the artist to please her audience, and the writer to please her reader.

Alice's mother suggests that Alice is the girl in the painting who hides (258). If we are to also identify Munro with the girl in the painting, then she hesitates to come to Jesus because she resists aligning herself with linear notions of time associated with Christianity. Even the counting of years in Western teleology, for instance, begins with the moment of

Christ's death. Yet this is not the only moment in the story where Munro employs religious language. Alice rejects her peers at Sunday school in favour of her new babysitter: "Instead, I worshipped Sadie. I heard my mother say to my father, 'She worships Sadie.'" Her father responds by saying that Sadie "was a godsend" (263). Here, Alice blurs the boundaries between her own perception and her mother's. Moreover, she exemplifies her mother's anxiety that Alice worships an idol over Christ, and Munro shows that Alice turns away from Christianity and toward a more female-centred religion. Alice's father's statement that Sadie "was a godsend" (263) confirms Sadie's association, for Alice, with the religious and the spiritual: it is as though God sends Sadie to her. As in "Corrie," Alice rejects the old patriarchal ways in favour of the newly emerging feminine ones.

In "The Eye," it is precisely Sadie's independence, this refusal to be "caught" (262) by a man, that appeals to young Alice. Moreover, Sadie embraces economic independence. "You paid a dime for a dance," Alice explains, but Sadie "always liked to pay her own dime, not to be beholden" (261). Sadie actively strives and works for this independence, since it goes against the town's norms. Though she liked to pay for her own dances, for instance, "sometimes a fellow got to her first" (261). If the fellow could not dance well, then Sadie would "[break] off and [leave] him stranded, danced by herself—which was what she liked to do anyway" (261). The imminent danger for a woman who pursues such independence is clear: Sadie tells young Alice that, though some are better dancers that others, "it was not always the feet you had to look out for. It was where they wanted to get hold of you" (261-62). When Alice looks frightened at Sadie's statement that she didn't want to get "caught," Sadie says, "There's nothing in this world to be scared of, just look out for yourself" (262). Sadie's implicit warning to Alice that she must look out for men's licentious behaviour, made ironic by the phrase "just look out for yourself," contrasts starkly with the townsfolks' interpretation of Sadie's behaviour. In their view, it is not the men who are morally suspect but Sadie herself. They interpret her death, which occurs because a driver hit her in the parking lot of the dance, as her own fault: "Sadie scurrying along without even a flashlight would behave as if it was everybody's business to get out of her way. 'A girl without a boyfriend going to dances on foot,' said the woman who was still being friends with my mother...'It was asking for trouble'" (267).

Moreover, the driver who hits Sadie is never prosecuted: "My mother wanted something done that might have had to do with Sadie and the car that hit her, but my father said to leave it alone. We've got no business in town, he said" (267). Munro highlights the alternative trajectory that Sadie follows and that young Alice admires, but she also shows the tragedy and unfairness that, for Sadie, is its result.

Despite Sadie's fate, it is an alternative time trajectory, one that does not follow the town's and her mother's expectations for women, that Alice seems to desire. Her movement away from her mother, exemplified in part by her rejection of her mother's religion, is also a movement toward herself, a coming of age, an awakening into her own being and identity. To understand this movement, we must turn to the climactic scene in "The Eye," the scene in which Alice has a spiritual awakening and comes to know herself. In "Corrie," the rejection of Christianity awakening to a new life occurs in a church—at a funeral—and the same is true in "The Eye." Unlike in "Corrie," however, in "The Eye," this awakening includes both a struggle for Alice to separate from her mother and a discovery of herself. When they arrive at the funeral, young Alice does not want to view Sadie's body in the coffin, but she must do so at her mother's bidding: "Yes, my mother was saying. Of course we must see Sadie. Dead Sadie...'Come now,' she said to me" (268). Alice is the girl in the painting who hides around the corner because she is too shy to meet Jesus, but in this instance, it is not Jesus she is reluctant to see but Sadie. When they approach the coffin, Alice keeps her "eyes squeezed shut" while her mother holds her hand (268). The moment that she frees her hand from her mother's is the moment that she is able to open her eyes and look into the coffin. What she sees there exemplifies Kristeva's notion of the "abject"—that which falls away from bodies so they can enter a social and ordered world (Grosz, *Volatile Bodies* 192). Sadie's dead body, much like the dead cow that Del examines in *Lives of Girls and Women*, is, in Kristeva's terms, "a typology of personalized horror" (quoted in Grosz, *Volatile Bodies* 192). It is what the social body must expunge to be whole. The simultaneous attraction and repulsion that is characteristic of Kristeva's notion of the abject is also evident in Alice's reaction: "I shut my eyes quickly but found myself unable to keep from looking again" (269). What Alice sees when she peers into the coffin also exemplifies Lacan's notion of the self in the mirror stage—a fictional, unified whole with whom the newly formed subject identifies. When she looks at Sadie, she sees herself as though in a mirror. She recognizes herself in a whole and unified image; yet that image is fictional, elusive, and situated outside of and apart from her own body.

Indeed, when young Alice sees Sadie, she momentarily experiences being her. She becomes the Other she deliberates and imagines, even as she dissociates from that identification through the use of second-person narration: "if you were her, if you were inside her, to be able to see out through the lashes, just to distinguish maybe what was light outside and what was dark" (269). Alice momentarily experiences clarity, expressed in metaphorical and religious terms: she is able to distinguish between "light"—what is true, real, and ethical—and its opposite, what is "dark." The moment of epiphany is fleeting, just as it is for Narcissus in Ovid's *Metamorphoses*. Narcissus peers into a pond to see his own reflection just as Alice peers into Sadie's coffin to see her own, but that image slips away. According to Ovid, for Narcissus, "Only the glancing mirror / Of reflections filled his eyes, a body / That had no being of its own, a shade / That came, stayed, left with him—if he could leave it" (98). Alice's self-recognition in Sadie, like Narcissus's, is illusory and momentary. Soon, her mother takes her hand again, and she is no longer inside of Sadie—"before any time had passed, as it seemed to me, we found ourselves *outside*" (269, emphasis added).

When Alice peers into Sadie's coffin and looks at her body, she sees her open her eye, a rational impossibility, since Sadie is dead. "Something moved. I saw it, her eyelid on my side moved...And I did not dream of calling anybody else's attention to what was there, because it was not meant for them, it was completely for me" (169). Here, the language shifts as Alice moves from *identifying* with Sadie to *receiving* something from her. Sadie's act of opening her eye for Alice—of winking at her—is a moment of intimacy, to use Morra's term, between Sadie and Alice. Bobby Sheriff's performative dance at the end of *Lives of Girls and Women* is a gift for Del, "not shared with me so much as displayed for me" (237), and in "The Eye," Alice perceives Sadie's eyelid flutter as "performed completely for me" (269). Whereas Bobby's dance is "the only special thing he ever did for me" (*Lives* 236), Sadie's wink is a "special experience" (*Dear Life* 269). In *Lives*, Bobby's dance "seemed also to have a concise meaning, a stylized meaning—to be a letter, or a whole world, in an alphabet I did not know" (237). It situates him as Del's muse figure, providing her with the material out of which she, and implicitly Munro, will carve their stories—even as the act he performs remains essentially mysterious. Likewise, in "The Eye," Sadie is a muse figure for Alice, remembered by Munro all these years later, a feminist figure who takes various characterizations and forms through the corpus of Munro's work. Of course, key to the young Alice's "special experience" (269)—witnessing Sadie's open eye—is also witnessing the "I" and a moment of knowledge; a moment when Alice has an "open eye," so to speak, and can see. The "I" that is witnessed is complex: the young Alice sees Sadie for who she is, her "I"; she sees her own "I," herself, newly emerged; and Munro sees Alice's "I"—the author, that is, looks back at her child-self anew.

According to Lewis Hyde, a gift "is a thing we do not get by our own efforts" (xxxii), and it must be constantly given away, kept in motion through time. "Sometimes the embodied gift—the work," Hyde maintains, "can reproduce the gifted state in the audience that received it. Let us say that the 'suspension of disbelief' by which we become receptive to a work of the imagination is in fact belief, a momentary faith by virtue of which the spirt of the artist's gift may enter and act upon our being" (195-96). Like Bobby's performative dance, Sadie's wink, meant especially for Alice, is a gift that she receives and passes forward through time, giving it away in the form of Munro's own writing to her readers. They, like her, are to receive it and then give it away. Munro incorporates works of previous writers like Joyce and Brontë in books such as *Lives of Girls and Women*, receiving them as gifts and engaging in literary allusion and intertextuality. Similarly, present and future writers will receive Munro's gift of writing, build upon it, and give it away. This dynamic of the giving and receiving of art through time was, perhaps, what poet Ezra Pound meant when he spoke of a living literary tradition. Yet Hyde speaks not only of ongoing giving and receiving, but also of a "suspension of disbelief," and he asserts that such "suspension of disbelief" is in fact a "momentary faith" (195). "The work will induce a moment of *grace*," he explains, "a communion, a period during which we too know the hidden coherence of our being and feel the fullness of our lives" (196, emphasis added).

In "The Eye," Alice must engage in a "suspension of disbelief" to receive the gift of Sadie's wink. She must dismiss the rational notion that Sadie cannot wink at her, since she is dead. That "suspension of disbelief" is a kind of faith, but as in "Corrie," it is not the same as the Christian faith to which she is expected to adhere, but rather a newly emerging, feminine and feminist one, only fitting as Sadie herself exemplifies an independence from patriarchy and traditional modes of being. Furthermore, just as her identification with Sadie is a momentary experience by which she seems to embody Sadie's dead body and see through her eyes, so too is her receiving of Sadie's gift of the wink also fleeting, a "momentary faith." Later, Alice no longer believes what she saw: "one day when I may even have been in my teens, I knew with a dim sort of hole in my insides that now I didn't believe it anymore" (270). Yet she believes for a long time, and so the grace that is Bobby's dance in *Lives* and Sadie's wink in "The Eye" is both the grace of style and the grace of time—a period of delay, a grace period by which Alice maintains her faith. Alice's loss of belief is also her release into mourning, not only for Sadie, but for her own childhood, now written, now gone.

"Dear Life"

In "'Don't Take Her Word for It': Autobiographical Approximation and Shame in Munro's *The View from Castle Rock*," Morra states that the second half of *Castle Rock* "deals more closely with the narrator's personal life, thereby suggesting that one's identity is connected to an understanding of one's past and a sense of connection to familial lineage" (257). In Munro's "Dear Life," the title story and the ending to the collection, Munro addresses familial lineage. The story, much like "The Eye," is in part about Munro's relationship with and memories of her mother, but it also examines a different kind of lineage, one that deals with place rather than genealogy. Specifically, Munro returns to the places of her childhood: the land, the town, and the house. She examines the town's history and its residents as though they are ancestors, carrying their gifts from the past into the present. "Dear Life" investigates the occupation of places through time. For Munro, *home* is located in her childhood house, her own body, and in her return to her mother since, as Yann Martell acknowledges, "At first, home is a body, the mother's body" (171). In Munro's stories, the home is never static but always dynamic, moving and unsettled in both place and time.

The story begins with a description of Alice's hometown and neighbourhood, and discusses the separation of the town by the river: one side of the river was more run down than the other, indicating a class division. She discusses her childhood friendship with a girl, Diane,[3] who lives in the disreputable part of the town, in a house that Alice's mother does not want her to enter, since Diane's mother, who has died, was a prostitute. The story muses on Alice's mother's disapproval of Diane and the fact that Diane later mysteriously moves away, suggesting that she might follow the same allegedly immoral fate as her mother. The story then shifts to a discussion of Alice's childhood home. Alice experiences an epiphany when she reads a newspaper account—much later in her life—that reveals who owned her home before her own family did. As it turns out, she knew of the family who owned it, the Netterfields, and she remembers that when she was a child, an elderly Mrs. Netterfield visited their home. The story is a meditation both on place and time, the places in which we reside, through generations, and the remembering and disremembering of them. By the end of "Dear Life," Alice seems to have come to a new understanding of herself, her mother, and her past, though in typical Munro style, that understanding is always ambiguous and never definitive or resolved.

In "Dear Life," there is a sense of repetition through time, whereby "newness" is conceived as a paradigm shift, a change in perspective. The new is radically different from the old and yet intimately tied to it. Each repetition is also an approximation. This repetition suggests that Munro represents her own life, even as that representation continually misses the mark, approximates as it creates. The story begins with a description of the road where the young Alice lived, "the end of a long road, or a road that seemed long to me" (299). The "real town" is "back behind" her as she walks home from school (299), suggesting a separation between her house and the town, but also between what she represents and what is "real." The "long road" and two bridges that Alice mentions early in the story are her journey through both place and time—the road a metaphor for her life, the bridges a metaphor for life's crossings.

Correspondingly, the places and landscapes Alice occupies seem to have outward appearances that are disjunct from their inner realities. The wooden walkway on one of the bridges, for instance, "occasionally had a plank missing, so that you could look right down into the bright, hurrying water" (299). The missing plank enables Alice to see what runs underneath, to delight in the river's beauty and danger—"[it] was deep enough to drown you" (299). Yet that vantage point is quickly covered: "someone always came and replaced the plank eventually"

(299). Similarly, she likens her own rural landscape to the one in L.M. Montgomery's *Anne of Green Gables*, but recognizes that she "purifie[s]" (305) it: "Fresh manure was always around, but I ignored it, as Anne must have done" (305).[4] Munro unmasks the "life" she addresses in the title of her story, though she holds that life "dear." At times, she covers what she knows is true to protect others, changing the name of her childhood friend to Diane, for example (301). At other times, however, she unmasks the truth, and she is unapologetic in her departure from storytelling conventions. For instance, she mentions that a man named Roly Grain who owned a house near her childhood home, but then she does not mention him again. In a moment of self-reflexivity and meta-narrative, of acknowledging that she writes autobiographically, she says, "he [Roly Grain] does not have any further part in what I'm writing now...because this is not a story, only life" (307).

The story of Alice's childhood friendship with Diane is also a story of outward appearances and inner realities, even as Munro problema-tizes any definitive version of the truth. Young Alice goes to her friend's house after school one day so that Diane can teach her the Highland Fling, but when Alice's mother finds out, she picks her up and tells her "never to enter that house again" (301). When Alice explains to her mother that Diane was teaching her to dance, her mother says that she "might learn it properly sometime, but not in that house" (302). On the one hand, Diane and Alice's friendship is innocent, but on the other, underlying its outward appearance is Munro's mother's knowl-edge and moral judgement of Diane's mother's past as a prostitute. Alice's mother therefore perceives a moral danger in her daughter's association with Diane. Like the running water underneath the bridge that is "deep enough to drown you" (300), from Alice's mother's van-tage point—which differs from Alice's—there is an underlying risk. Interestingly, her mother's moral judgement is displaced from Diane to the house in which she lives. Her mother does not tell her not to asso-ciate with Diane but rather "never to enter that house again" (301). This emphasis on place rather than person, as though the places one occu-pies determine one's character, is consistent with the story as a whole. For instance, when discussing the history of the town and its con-struction, Munro notes that once a bridge was built across the river, "it began to dawn on people how much more convenient it would be to live over on the other side, on higher ground, and the original settlement dwindled away to the disreputable" (306). The "higher ground" of which Munro speaks refers both to physical geography and moral character. Likewise, when Alice's parents do renovations to their home, the new room alters young Alice's painful memories of her father beating her there. "My father's beatings of me had taken place in the old room, with me wanting to die for the misery and shame of it all," Alice notes. "Now the difference in the setting made it hard even to imagine such a thing happening" (308). Thus, Munro associates places with feelings through time. Both in the case of the town and the room, the place itself changes through time, as new appearances cover but relate to past ones: "original settlements dwind[le] away" (306), and rooms take on a new character divorced from the old.

There are two stories about Mrs. Netterfield in "Dear Life," both of which Alice hears from her mother. In the first story, Mrs. Netterfield chases the delivery boy "with a hatchet" (312). In the second, young Alice is sleeping in her baby carriage at the front of the house when Mrs. Netterfield approaches. Alice relays the account of Mrs. Netterfield as her mother told it to her, and so in a sense it is her mother's story, not hers. Before she begins, she says that she "seldom objected now to her [mother's] way of looking at things" (310). On the one hand, this statement recalls Alice's alignment with and departure from her mother's perspectives in "The Eye"; on the other hand, the statement is ironic, since the story of Mrs. Netterfield ultimately unveils Alice's interpretation as different from her mother's. Interestingly, Alice notes that her mother told her stories of Mrs. Netterfield "several times" (310), and then she draws our attention to the differences in her mother's versions of these stories (315). She also questions the details of the stories: "some things about this story were puzzling" (311). Typical of Munro's narration, the author continually reminds us that she is telling a story, revealing the story's construction in moments of self-reflexivity. She tells the story as she interprets and creates it, trying to get at the truth. Alice's role as the interpreter of her mother's stories is highlighted when she explains that after her mother got Parkinson's disease, she had to explain to other people what her mother was saying: "I was her interpreter, and sometimes I was full of misery when I had to repeat elaborate phrases or what she thought were jokes" (315). The notion of being her mother's interpreter echoes one of Munro's other stories, "The Peace of Utrecht." In "Dear Life," Alice interprets her mother's stories about Mrs. Netterfield; similarly, Munro's readers interpret her writing. Each work is repeated as it is passed on to the next recipient. The story is Alice's mother's, then hers, and then ours. It is reworked and reimagined, and then passed on yet again.

This *mise en abyme* is evident in Munro's storytelling technique: the stories of Mrs. Netterfield are within the story of "Dear Life," and Alice's mother's stories are interpreted and retold by Munro, then received and interpreted yet again by her readers. It is also evident in Munro's emphasis on houses and their occupants throughout the text: one occupant replaces the next in a continual and ongoing cycle. As we have seen, the author takes great care to describe the placement of the houses in the town and to explain how they represent class. In addition, she demonstrates how houses—according to the townsfolk and her mother—are seen to hold moral character, for example in the case of Diane. When Alice begins to speak of Mrs. Netterfield, unsurprisingly, she begins not with the person but her house. "Several times," she notes, "[my mother] told me a story that had to do with the house that now belonged to the war veteran named Waitey Streets. The story was not about him," she continues, "but about someone who had lived in that house long before he did, a crazy old woman named Mrs. Netterfield" (310). Munro draws attention here to the person who lives in Netterfield's house now to highlight the difference between the present and the past, what is outwardly apparent and inwardly hidden. Presently, Waitey Streets owns the house that was previously Mrs. Netterfield's, just as Mrs. Netterfield, Alice later finds out, owned the house that was later her childhood home. As stories are dynamic, moving from writers to listeners, so too are houses, occupied by one resident and then later by another, continually repeating the holding and shaping of lives, but each time different, with a trace of the old left behind.

The most intriguing part of "Dear Life" is the story of Mrs. Netterfield and her visit to Munro's childhood home, a story within the story. It is clear from Alice's mother's version of the story that she felt Mrs. Netterfield was dangerous: she implies that she was there to kidnap young Alice. Munro's mother runs "out the kitchen door to grab [Alice] out of [her] baby carriage" (313), and then "grab[s] [her] for dear life" (318). "Did it cross her mind that the old woman might just be paying a neighbourly visit?" Alice asks. "I don't think so," her mother answers

(313). Further punctuating her mother's story, Munro explains that Mrs. Netterfield then walked all around the house, peering into the windows and "press[ing] her face against every pane of glass" (314). However, later in life, Alice discovers that Mrs. Netterfield lived in the house before their own family did. She experiences a shift in her reception of this story that she had heard from her mother so long ago and believed for a long time. Both Munro and her readers now realize that Mrs. Netterfield was likely coming to take a look at her old home. Many other mysteries about Mrs. Netterfield remain—"who was it who came and took her away, as my mother said?" (318)—but one revelation is resolved. Mrs. Netterfield may not have been a "crazy woman" (312) at all, but simply someone who wanted a glimpse of her past.

As in "Corrie," then, the protagonist, who is here none other than the author herself, experiences an epiphany at the end of the story, an understanding that historical realities are not necessarily what they seem. Munro challenges the idea that she and her family are the rightful and sole owners of the house. Instead, she foregrounds the ways in which the occupation of places changes through cycles of time. "I have found that several different families owned that house between the time that the Netterfields sold it and the time that my parents moved in" (318), she explains. Whereas Alice is not allowed *in* Diane's house because of her mother's perception of immorality there, Mrs. Netterfield is kept *out* of their house because of Alice's mother's perception of the same: just as Diane's mother is deemed immoral, Mrs. Netterfield is deemed "crazy" (312). Huebener explains that imperial time "fails to do justice to many members of society because it represents subaltern groups as 'backward' or simply fails to acknowledge their experiences" (*Timing* 29). Both Diane and Mrs. Netterfield—against the framework of progress—might occupy the subaltern, and their experiences are denied or unacknowledged. Both are women who, in McClintock's words, are "ambiguously placed on the imperial divide (nurses, nannies, governesses, prostitutes, and servants)" and serve as "boundary markers and mediators" (48). In "Dear Life," the boundary that determines whether one goes *in* or *out* is the house itself, a contested place occupied by successions of people over time. The boundary of the house is mirrored by the boundary of the river in the town, where, on one side, the houses are on "higher ground" (306) than on the other.

Indeed, Munro problematizes the notion of ownership. As Benny and then Del proclaim ownership of the riverbank in the opening of *Lives of Girls and Women*, Munro also proclaims ownership of the places she occupies in "Dear Life." Alice only discovers that Mrs. Netterfield previously owned her childhood home when she reads a poem that refers to the home, written by Mrs. Netterfield's daughter and published in the newspaper. As she reads it, she comes to an awareness that the house and the landscape surrounding it was not only hers but also Netterfield's: "as I read I began to understand that she was talking about the same river flats that I had thought *belonged to me*" (316, emphasis added). When she reads about the riverbank in the poem, she states, "that was our bank, my bank" (317), and when she reads about her own house as Netterfield's, she states, "our house" (318). The recognition that the house had not always been hers is an unravelling of the logic of imperial time: ownership is temporary, not permanent; places and the memories they hold are shared, not coveted.

That Alice's mother calls Mrs. Netterfield's presence at their house a "visitation" (315), as though she is a ghost, suggests a blurring of boundaries between the past and the present, a moment of what Grosz calls the "untimely." Grosz explains that we can think of time "only in passing moments, through ruptures, nicks, cuts, and in instances of dislocation" (*Nick of Time* 5). Mrs. Netterfield's "visitation" is such a rupture. Like Sandy's ghost who comes to visit Uncle Benny in *Lives of Girls and Women*, Netterfield's visit to her old house, as Munro later understands it, is a moment in which the past exists in the present. It is an event that makes up "the unpredictable emergences of our material universe" (Grosz, *Nick* 5), and undoes imperialist logic. Furthermore, because such logic is aligned with that of patriarchy, when Munro challenges imperialist values, she challenges patriarchal ones as well. Alices's realization that Mrs. Netterfield was not a crazy woman, but was simply looking at her old home, is the undoing of patriarchal values that would deem women as unsound. Likewise, retrospectively, Alice departs from her mother's idea that Diane's house was immoral because of her mother's work as a prostitute.

When Mrs. Netterfield returns to her old home and peers into the windows, she is not only looking back at her past but also at herself. Thus, Munro thematizes the examination of the self in autobiography—"the split of the 'je' and 'moi' that in Lacan's work defines subjectivity" (Benstock, "Theories" 7). Netterfield looks into the mirror of the windowpanes at her home to see herself, unified and whole. Like Narcissus in the legend of Echo and Narcissus, Mrs. Netterfield peers into the self in her reflection. Finding she is not let *in*, "impatience or anger [takes] hold and then the rattling and the banging came" (315). As storytelling and home ownership appear as *mise en abymes* in "Dear Life"—each continually replaced through time with another—so too is one's perception of the self. Netterfield's act of peering into the windows of her home to see her own reflection, in other words, is displaced onto Alice's act of seeing herself in the poem that Mrs. Netterfield's daughter writes. In "The Eye," Alice refuses to see herself in certain artistic representations, such as the painting of the children with Jesus. Yet, here, she recognizes her place and her home in the poem right away. Importantly, as she receives the poem's story, she revises it, making it her own, and attempting to know the truth. "Another verse was about a stand of maples," she notes, "but there I believe she was remembering it wrong—they were elms, which had all died of Dutch elm disease by now" (317). Young Alice looks into the poem and sees herself: "I had once made up some poems myself, of a very similar nature" (317). Presumably, we readers might also see ourselves in Munro's writing, our small towns like hers; our experiences, perhaps, alike. In the movement through time, stories are told and retold, houses are lived in by different people, and present identities are tied to historical ones—they are communal and connected to those "visitations" of the past, rather than solely individual. Shari Benstock explains that "for Gusdorf, autobiography 'is the mirror in which the individual reflects his own image'" ("Authorizing" 15). But what if it is not an individual's image that determines the autobiographical self, but a collective one? In this view, Mrs. Netterfield's "rattling and banging" is an "impatience" (315) to get in to the self as much as it is to get in to the house, an endeavour that needs the acknowledgement of another, that requires not singularity but multiplicity.

To understand the final pages of "Dear Life," we might turn, as I did for my interpretation of "The Eye," to Hyde's notion of the gift. Hyde states that "the spirt of the artist's gifts can wake our own" (xxxiii). If this is the case, then Alice accepts the gift of Mrs. Netterfield's daughter's poem, recognizing herself in it and passing it on in the gift of her own writing to us. Yet "the spirit of the gift is kept alive by its constant donation" (xxxv), and as such, we must neither covet or keep it, for it is not ours except to give away. At the end of the story, Alice speaks of writing a letter to Mrs. Netterfield's daughter, who wrote the poem, but she does not act on that possibility: "the person I really would have liked to talk to then was my mother," she notes, "who was no longer available" (318). She explains that just as she did not pursue a visit to Netterfield's daughter, she also declined to attend her mother's funeral, which she regrets. The story ends, then, not by musing on the idea of the gift, but rather on forgiveness, and specifically, Munro's forgiveness of herself: "we say of some things that they can't be forgiven, or that we will never forgive ourselves. But we do—we do it all the time" (319). The letter that Alice does not write to Mrs. Netterfield's daughter is displaced by the letter that Munro writes to her readers, the story itself. In it, she addresses her life directly, evident in the story's title. She looks back on her life directly as though looking in the mirror or a pool of water. Yet she finds that she cannot, ultimately, go home, much as she would like to. Her mother is "no longer available" (319), and neither is her childhood. Unable to go back, Munro leaves her stories in the hands of her readers, who—however imperfectly—will pass the gift on, revising and recreating as they do.

Patrick Grant notes that "the notion that we have a single, unitary self is yet another ideal that we do not and cannot live up to" (5). There is "a sense of the self as an autonomous agent and the bearer of responsibilities," he explains, "in the gap between people's actual imperfections and the ideals to which they aspire" (5). In the final two chapters of this book, I have discussed how Munro addresses the ethics of responsibility, including the guilt she seems to feel at the end of *Dear Life* for not attending her mother's funeral. Munro emphasizes failure throughout her corpus of work. Even at the end of her final collection, she says that her writing was "invariably unsatisfactory" (318). Yet it is precisely within this failure and imperfection that the potential for epiphany emerges, even as it is a fleeting moment of time. We can experience the world anew; removed, in moments of grace, from the stagnancy that is linear and normative time. Like Corrie, we walk around our rooms, taking in our new perceptions and letting go of the old. Like Alice in "The Eye," we receive the gift of Sadie's wink, and we believe, not in individual morality, not in the striving for perfection, but

Time and Life Writing 189

in a dynamic movement through time that awakens us to those with whom we are connected, to identities that are communal and inclusive of the past, present, and future.

Conclusion

AS WE DRAW TOGETHER the final threads of our exploration of Alice Munro's relationship with the concept of time, we might note that her legacy stands as a testament to the enduring power of storytelling. Munro's stories reverberate across generations, reminding us that "ordinary lives," as she has said, are indeed "extraordinary" ("From the Archives"). The notoriety she has garnered is not simply a product of her prose or her astute observations of human nature, but a result of her ability to wield time as a central narrative tool, inviting readers into a realm where chronology bends and narrative boundaries expand. Narrative time, so often overlooked or relegated to mere backdrop, flourishes under Munro's pen. The moments of choice, regret, and transformation that weave through her narratives often become a mirror for our own experiences, urging us to examine the multifaceted nature of existence and the interplay of decisions that become our destinies.

Curiously, while Munro's exploration of time is a cornerstone of her storytelling, scholarly discourse has often gravitated toward her vivid sense of place: her rural landscapes evoke the essence of her Canadian upbringing in small-town Ontario. However, as we delve deeper into her work, it becomes evident that Munro's manipulation of time serves as the undercurrent that propels her narratives, allowing for a layering of emotions and perspectives that amplify the resonance of her tales. While her landscapes are undeniably evocative, they are, in a sense, vehicles through which she explores time. As we have seen in Munro's writing, the author skilfully shows how time and place are intimately intertwined. Homes and houses, spaces and places, are front and centre in Munro's work—from the living room where Rose's father beat her in *Who Do You Think You Are?* to the schoolhouse where Cora calls to her from above, to Stella's beach house in "Lichen," and to Munro's own childhood home, formerly owned by Mrs. Netterfield in the author's autobiographical story, "Dear Life." Markers of both place and time, such as maps, clocks, old photographs, and letters, are prominent in her work, and they are uniquely relevant in each of the stories she tells. Places are dynamic; they move through time, as do our perceptions and memories of them.

I have argued in this book that Munro's stories examine the meaning of art and literature in time. The author recognizes the revolutionary potential that "monumental time," to use Friedrich Nietzsche's phrase, has to disrupt linearity, and she identifies the fissures and limitations of linear time. Monumental time, as Kristeva explains, is more closely associated with anthropology than chronological history. It involves unearthing artifacts and moments that enable us to see the world anew. Munro taps into monumental time in her stories, identifying the layers of the past in any given moment and challenging the closed stories of singular and traditional histories. Throughout this book, we have seen how this disruption of linear time works in selected stories.

Through literary allusions, for instance, the author demonstrates layers of time. The character of Del in *Lives of Girls and Women* is an aspiring writer who "stands on the shoulders of giants" as she negotiates works written by the Brontë sisters. Del hides her writing in the folds of Emily Brontë's *Wuthering Heights*, and this act symbolizes a disruption in linear time: Del replaces Craig's linear history with women's literature and voice. Garson has studied the extent to which Munro alludes to Charlotte Brontë's *Jane Eyre* in *Lives of Girls and Women*, showing how Munro herself, like her character of Del, builds upon both a male and a female literary tradition. Munro further contests time in *Lives* with the genre of the work. The book could be considered either a novel or a collection of short stories—critics have differed on their opinion in that regard. It is also both a coming-of-age story and a contestation of the conventions of that genre. In *Lives*, Munro thwarts the linear narrative that would have a girl come into adulthood by getting a basic education, marrying, and having children. She plays with narrative dissent and contests linearity in this collection and throughout her corpus of work.

In *Who Do You Think You Are?*, Munro takes her protagonist well beyond her coming-of-age years, even as that collection, in many ways, still adheres to the Bildungsroman genre. Munro brings us along with the character of Rose as she moves from her childhood into middle age. Whereas *Lives* concludes when Del is in her late teens, *Who* concludes when Rose is in her forties. Literary critics such as Carrington, Duncan, Howells, and Thacker have addressed narrative time in Munro's stories, explaining how the author demonstrates a split point of view as the adult narrator perceives her childhood past. Munro layers narrative perspectives regarding the time span of her characters' lives. Yet, we might consider another kind of split narrative that manifests in *Who*—the one that Munro wrote before she pulled the manuscript from production. As Hoy explains, Munro realized at the last minute that the two main characters, Rose and Janet, were really one person, and she asked her publisher to halt production so that she could revise the work. In the end, Rose became the protagonist of *Who* and Janet became the protagonist of *The Moons of Jupiter*, Munro's subsequent collection of stories. It is important to note that in draft manuscripts, Janet is a writer who creates the character of Rose, though this fact is not revealed until the end. Much like the epilogue of *Lives*, Munro's writing process shows her commitment to metafictional elements and self-reflexivity. *Who*, like *Lives*, both adheres to and resists the Bildungsroman. The publication history of *Who*, in particular the fact that its publication was delayed for revision, foregrounds Munro's process as embedded in time. The production history of the book reveals how Munro's characters in her mind are never static but always moving through time, always in flux.

The Progress of Love, the collection of stories that I discuss in chapter three, highlights and ironizes time. The title, of course, is itself ironic. Munro does not see love as progressive. Rather, she shows its randomness, its non-linearity, and its resistance to chronology and logic. In this collection, Munro shifts from writing coming-of-age stories to writing stories that are about ageing, highlighting corporeality. Images of ageing bodies and ageing material objects fuse, as in the instance when Stella contemplates a fading photograph of David's nude lover, Dina, in the story "Lichen." In that story, Munro refers to the Book of Kells and highlights it as a found treasure. In so doing, she suggests that there is power in the ancient world of literature and art, and that this power manifests in the present. As she does in *Lives* and *Who*, Munro highlights how artists build upon and incorporate the genius of their predecessors in a pattern of continual disintegration and displacement that ultimately results in renewal and creativity. In "White Dump,"

Conclusion   193

the dump sparkles like a treasure: it is similar to the Book of Kells in "Lichen." It is also a place of discovery and creativity, just as it is one of waste and excess. The story highlights Isabel's "progress of love" as she moves from her first husband to her affair with the pilot, seeing a "glint" in his eye that is likened to the sparkle of the white dump. Like *Lives*, which incorporates allusions to previous works of literature, stories in *The Progress of Love* highlight ancient sacred works such as The Book of Kells and emphasize moments in historical time such as the moon shot. In her stories, Munro draws attention to glimpses of history—glints or sparkles or treasures that serve as moments of insight. These moments are fissures in and challenges to the accepted trajectory of time and offer us new ways of understanding. While Armstrong's walk on the moon might be seen as a moment of "progress," Munro turns the tables on that idea and instead offers notable and important but often unrelated moments in time.

Between the publication of *Who* and *The Progress of Love*, Munro's renown burgeoned. Her stories found homes in esteemed literary magazines such as *The New Yorker* and *Saturday Night*, while her collection of stories, *Moons of Jupiter*, also debuted in this period. Additionally, Munro's personal life transformed. She left and divorced Jim Munro in the 1970s, after the publication of *Lives*, and began a relationship with Gerald Fremlin, which precipitated her move back to rural Ontario. When *Friend of My Youth* was published in 1990, eight of the ten stories in the collection had already been published in *The New Yorker* (Thacker, *Alice Munro* 370). In *Friend*, mother-daughter dynamics emerge as a recurring motif, echoing Munro's complicated relationship with her own mother, who had Parkinson's disease. In the midst of this thematic exploration, the story "Friend of My Youth" introduces a multifaceted narrator who, while seemingly drawn to unravel the enigma of her mother's friend, Flora, yearns, at a deeper level, to understand her relationship with her own mother. In the story "Meneseteung," Munro's narrator delves into the life of the local poet Almeda Roth, mirroring her intrinsic fascination with the desire to glean insights from the past—an enigmatic pursuit that teeters on the precipice of elusiveness. In both stories, and in the collection as a whole, the author explores relations between women figures of the past and the present, both in historical and maternal realms.

That Munro's mother suffered from Parkinson's disease is interesting in terms of Munro's consideration of characters with disabilities in stories such as "Child's Play" in *Too Much Happiness* and "Corrie" in *Dear Life*. The author's treatment of mother figures and characters with disabilities is never simple or reductive. Rather, she provides complex characters with layers of their own personal histories, and she considers both the characters' dilemmas themselves as well as the townspeople's and outsiders' judgemental and mistaken perceptions of them. Many of the stories in *Too Much Happiness* feature adult narrators who look back on their childhood, demonstrating split selves. The collection considers ethical decisions when looking back on one's past, whether that past involves regret and nostalgia, as in "Fiction," or crime and guilt, as in "Child's Play." By the time *Too Much Happiness* was published in 2009, Munro had already published her autobiographical book about her ancestors and herself, *The View from Castle Rock* (2006), and was well established in her career. In *Too Much Happiness*, she continued to exemplify her brilliant style. Each story goes back and forth in time, showing the characters' propensity for looking back upon their lives and misremembering it either through nostalgia or regret. In "Fiction," Munro plays with the fine line between fiction and nonfiction when her protagonist, Joyce, encounters a story that seems to mirror aspects of her own life. This "story within a story," written by Christie O'Dell from Joyce's own past, is presumably fiction. But to Joyce, it represents her truth—she is the very character in the story that she contemplates. In "Child's Play," Marlene tries to make amends for the crime she committed as a child, with limited success: she cannot confess. In that story, Munro contemplates our expectations of ethical responsibilities and what happens when we fail to meet them. Munro analyzes time in these stories as she delineates various mismatches between remembered realities and remembered selves, guilt and regret-ridden presents and covetous and raucous pasts.

Dear Life, Munro's final collection of short stories and the one that I address in the final chapter of this book, incorporates four stories—the "Finale"—that look back on Munro's own life. Autobiographical in nature and bearing Munro's typical style of writing fiction, these stories blur the boundaries between fact and fiction, reality and illusion, lives lived and lives written. In "Corrie," which is not part of the

"Finale," Munro writes a fictional character who is stuck in the past, exemplifying stagnancy even as the world continues to turn. Munro relays linear time in this story through references to the so-called march of progress in Corrie's father's boot factory. Yet that establishment crumbles and Corrie's father passes away, marking the possibility of toppling the patriarchal system within which Corrie and her town are embedded. The story explores Corrie's place in this dynamic landscape as she becomes the victim of blackmail and the mistress to her father's friend. In "The Eye," the first of the four autobiographical stories in the collection, Munro plays with the homonym "Eye/ I" to tease the reader as the author writes about herself, her own "I," while metaphorically looking the reader in the "eye." The wink that occurs in the story can be read as Munro's wink to her readers, as she offers just glimpses of her personal past. On the one hand, the "Finale" is a departure for Munro from her typical style, since it consists of stories that are autobiographical rather than fictional. On the other hand, it is an arrival for the author, since there are echoes of her own self and relationships throughout her oeuvre. That is, Munro has been writing autobiographically all along.

During the 1970s, some people felt that Munro's *Lives of Girls and Women* should be banned. This movement to ban her books was occurring at the same time that Margaret Laurence's *The Diviners* was also under fire. In a letter to her publisher Jack McClelland on February 14th, 1976, Laurence expressed her feelings of helplessness about not being able to do anything about the situation. In her comment, she refers to Munro and the fact that both authors were being attacked at the same time: "I feel personally I can't do much as it is my book. I also can't, unfortunately, speak up for Alice's book, as I'm personally involved through my own novel" (Davis and Morra 376).

In an interview about the movement to censor *Lives of Girls and Women* from schools, Munro made the following comment: "As far as I can tell from the talk of the people who are against the books they somehow think that if we don't write about sex, it will disappear, it will go away. They talk about *preserving* their seventeen-year-old and eighteen-year-old children, protecting them. Well, biology doesn't protect them. They don't need to read books" ("Nobel Prize Winner Alice Munro," emphasis added). Those who wanted the book to be censored met with some success, albeit temporarily. *Lives of Girls and Women* was banned from one high school in Peterborough, near where Laurence lived and where the censorship saga continued to thrive around her own book. According to the *Kingston Whig-Standard*, *Lives* was also banned by the school board in Munro's home county from the grade thirteen reading list, and in "dozens of school districts across Canada" (Simonds "Free"). Such movements toward banning books are themselves, of course, historically contextual. In his book-length study of censorship in Canada, Mark Cohen explains that Canadian literature bourgeoned in the 1970s. Many of these new works of Canadian literature were put on school curricula, which led "to the increase in the prominence of the issue of censorship in Canada" (viii). While Munro's writing can be considered in relation to the place and time in which it was produced, in many ways, the author was ahead of her time. Munro's work, as it highlighted what we might call "women's time," to use Kristeva's phrase, met resistance amongst her conservative readers.

McGill argues that Munro's career "has been marked more by continuity and recursion than by transformation" ("Alice Munro" 137). In this respect, as McGill also points out, "her career trajectory mirrors an approach to life and art that her stories recurrently, if implicitly advocate: namely, one of return and revision" (137). In her stories, Munro demonstrates the non-linearity of time, the problem in the construction of linear progress and closed narratives. In her life, too, Munro resists the notions of linearity and transformation. Munro's tendency to revise her own stories—seeing them as never finished, never having "arrived"—corroborates this view. In "Meneseteung," the ending that she submitted to *The New Yorker* and that they cut for publication was restored for the story's publication in the collection, *Friend of My Youth* (Thacker, *Alice Munro* 435). We have seen similar instances with regard to Munro's writing process: the pulling of *Who Do You Think You Are?* from its production to revise it, as well as the different endings to her story "Corrie," published in *The New Yorker* and *Dear Life*.

If Munro emphasizes non-linearity, flashes of time, and circularity in her stories, then she mirrors those qualities in her own process of writing too. Another example of Munro's career trajectory and its resistance to the idea of development and transformation is the fact that she did not write novels. As McGill puts it, "A myth of artistic development substantially overturned by Munro's career is that writing short fiction is only a stepping-stone for authors on the way to writing novels"

Conclusion   197

("Alice Munro" 139). That she never wrote a novel—unless one considers *Lives* to be a novel rather than a collection of short stories—is testament to the short story and its value as a literary form. One does not graduate, so to speak, from writing short stories to writing a novel, as many in Munro's time believed. One might argue that Munro's winning of the Nobel Prize in Literature in 2013 is itself an example of how her career has progressed, but as McGill explains, Munro was successful from the start, winning a Governor General's Award for her first collection of short stories, *Dance of the Happy Shades* (139). Thus, to ascribe phases of development to Munro's career is to force it into a linear and progressive chronology that she herself resisted both in her writing and in her life. Instead, we might view Munro's life in the same way that she views the lives of people, as flashes or moments of insight and delight, strife and imperfection.

As Thacker puts it in *Reading Alice Munro: 1973-2013*, Munro has written out of her own life and her own place; she writes "of being alive, of just being human, of wondering, of trying to understand, of trying to maintain" (244). Though she began writing in the 1950s, critics of her work did not emerge until after the publication of *Dance of the Happy Shades*, and these were reviews and newspaper articles. In the mid-1970s, after the publication of *Lives of Girls and Women*, scholars started to write about her work. Hoy's 1980 article, "Dull, Simple, Amazing and Unfathomable: Paradox and Double Vision in Alice Munro's Fiction," "directed critical attention away from thematics and toward language, structure, and style in Munro's stories" (Thacker, *Reading* 247), which inspired other critics to examine the process and product of her writing. Through the 1990s, as Munro continued to publish fiction, writers focused on analyzing individual works, and they turned to literary theory to interpret the author's work. Nunes's essay, "Postmodern 'Piecing': Alice Munro's Contingent Ontologies," is exemplary in this regard, and is an important essay as it situations Munro as a postmodern writer (Thacker, *Reading* 250-51). "The frequency and number of critical articles on Munro published since 2000," Thacker states, "certainly suggest that interest in her work not only continues but shows no sign of abating" (*Reading* 253). Thacker points to influential articles on "classical and mythological allusions," such as those by Garson and Luft (253). He acknowledges the "succession of Alice Munro tribute volumes" (254), such as those volumes produced out of academic conferences on

Alice Munro, including one in the Canadian literary journal, *Open Letter*, in 2003-2004, and *Reading Alice Munro in Italy*, in 2008. Thacker further points to the story "Meneseteung," noting how much scholarly attention it has drawn, including important essays by Ware and Duffy (254-58).

Yet if scholarly work on her writing has been constant throughout Munro's career, it has also been embedded in time, demonstrating the various emphases of literary scholarship throughout the decades. Her work is a staple in Canadian literature, but she is also one of the few Canadian writers to have garnered international attention. Notably, Munro secured an American literary agent, Virginia Barber, and stayed with that agent throughout her life. In the 1950s and 60s, when Munro began to publish her stories, there were not many Canadian literary agents, publishers, or magazines to place one's work. Notwithstanding her obvious talent, the lack of literary opportunities in Canada at that time may be why she began with an American agent and how she started her career in America and beyond.

Munro's journey was also guided by mentors and pivotal literary connections within Canada, most notably Robert Weaver, an instrumental figure at the Canadian Broadcasting Corporation (CBC), and the sagacious editor, Douglas Gibson. Weaver's influence came to the fore when he assumed stewardship of the "Canadian Short Stories," a fifteen-minute weekly radio program that he curated through the solicitation of narratives from all corners of the nation (Thacker, *Alice Munro* 109-10). Thacker notes that "connecting with Robert Weaver was a key moment for Alice Munro, and a very lucky one" (110). Similarly, meeting Gibson in 1974 was an important moment for the author. Writing about the first time he met Munro, Gibson explained, "it was in 1974 that we met in London, Ontario, when Alice had left Victoria and her marriage...I knew that her career was bound for great success." When Munro told Gibson that others were encouraging her to write a novel, Gibson said, "You're a great short story writer. You must keep on writing them. I'm a publisher, and I'd be very pleased if you came with me and went on writing short stories for the rest of your career. And you'd never, ever, find me asking you for a novel." Both Weaver and Gibson would be influential for Munro throughout her career. Gibson remained her publisher and editor not only at Macmillan of Canada, but also at McClelland & Stewart. Both Weaver's and Gibson's steadfast belief in Munro was unwavering.

Conclusion   199

From personal and professional interactions, to her influence on Canadian literature, to her melding of the fictional with the autobiographical, Munro has inspired her readers near and far, at home and abroad. Her stories suggest a way of understanding time that is more woman-centred and focused on the corporeal over the cerebral, the cyclical over the linear. I have argued in this book that Munro challenges traditional narratives, embracing a new kind of narrative time that resists linearity and easy, resolved endings. Instead, the author engages in innovative narrative techniques that include *mise en abyme*, self-reflexivity, and cyclicality. In so doing, Munro offers us the opportunity to consider a different way of understanding the world, one that might cause us to move through and occupy our places and times in novel ways. Studying Munro's stories and her depiction of time within them is important because it helps us to understand the problems and complexities of the places and times in which we live. Many have already begun the work of re-evaluating how we relate to time in the contemporary world—by engaging in slow movements or by resisting neoliberalism's call to constantly be more productive and speedier, measuring time in terms of money, always doing *more*. We need a new way of thinking to guide us in a world that is threatened by global uncertainty. Munro, among others, offers us a way to think about such a shift. She reaches back through time in her stories: to ancient, geological time in "Lichen"; to familial and ancestral time *Lives of Girls and Women* and *Dear Life*; and to personal time and childhood memories in "Child's Play." Munro asks us to consider how our assumptions about time and our ways of relating to it affect how we live in the world, how we remember, or how we wilfully forget. It's time for a new *time*. Munro is one author who can guide us toward it.

Notes

Introduction

1. In *Narcissistic Narrative: The Metafictional Paradox*, Linda Hutcheon draws upon the work of Jean Ricardou and Roland Barthes to explain the concept of *mise en abyme*. It is, she notes, a metafictional device that is similar to an extended allegory. It is a regress in infinitum that embeds and critiques its own text. It is based on a structural level of reflection by which an image or a narrative incident is embedded within another, and then another, seemingly in an infinite and endless pattern.

2. "The Bear Came Over the Mountain" was published by *The New Yorker* in the December 27, 1999 and January 3, 2000 issue of the magazine. When Munro won the Nobel Prize in Literature in 2013, *The New Yorker* reprinted the story as a tribute, printing the original version of it, rather than the *Hateship* version published in 2001.

3. "In Sight of the Lake" was first published in *Granta*, vol. 118, in 2012, and then in *Dear Life* in 2012.

4. Lorraine York's article, "'The Other Side of Dailiness': The Paradox of Photography in Alice Munro's Fiction," examines the juxtaposition of movement and statis, daily habit and unencountered events, comparing Munro's writing to her representations of photographs in her work. In "'What Happened to Marian?': Art and Reality in *Lives of Girls and Women*," Thomas Tausky considers the role that art and photography play in that book.

5. Lacan's notion of *jouissance* shifts over time in his various writings, but can be interpreted generally as akin to pleasure and play. French feminists such as Kristeva have appropriated this term, building upon Lacan's theories of it and applying them to feminine pleasure. For Kristeva, *jouissance* also has to do with the maternal, the semiotic, and the *chora*. The abject, by contrast, is a concept that Kristeva discusses in *Powers of Horror*, published in 1980. Here, Kristeva defines the abject as that which one rejects to maintain

subjectivity. The abject breaks down the barriers between self and Other, and therefore threatens subjectivity and the ego.

6. Freud's psychoanalytic theory discusses the id, the ego, and the superego. The id is the primitive, instinctive, and repressed part of the self, whereas the ego is a more public persona, and the superego its judgemental and moral overlay.

7. Northrop Frye was an influential Canadian literary theorist. In *The Bush Garden: Essays on the Canadian Imagination*, he argues that Canadian literature is marked by a sense of being outside of cultural centres, which leads to the question "Where is here?" Frye coined the phrase "garrison mentality" to depict a sense of isolation felt in small towns in harsh climates that depend upon and yet are apart from urban and cultural centres.

8. See Sergia Perosa's "Michael Ondaatje's *In the Skin of a Lion* and the Building of Cities" and Miles Chilton's "Atwood's *Cat's Eye* and Toronto as the Urban Non-Place."

9. See Laurence Ricou's "Field Notes and Notes in a Field: Forms of the West in Robert Kroetsch and Tom Robbins" and my *Margaret Laurence Writes Canada and Africa*.

10. See, for instance, Morra's "Don't Take Her Word for It: Autobiographical Approximation and Shame in *The View From Castle Rock*," and Thacker's "'As Truthful as Our Notion of the Past Can Ever Be': William Maxwell, His Ancestors, and Alice Munro's *The View from Castle Rock*."

1 | Genre, Narrative, and Time in *Lives of Girls and Women*

1. By referring to "unhomeliness" and the "uncanny," Sugars and Turcotte allude to both Homi Bhabha and Sigmund Freud. Bhabha defines the "unhomely" in "The World and the Home" as that which "captures something of the estranging sense of the relocation of the home and the world in an unhallowed place" (445). For Bhabha, in an unhomely moment, one feels outside of home, even when one is in the place of the home. It is a moment between home and world when the boundaries between the two become blurred. The uncanny, a similar Freudian concept upon which Bhabha builds, refers to an experience encountered that feels both familiar and unfamiliar, recognizable and horrifying ("Uncanny").

2. Huebener's analysis of "imperial time" is based on the work of Daniel Coleman, who draws upon Mikhail Bakhtin's philosophies. Coleman "borrows Bakhtin's literary model of the 'chronotope'—a cognitive image that arranges our conceptualizations of time's passage—and applies this concept more broadly to the sphere of social relations...The most dominant of these is Isochronic or Imperial Time, which underpins the Canadian invader-settler narrative and 'understands everyone in the world to be on a

single timeline, with some cultures being more advanced and leading the way into the future while others are more primitive and 'backward'" (Huebener, *Timing* 29).

3. Building on the work of Freud and Lacan, Kristeva explains that the symbolic order is that which the child enters when "he" (a male trajectory) enters the mirror stage and recognizes himself in the mirror as an Other. The symbolic order is an entrance into language and an alienation of the Other—the image—from the prior, fragmented being. By contrast, the semiotic, which is pre-Oedipal, is affiliated with prosody and fragmentation, fissure and dissolution. Kristeva locates "women's time" in the realm of the semiotic rather than the symbolic ("Women's Time").

4. As mentioned, "uncanny," according to Freud, involves a moment in which one encounters that which is at once familiar and unfamiliar, homely and unhomely. It constitutes a horrifying moment because one is seemingly ousted from the very home or root from which one comes. For instance, in gothic literature, the "uncanny" might be represented by a frightening doll that is like the self—a representation of the human—and yet horrifyingly unlike the self. In this instance, Del sees herself represented by Garnet, but does not like what she sees. She simultaneously recognizes and rejects the "self" that she witnesses.

2 | The Past and the Present in *Who Do You Think You Are?*

1. This trope relates to Munro's previous book, *Lives of Girls and Women*. It recalls the items that Uncle Craig has in his office, such as the Union Jack on his front veranda (*Lives* 28) in "Heirs of the Living Body," the second story in the collection.

2. This is one of a number of stories in which Munro draws upon her own life experiences in her fiction, and as such, her fiction is autobiographical. In her interview with Munro, Lisa Dickler Awano says to the author, "You keep coming back...to your relationship with your father, who was an accomplished writer and an extremely sensitive person, and a reader all his life...but then there's this immovable fact that you refuse to turn away from, which is that he hit you with a belt when you were growing up," and Munro responds, "That's true" (183).

3. In her article analyzing representations of women professors in Canadian literature, Wendy Robbins et al. point out that Munro wrote Dr. Henshawe's character in the 1970s, when representations of academic women foregrounded struggles between balancing a career with marital and parental duties. She points to Henshawe's mentorship of Rose and other women scholars, and the fact that Henshaw discourages Rose from her romantic relationship with Patrick (55). In this way, we might compare

Notes   203

Henshawe with Del's mother in *Lives*, since they both see a disjunction between romantic relationships and scholarly pursuits, as though they cannot see the two going together. It is noteworthy, too, that these two women characters—Ada and Dr. Henshawe—are from the same generation of women, even as they are in different social classes.

4. In a 2013 interview, Munro articulates this shame in relation to her own experience of being beaten by her father. "I still reject it and feel a kind of horror about it to myself. I feel that I was an unworthy person, and that's what it makes you feel. But also I realize that this is what happened at the time, and you can't shy away from that" (Awano 183).

5. According to Lacan, the infant progresses from oneness with the mother to a recognition of the self as separate from the mother. Feminists such as Nancy Chodorow, among others, have contested this view and have resisted such a progression, suggesting that females retain the oneness with the mother. That oneness, for such feminists, is not regressive but nonetheless contests the so-called progressive timeline that Lacan posits. I suggest that Munro implicitly aligns herself with such feminists by demonstrating an ongoing infusion of Rose's past with Flo in her present.

6. Munro's stepmother attended the Governor General's Awards ceremony in 1969 when Alice Munro won it for *Dance of the Happy Shades*, and may have been the basis for this scene (Thacker, *Alice Munro* 198).

7. In "Simulacra and Simulation," Jean Baudrillard argues that simulacra are copies that no longer have an original. The idea of simulacra is relevant to Munro's story because Rose is increasingly removed from the so-called original—Milton's performances of baptism.

8. This relationship, while fictional, reflects Munro's own relationship with her mother. When her mother was suffering from Parkinson's disease, Munro was the one to look after and care for her. Like a mother caring for her child, their roles were reversed.

3 | Time and Corporeality

1. Linguist and philosopher Jacques Derrida discusses his concept of *différance* in "Structure, Sign, and Play in the Discourse of the Human Sciences," an essay that marks the beginning of post-structuralism. The essay, which Derrida first presented as a lecture at Johns Hopkins University in 1966, articulates his concept of *différance* as a deviation from "difference" and "deferral." He explains that meaning in language is generated from a word's difference from other words, and at the same time, that meaning is infinitely deferred or postponed.

2. As Thacker explains in *Alice Munro: Writing Her Lives*, Munro's editor at *The New Yorker*, Charles McGrath, asked her to tone down some of the "crotch

imagery" in "Lichen," saying: "The real magic of this story, it seems to me, is the way it earns and then miraculously effects that transformation of pubic hair into lichen, but I think it should happen effortlessly and almost invisibly" (410). Later, Munro's agent, Virginia Barber, "laughing at this exchange," wrote to Munro: "So, you've a dirty mind, Alice Munro, but it's a talented dirty mind and that's O.K." (quoted in Thacker 410).

4 | Time and Narrative Framing

1. Daniel Menaker worked as an editor at *The New Yorker* for twenty-six years before becoming the executive editor-in-chief at Random House, where he "published such best-selling authors as Salmon Rushdie, Colum McCann, Billy Collins, and Elizabeth Stout" (McGrath). He began at *The New Yorker* as "a fact checker in 1968, then became a copy editor, and for nineteen years was an editor in the fiction department, where he worked on the stories of Alice Munro, Mavis Gallant, Michael Cunningham and Michal Chabon, among many others" (McGrath).

2. Wee Macgregor is a series of short stories about the title character, a young boy. It was written by J.J. Bell and first published in 1933. The stories are written in Scottish dialect and are humorous, often engaging in playful language. That Munro cites this work is significant, given her own attention to language and miscommunication.

3. Critics interpret the character of Jarvis Poulter in various ways. As Ware points out, for Dermot McCarthy, "Jarvis Poulter is not simply an unsuccessful suitor, he is an 'imaginative patriarch'...[who] represents the 'considerable respectability' of Dufferin Street" (69-70). Other critics, such as Deborah Heller, focus on the confinement that Jarvis represents and Almeda Roth's rejection of him, noting that Jarvis's "contemptuous treatment of [the other woman] signals the end of Almeda's romantic interest in *him*" (quoted in Ware 70). Ildikó de Papp Carrington suggests that Almeda's rejection of Jarvis Poulter is a rejection of "'masochism' to which some of Munro's 'earlier heroines' yield'" (quoted in Ware, 68).

4. The Munro Tract is an area of land in Ontario named after Munro since she lived there and set many of her stories in that area. It is "bounded on the west and south by Lakes Huron and Erie, on the north by the town of Goderich, on the east by London" (Baird para. 4).

5 | Memory and Retrospect

1. As Thacker explains in *Alice Munro: Writing Her Lives*, Munro made a special request to her publisher to have the book printed on environmentally friendly, recyclable paper: "Munro's decision had a widespread impact on

the Canadian book trade; many other authors and publishers have followed suit" (499).

2. The philosopher René Descartes famously said, "Cogito, Ergo Sum," which can be translated from Latin to English to mean, "I think, therefore I am." Feminist philosophers such as Grosz, among others, have pointed out that Descartes's pronouncement privileges the mind over the body. In Western culture and philosophy, however, women have often been associated with the body. Some feminist philosophers have sought to challenge Descartes's mind-body split, suggesting not only that the mind and body are one, but also that the mind does not dominate over the body. They emphasize the body and corporeality as essential to the subject and subjectivity.

3. We might consider reading this story in light of Skinner's revelation. Munro was implicated in the abuse of her daughter in that she did not leave Fremlin to stand by Skinner. Though Munro may have felt guilt for this refusal to support her daughter, she never reconciled with her, nor did she ever confess her "sin" publicly.

4. The phrase "compulsory heterosexuality" became known when Adrienne Rich published her essay called "Compulsory Heterosexuality and Lesbian Existence" in 1980 and has been discussed and employed by feminists such as Judith Butler and others since that time. In that early essay, Rich explains that sociological structures deem heterosexuality the norm and homosexuality as deviant. Such structures cause people to adopt heterosexuality regardless of their own sexual preferences. This concept is relevant to "Child's Play," since Marlene negotiates and is embedded within dominant sociological structures—imperialism, heterosexuality—even as she explores that which is Other to those structures.

6 | Time and Life Writing

1. In my discussion of Munro's two autobiographical stories, "The Eye" and "Dear Life," I use "Alice" to refer to the narrator and "Munro" to refer to the author.

2. In Sigmund Freud's influential essay, "The Uncanny," he introduces the idea of the "double" or the "doppelgänger." On Freud's view, an encounter with a double results in an uncanny experience, one in which a person senses both the "familiar" and the "unfamiliar" (or *heimlich* and *unheimlich* in German). It is Freud's notion of the doppelgänger that I refer to here, in Sadie's representation of that which is forbidden to young Alice— independence, creativity, celebrity, and perceived promiscuity—even as Sadie is also familiar and desirable to her, someone Alice wants to emulate, to be.

3. As mentioned, Alice Munro read and admired L.M. Montgomery's *Anne of Green Gables*, and so the name of Alice friend, Diane, could be a reference to Anne's friend, Diana, in that book.

4. As Thacker explains in *Alice Munro: Writing Her Lives*, Montgomery was a strong influence on Munro. Montgomery "paid a visit [to Wingham, Ontario, where Munro lived] and spoke at St. Andrew's Presbyterian church there" (64). "By the time of Montgomery's visit," Thacker explains, when Munro was only eight years old, "Munro had read *Anne of Green Gables* while, for her part, her mother had read all of Montgomery's books" (65).

Works Cited

Alaimo, Stacy, and Susan Hekman. "Introduction: Emerging Models of Materiality in Feminist Theory." *Material Feminisms*, edited by Stacy Alaimo and Susan Hekman, Indiana UP, 2008, pp. 1-19.

Anderson, Benedict. *Imagined Communities.* 1983. Verso, 2003.

Antonova, Anna. "Three Faces of the Monster: Interpreting Disability and Creating Meaning in Translations of Alice Munro's 'Child's Play.'" *TransUlturAl,* vol. 11, no. 1, 2019, pp. 85-103, https://doi.org/10.21992/tc29400.

Atwood, Margaret. *Survival: A Thematic Guide to Canadian Literature.* Anansi, 1972.

Atwood, Margaret. *"Lives of Girls and Women:* A Portrait of the Artist as a Young Woman." *The Cambridge Companion to Alice Munro*, edited by David Staines, Cambridge UP, 2016, pp. 96-115.

Awano, Lisa Dickler. "An Interview with Alice Munro." *The Virginia Quarterly Review*, vol. 89, no. 2, Spring 2013, pp. 180-84.

Baird, Daniel. "Alice Munro." *The Canadian Encyclopedia, 2024,* https://www. thecanadianencyclopedia.ca/en/article/alice-munro#:~:text=Her%20 numerous%20and%20award%2Dwinning,William%20Faulkner's%20 Yoknapatawpha%20County%20or.

Barry, Elizabeth. "Putting it Down to Experience: Ageing and the Subject in Sartre, Munro and Coetzee." *European Journal of English Studies*, vol. 22, no. 1, 2018, pp. 13-27.

Baudrillard, Jean. *Simulacra and Simulation*. Translated by Sheila Glaser, University of Michigan Press, 1994.

Benstock, Shari. "Authorizing the Autobiographical." *The Private Self: Theory and Practice of Women's Autobiographical Writings*, edited by Shari Benstock, University of North Carolina Press, 1988, pp. 10-33.

Benstock, Shari. "Theories of Autobiography." *The Private Self: Theory and Practice of Women's Autobiographical Writings*, edited by Shari Benstock, University of North Carolina Press, 1988, pp. 7-9.

Beran, Carol L. "Images of Women's Power in Contemporary Canadian Fiction by Women." *Studies in Canadian Literature*, vol. 15, no. 2, 1990, pp. 55-76, https://journals.lib.unb.ca/index.php/SCL/issue/view/727.

Beran, Carol L. "The Pursuit of Happiness: A Study of Alice Munro's Fiction." *The Social Science Journal*, vol. 37, no. 3, 2000, pp. 329-45.

Beran, Carol L. "Beautiful Girlhood, a Double Life: Lucy Maud Montgomery, Margaret Laurence, and Alice Munro." *American Review of Canadian Studies*, vol. 45, no. 2, 2015, pp. 148-60.

Berndt, Katrin. "The Ordinary Terrors of Survival: Alice Munro and the Canadian Gothic." *Journal of the Short Story in English*, vol. 55, 2010, https://journals.openedition.org/jsse/1079.

Berndt, Katrin. "Trapped in Class? Material Manifestations of Poverty and Prosperity in Alice Munro's 'Royal Beatings' and 'The Beggar Maid.'" *Neohelicon*, vol. 47, 2020, pp. 521-35, https://doi.org/10.1007/s11059-020-00550-1.

Besner, Neil. "Remembering 'Every Last Thing': Alice Munro's Epilogue to *Lives of Girls and Women*." *Alice Munro Everlasting: Essays on Her Works II*, edited by J.R. (Tim) Struthers, Guernica Editions, 2020, pp. 157-71.

Bhabha, Homi K. "The World and the Home." *Dangerous Liaisons: Gender, Nation, and Postcolonial Perspectives*, edited by Anne McClintock et al., University of Minnesota Press, 1997, pp. 445-55.

Bigot, Corinne. "Marooning on Islands of Her Own Choosing: Inscribing Place and Instability in Alice Munro's 'Deep-Holes.'" *Commonwealth Essays and Studies*, vol. 42, no. 2, 2020, https://doi.org/10.4000/ces.1882.

Blin, Lynn. "Alice Munro's Naughty Coordinators in 'Friend of My Youth.'" *Journal of the Short Story in English*, vol. 55, 2010, https://journals.openedition.org/jsse/1112

Blodgett, E.D. *Alice Munro.* Twayne, 1988.

Bowen, John. "The Gothic." *YouTube,* uploaded by The British Library, 6 Jun. 2014, https://www.youtube.com/watch?v=gNohDegnaOQ.

Brandt, Stefan L. "'Not a Puzzle so Arbitrarily Solved: Queer Aesthetics in Alice Munro's Early Short Fiction.'" *Zeitschrift fur Kanada-Studien*, vol. 36.1, no. 65, pp. 28-41.

Burges, Joel. "Obsolescence/Innovation." *Time: A Vocabulary of the Present*, edited by Joel Burges and Amy J. Elias, New York UP, 2016, pp. 82-96.

Burges, Joel, and Amy J. Elias. "Introduction: Time Studies Today." *Time: A Vocabulary of the Present*, edited by Joel Burges and Amy J. Elias, New York UP, 2016, pp. 1-32.

Burszta, Jędrzej. "Images of Past and Present: Memory and Identity in Alice Munro's Short-Story Cycles." *Alice Munro: Understanding, Adapting and Teaching*, Springer International Publishing Switzerland, 2016, pp. 23-35.

Butler, Judith. *Gender Trouble: Feminism and the Subversion of Identity.* Routledge, 1990.

Butler, Judith. *Bodies That Matter: On the Discursive Limits of "Sex."* Routledge, 1993.

Butt, William. "Southwestern Ontario, the Narrator, and 'Words with Power' in Alice Munro's 'Meneseteung.'" *Short Story*, vol. 21.1, no. 3, pp. 13-43.

Carrington, Ildikó de Papp. *Controlling the Uncontrollable: The Fiction of Alice Munro.* Northern Illinois UP, 1989.

Carroll, James. "Who Was Mary Magdalene?" *The Smithsonian Magazine*, June 2006, https://www.smithsonianmag.com/history/who-was-mary-magdalene-119565482/

Chilton, Myles. "Atwood's *Cat's Eye* and Toronto as the Urban Non-Place." *The Image of the City in Literature, Media, and Society*, edited by Will Wright and Steven Kaplan, Society for the Interdisciplinary Study of Social Imagery, 2003, pp. 154-60.

Chodorow, Nancy. *The Reproduction of Mothering: Psychoanalysis and the Sociology of Gender.* University of California Press, 1999.

Cohen, Leah Hagar. "Alice Munro's Object Lessons." Review of *Too Much Happiness*. *New York Times*, 7 Nov. 2009, https://www.nytimes.com/2009/11/29/books/review/Cohen-t.html.

Cohen, Mark. *Censorship in Canadian Literature.* McGill-Queen's UP, 2001.

Coleman, Philip. "*Friend of My Youth*: Alice Munro and the Power of Narrativity." *Critical Insights: Alice Munro*, edited by Charles E. May, Salem Press, 2012, pp. 160-74.

Conde, Mary. "'True Lies': Photographs in the Short Stories of Alice Munro." *Études canadiennes / Canadian Studies*, vol. 32, 1992, pp. 97-110.

Cotterell, Arthur, and Rachel Storm. *The Ultimate Encyclopedia of Mythology: An A-Z guide to the Myths and Legends of the Ancient World.* Hermes House, 2003.

Crouse, David. "Resisting Reduction: Closure in Richard Ford's *Rock Springs* and Alice Munro's *Friend of My Youth*." *Canadian Literature*, vol. 146, 1995, pp. 51-64.

Davis, Laura K. *Margaret Laurence Writes Africa and Canada.* Wilfrid Laurier UP, 2017.

Davis, Laura K., and Linda M. Morra, editors. *Margaret Laurence and Jack McClelland, Letters.* University of Alberta Press, 2018.

DeFalco, Amelia. "Caretakers/Caregivers: Economies of Affection in Alice Munro." *Twentieth Century Literature*, vol. 58, no. 3, Fall 2012, pp. 377-98.

Derrida, Jacques. "Structure, Sign, and Play in the Discourse of the Human Sciences." *Modern Criticism and Theory: A Reader*, edited by David Lodge, Longman, 1993, pp. 108-23.

Diemert, Brian. "Out of the Water: The Presence of Virginia Woolf in Alice Munro's *Lives of Girls and Women*." *Eureka Studies in Teaching Short Fiction*, vol. 6, no. 2, 2006, pp. 120-30.

Duffy, Dennis. "Too Little Geography; Too Much History: Writing the Balance in 'Meneseteung.'" *National Plots: Historical Fiction and Changing Ideas of Canada*, edited by Andrea Cabajsky and Brett Josef Grubisic, Wilfrid Laurier UP, 2010, pp. 197-213.

Duffy, Dennis. "Alice Munro's Narrative Historicism: 'Too Much Happiness.'" *American Review of Canadian Studies*, vol. 45, no. 2, 2015, pp. 196-207.

Duncan, Isla. *Alice Munro's Narrative Art*. Palgrave Macmillan, 2011.

Duncan, Isla. "'A Cavity Everywhere': The Postponement of Knowing in 'Corrie.'" *Commonwealth Essays and Studies*, vol. 37, no. 2, 2015, pp. 57-67, https://doi. org/10.4000/ces.5057..

Dutoit, Thomas. "Boring Gravel: Literary Earth, Alice Munro's Ontario Geolithic." *Études canadiennes / Canadian Studies*, vol. 77, pp. 77-109.

Dvorak, Marta. "The Other Side of Dailiness: Alice Munro's Melding of Realism and Romance in *Dance of the Happy Shades*." *Études Anglaises*, vol. 67, no. 3, 2014, pp. 302-17.

Elliott, Gayle. "'A Different Tack': Feminist Meta-Narrative in Alice Munro's 'Friend of My Youth.'" *Journal of Modern Literature*, vol. 20, no. 1, 1996, pp. 75-84.

Ferguson, Suzanne. "Sequences, Anti-Sequences, Cycles, and Composite Novels: The Short Story in Genre Criticism." *Journal of the Short Story in English*, vol. 41, 2003, pp. 103-17.

Felski, Rita. *Doing Time: Feminist Theory and Postmodern Culture*. New York UP, 2000.

Francesconi, Sabrina. "Memory and Desire in Alice Munro's Stories." *Textus: English Studies in Italy*, vol. 29, no. 9, 2009, pp. 341-60.

Freud, Sigmund. "The Uncanny." *The Complete Psychological Works, Vol. XVII*. Hogarth Press, 1955, pp. 217-56.

Freud, Sigmund. "Civilization and Its Discontents." *The Freud Reader*, edited by Peter Gay, W.W. Norton, 1995, pp. 722-72.

"From the Archives: Rex Murphy Interviews Alice Munro (1990)." *YouTube*, uploaded by CBC *The National*, 10 Oct. 2013, https://www.youtube.com/ watch?v=4gkJNw6lWU8.

Frye, Northrop. *The Literary History of Canada*, University of Toronto Press, 1965.

Frye, Northrop. *The Bush Garden: Essays on the Canadian Imagination*. Anansi, 1971.

Garner, Lee, and Jennifer Murray. "From Participant to Observer: Theatricality as Distantiation in 'Royal Beatings' and 'Lives Of Girls and Women' by Alice Munro." *Journal of the Short Story in English*, vol. 51, 2011, pp. 1-9.

Garson, Marjorie. "Alice Munro and Charlotte Brontë." *University of Toronto Quarterly*, vol. 69, no. 4, 2000, pp. 783-825.

Garson, Marjorie. "Synecdoche and the Munrovian Sublime: Parts and Wholes in *Lives of Girls and Women.*" *English Studies in Canada*, vol. 20, no. 4, 1994, pp. 413-29.

Gault, Cinda. "The Two Addies: Maternity and Language in William Faulkner's *As I Lay Dying* and Alice Munro's *Lives of Girls and Women.*" *American Review of Canadian Studies*, vol. 36, no 3, 2006, pp. 440-57. doi:10.1080/02722010609481402.

Gibson, Douglas. "Douglas Gibson on Alice Munro." *The Belfry Theatre*, Victoria, BC, 29 Mar. 2017, https://archive.belfry.bc.ca/newsdouglas-gibson-alice-munro-stories/.

Godard, Barbara. "'Heirs of the Living Body': Alice Munro and the Question of a Female Aesthetic." *The Art of Alice Munro: Saying the Unsayable*, edited by Judith Miller, University of Waterloo Press, 1984, pp. 43-71.

Goldman, Marlene. *Dispossession: Haunting in Canadian Fiction.* McGill-Queen's UP, 2012.

Goldman, Marlene. "Alice Munro's Dramatic Fictions: Challenging (Dis)Ability by Playing with *Oedipus the King* and Embracing the Queer Art of Failure." *Ethics and Affects in the Fiction of Alice Munro*, edited by Amelia DeFalco and Lorraine York, Palgrave Macmillan, 2018, pp. 79-108.

Goldman, Marlene, and Sarah Powell. "Alzheimer's, Ambiguity, and Irony: Alice Munro's 'The Bear Came Over the Mountain' and Sarah Polley's *Away from Her.*" *Canadian Literature*, vol. 225, Summer 2015, pp. 82-99.

Gonzales, María Luz, and Juan Ignacio Olivia. "Alice Munro and the Evolving Construction of The Female Self." *Insights and Bearings*, edited by M. Brito and M.M. Gonzales, Universidad de La Laguna, 2007, pp. 179-90.

Grace, Sherill. *Landscapes of War and Memory: The Two World Wars in Canadian Literature and the Arts, 1977-2007.* University of Alberta Press, 2014.

Grant, Patrick. *Imperfection.* Athabasca UP, 2012.

Grosz, Elizabeth. *Volatile Bodies: Toward a Corporeal Feminism.* Indiana UP, 1994.

Grosz, Elizabeth. *Space, Time, Perversion.* Routledge, 1995.

Grosz, Elizabeth. *The Nick of Time: Politics, Evolution, and the Untimely.* Duke UP, 2004.

Grosz, Elizabeth. *Time Travels: Feminism, Nature, Power.* Duke UP, 2005.

Harde, Roxanne. "Teaching Women's Story Books: Genre and Gender Politics in *Lives of Girls and Women.*" *Eureka Studies in Teaching Short Fiction*, vol. 6, no. 2, 2006, pp. 54-61.

Harris, Margaret. "Authors and Authority in *Lives of Girls and Women.*" *Sydney Studies in English*, vol. 12, 1986, pp. 101-13.

Hay, Elizabeth. "The Mother as Material." *The Cambridge Companion to Alice Munro*, edited by David Staines, Cambridge UP, 2016, pp. 178-92.

Heble, Ajay. *The Tumble of Reason: Alice Munro's Discourse of Absence.* University of Toronto Press, 1994.

Heller, Deborah. "Getting Loose: Women and Narration in Alice Munro's *Friend of My Youth.*" *Essays on Canadian Writing*, vol. 66, 1998, pp. 60-80.

Houle, Karen. "Ending Things Well: Alice Munro's 'White Dump.'" *Alice Munro Everlasting: Essays on Her Works II*, edited by J.R. (Tim) Struthers, Guernica Editions, 2020, pp. 217-28.

Houston, Pam. "A Hopeful Sign: The Making of Metonymic Meaning in Munro's 'Meneseteung.'" *The Kenyon Review*, vol. 14, no. 4, 1992, pp. 79-92.

Howells, Coral Ann. *Private and Fictional Words: Canadian Women Novelists of the 1970s and 1980s.* Methuen, 1987.

Howells, Coral Ann. *Alice Munro.* Manchester UP, 1998.

Howells, Coral Ann. "The Telling of Secrets / The Secrets of Telling." *Open Letter*, vol. 11, no. 9, and vol. 12, no. 1, 2003-2004, pp. 39-54.

Hoy, Helen. "'Rose and Janet': Alice Munro's Metafiction." *Canadian Literature*, vol. 121, Summer 1989, pp. 59-83.

Huebener, Paul. *Timing Canada: The Shifting Politics of Time in Canadian Literary Culture.* McGill-Queens UP, 2015.

Huebener, Paul. *Nature's Broken Clocks.* University of Regina Press, 2020.

Hutcheon, Linda. *Narcissistic Narrative: The Metafictional Paradox.* Wilfrid Laurier UP, 1975.

Hutcheon, Linda. *The Canadian Postmodern: A Study of Contemporary English-Canadian Fiction.* Oxford UP, 1988.

Hyde, Lewis. *The Gift: How the Creative Spirit Transforms the World.* 1980. Penguin Random House, 2019.

Jamieson, Sara. "Surprising Developments: Midlife in Alice Munro's *Who Do You Think You Are?*" *Canadian Literature*, vol. 217, 2013, pp. 54-69, https://doi.org/10.14288/cl.v0i217.192673.

Jarret, Mary. "Women's Bodies in Alice Munro's *The Progress of Love.*" *Recherches Anglaises et Nord-Americaines*, vol. 22, 1989, pp. 83-88.

Jernigan, Kim. "Narrative Hauntings in Alice Munro's 'Meneseteung.'" *Short Story*, vol. 21.1, no. 2, 2013, pp. 44-69.

Johnson, Brian. "Private Scandals / Public Selves: The Education of a Gossip in *Who Do You Think You Are?*" *The Dalhousie Review*, vol. 78, no. 3, 1998, pp. 415-35.

Kamboureli, Smaro. "The Body as Audience and Performance in the Writing of Alice Munro." *Amazing Space: Writing Canadian Women Writing*, edited by Shirley Neuman and Smaro Kamboureli, NeWest Press, 1988, pp. 31-38.

Kealey, Josephene. "Religion in Alice Munro's *Lives of Girls and Women* and *Who Do You Think You Are?*" *Alice Munro's Miraculous Art*, edited by Janice Fiamengo and Gerald Lynch, University of Ottawa Press, 2017, pp. 207-17.

Kristeva, Julia. *Powers of Horror: An Essay on Abjection*. Translated by Leon S. Roudiez, Columbia UP, 1982.

Kristeva, Julia. "Revolution in Poetic Language." *The Kristeva Reader*, edited by Toril Moi, Columbia UP, 1986, pp. 90-136.

Kristeva, Julia. "Stabat Mater." *The Kristeva Reader*, edited by Toril Moi, Columbia UP, 1986, pp. 160-86.

Kristeva, Julia. "The System and the Speaking Subject." *The Kristeva Reader*, edited by Toril Moi, Columbia UP, 1986, pp. 24-33.

Kristeva, Julia. "Women's Time." *The Kristeva Reader*, edited by Toril Moi, Columbia UP, 1986, pp. 187-213.

Lacan, Jacques. "The Mirror Stage as Formative of the Function of the I." *Ecrits: A Selection,* translated by Alan Sheridan, W.W. Norton, 1977, pp. 1-7.

Lesk, Andrew. "Playing the Parts: The 'Corps Morcelé' in Alice Munro's *Lives of Girls and Women*." *Studies in Canadian Literature*, vol. 32, no. 1, 2007, pp. 141-53.

Levene, Mark. "Alice Munro's *The Progress of Love:* Free (and) Radical." *Critical Insights: Alice Munro*, edited by Charles E. May, Salem Press, 2012, pp. 142-59.

Lorre-Johnston, Christine, and Eleonora Rao. "Introduction." *Space and Place in Alice Munro's Fiction*, edited by Christine Lorre-Johnston and Eleonora Rao, Camden, 2018, pp. 1-14.

Löschnigg, Maria. "Oranges *and* Apples: Alice Munro's Undogmatic Feminism." *The Cambridge Companion to Alice Munro*, edited by David Staines, Cambridge UP, 2016, pp. 60-78.

Löshnigg, Maria. "Carried Away by Letters: Alice Munro and the Epistolary Mode." *Alice Munro's Miraculous Art: Critical Essays*, edited by Gerald Lynch and Janice Fiamengo, University of Ottawa Press, 2017, pp. 97-114, https://dx.doi.org/10.1353/book52686.

Luft, Joanna. "Boxed In: Alice Munro's 'Wenlock Edge' and *Sir Gawain and the Green Knight*." *Studies in Canadian Literature*, vol. 25, no. 1, 2010, pp. 103-26.

Lutz, Catherine A., and Jane L. Collins. *Reading National Geographic.* University of Chicago Press, 1993.

Mallinson, Jean. "Alice Munro's *The Progress of Love.*" *West Coast Review*, vol. 21, no. 3, 1987, pp. 52-58.

Mark, Joshua. "Book of Kells." *World History Encyclopedia*. 30 Jan. 2018. https://www.worldhistory.org/Book_of_Kells/.

Marrone, Claire. "States of Perception and Personal Agency in Alice Munro's *Dear Life*." *Journal of the Midwest Modern Language Association*, vol. 50, no. 2, 2017, pp. 85-101.

Martell, Yann. "Musings on the Meaning of Home." *Writing Home: A PEN Canada Anthology*, edited by Constance Rook, McClelland & Stewart, 1997, pp. 171-80.

Martin, W.R. *Alice Munro: Paradox and Parallel.* University of Alberta Press, 1987.

Mathews, Lawrence. *"Who Do You Think You Are?*: Alice Munro's Art of Disarrangement." *Alice Munro Everlasting: Essays on Her Works II,* edited by J.R. (Tim) Struthers, Guernica Editions, 2020, pp. 183-95.

May, Charles, E., editor. *Critical Insights: Alice Munro.* Salem Press, 2012.

MacKendrick, Louis K. *Probable Fiction: Alice Munro's Narrative Acts.* ECW Press, 1981.

MacKendrick, Louis K. "Giving Tongue: Scorings of Voice, Verse, and Flesh in Alice Munro's 'Meneseteung.'" *Short Story,* vol. 21, no. 1, 2013, pp. 70-87.

McCarthy, Dermot. "The Woman Out Back: Alice Munro's 'Meneseteung.'" *Studies in Canadian Literature,* vol. 19, no. 1, 1994, pp. 1-19, https://journals.lib.unb.ca/index.php/SCL/article/view/8191.

McClintock, Anne. *Imperial Leather: Race, Gender, and Sexuality in the Colonial Contest.* Routledge, 1995.

McGill, Robert. "'Daringly Out in the Public Eye': Alice Munro and the Ethics of Writing Back." *University of Toronto Quarterly,* vol. 76, no. 3, 2007, pp. 874-89.

McGill, Robert. "Alice Munro and Personal Development." *The Cambridge Companion to Alice Munro,* edited by David Staines, Cambridge UP, 2016, pp. 136-53.

McGrath, Charles. "Remembering Daniel Menaker, a Lighthearted Champion of His Writers." *The New Yorker,* 29 Oct. 2020, https://www.newyorker.com/culture/postscript/remembering-daniel-menaker-a-lighthearted-champion-of-his-writers.

McWilliams, Ellen. "Alice Munro's *Lives of Girls and Women*: A Case Study in Literary Influence." *Eureka Studies in Teaching Short Fiction,* vol. 6, no. 2, 2006, pp. 150-53.

Micros, Marianne. "Et in Ontario Ego: The Pastoral Ideal and the Blazon Tradition in Alice Munro's 'Lichen.'" *Essays On Canadian Writing,* vol. 66, pp. 44-60.

Miller, Karl. "Humble Beginnings." Review of *The View from Castle Rock* by Alice Munro. *The Guardian* 28 Oct. 2006, https://www.theguardian.com/books/2006/oct/28/featuresreviews.guardianreview30

Mitchell, Lee Clark. *More Time: Contemporary Short Stories and Late Style.* Oxford UP, 2019.

Morra, Linda M. "'It Was[n't] All Inward': The Dynamics of Intimacy in the 'Finale' of Alice Munro's *Dear Life."* *Alice Munro,* edited by Robert Thacker, Bloomsbury, 2016, pp. 203-16.

Morra, Linda M. "'Don't Take Her Word For It': Autobiographical Approximation and Shame in Munro's *The View from Castle Rock."* *Alice Munro's Miraculous Art: Critical Essays,* edited by Janice Fiamengo and Gerald Lynch, University of Ottawa Press, 2017, pp. 255-69.

Morra, Linda M. "Introduction: Moving Archives: The Affective Economies and Potentialities of Literary Archival Materials." *Moving Archives,* edited by Linda M. Morra, Wilfrid Laurier UP, 2020, pp. 1-19.

Mulvey, Laura. "Visual Pleasure and Narrative Cinema." *The Audience Studies Reader*, Routledge, 2003, pp. 133-42.

Munro, Alice. *Dance of the Happy Shades.* 1968. Penguin, 2005.

Munro, Alice. *Lives of Girls and Women.* 1971. Penguin, 2005.

Munro, Alice. *Who Do You Think You Are?* 1978. Penguin, 1991.

Munro, Alice. *The Progress of Love.* 1986. Penguin, 2006.

Munro, Alice. *Friend of My Youth.* Penguin, 1990.

Munro, Alice. *Too Much Happiness.* Penguin, 2009.

Munro, Alice. "Corrie." *The New Yorker*, 10 Oct. 2010, https://www.newyorker.com/magazine/2010/10/11/corrie.

Munro, Alice. *Dear Life.* McClelland & Stewart, 2012.

Munro, Sheila. *Lives of Mothers and Daughters: Growing Up With Alice Munro.* McClelland & Stewart, 2001.

Murray, Jennifer. *Reading Alice Munro with Jacques Lacan.* McGill-Queen's UP, 2016.

Nath, Debarshi Prasad. "Reading Alice Munro's Early Fiction: A Kristevian Analysis." *Rupkatha Journal on Interdisciplinary Studies in Humanities*, vol. 4, no. 2, 2012, http://rupkatha.com/V4/n2/06_Alice_Munro_Early_Fiction.pdf.

New, W.H. *Landsliding: Imagining Space, Presence, and Power in Canadian Writing.* University of Toronto Press, 1997.

"Nobel Prize Winner Alice Munro on Banning Books: CBC Archives." *YouTube*, uploaded by CBC, 11 Aug. 2010, https://www.youtube.com/watch?v=fPhHkJKue2g&t=25s.

Nunes, Mark. "Postmodern 'Piecing': Alice Munro's Contingent Ontologies." *Studies in Short Fiction*, vol. 34, 1997, pp. 11-26.

"Old Norse language." *Encyclopedia Britannica,* 8 Oct. 2013, https://www.britannica.com.

Omhovère, Claire. "Stories in the Landscape Mode: A Reading of Alice Munro's 'Lives of Girls and Women,' 'Walker Brothers Cowboy,' and 'Lichen.'" *Alice Munro's Fiction: A Book with Maps in It*, edited by Christine Lorre-Johnston and Eleonora Rao, Camden House, 2018, pp. 82-99.

Orange, John. "Alice Munro and a Maze of Time." *Probable Fictions: Alice Munro's Narrative Acts*, edited by Louis K. MacKendrick, ECW Press, 1983, pp. 83-98.

Ovid. *The Metamorphosis.* Translated by Horace Gregory, Penguin, 1960.

Parr Traill, Catherine. *The Backwoods of Canada*, afterword by D.M.R. Bentley, New Canadian Library, McClelland & Stewart, 2010.

Peck, David. "Who Does Rose Think She Is? Acting and Being in *The Begger Maid: Stories of Flo and Rose*." *Alice Munro: Critical Insights*, edited by Charles E. May, Salem Press, 2022, 129-41.

Perosa, Sergio. "Michael Ondaatje's *In the Skin of a Lion* and the Building of Cities." *Imagination and the Creative Impulse in the New Literatures of English*, edited by Ted M. Bindella, Brill Academic Publishers, 1993, pp. 181-89.

Prentice, Christine. "Storytelling in Alice Munro's *Lives of Girls and Women* and Patricia Grace's *Potiki.*" *Australasian Canadian Studies*, vol. 8, no. 2, 1991, pp. 27-40.

Podnieks, Elizabeth, and Andrea O'Reilly. "Maternal Literatures in Text and Tradition: Daughter-Centric, Matrilineal, and Matrifocal Perspectives." *Textual Mothers, Maternal Texts: Motherhood in Contemporary Women's Literature*, edited by Elizabeth Podnieks and Andrea O'Reilly, Wilfrid Laurier UP, 2010, pp. 1-27.

Pound, Ezra, "In a Station at the Metro." *The Collected Poems of Ezra Pound*. 1948. New Directions, 1982.

Radu, Anca-Raluca. "Narrating New Worlds: Alice Munro's *Too Much Happiness*: Crisis in Goodness." *Narratives of Crisis—Crisis of Narrative*, edited by Martin Kuester et al., Wissner-Verlag, 2012, pp. 174-92.

Rak, Julie. "Introduction—Widening the Field: Auto/biography Theory and Criticism in Canada." *Auto/biography in Canada: Critical Directions*, Wilfrid Laurier UP, 2005, pp. 1-29.

Rao, Eleonora. "'Whose House Is That?': Spaces of Metamorphosis in Alice Munro's *Dance of the Happy Shades, Who Do You Think You Are?*, and *The View from Castle Rock.*" *Space and Place in Alice Munro's Fiction: A Book with Maps in It*, edited by Christine Lorre-Johnston and Eleonora Rao, Camden House, 2018, pp. 41-62.

Rainville, Lorie-Anne. "'When the Indians Were There': Memory and Forgetfulness in Alice Munro's *Dance of the Happy Shades.*" *La Clé des Langues*, March 2016, https://cle.ens-lyon.fr/anglais/litterature/litterature-americaine/litterature-contemporaine/when-the-indians-were-there-memory-and-forgetfulness-in-alice-munro-s-dance-of-the-happy-shades.

Raymond, Katrine. "'Deep Deep into the River of Her Mind': 'Meneseteung' and the Archival Hysteric." *English Studies in Canada*, vol. 40, no. 1, 2014, pp. 95-122.

Redekop, Magdalene. *Mothers and Other Clowns: The Stories of Alice Munro*. Routledge, 1992.

Redekop, Magdalene. "On Sitting Down to Read 'Lichen' Once Again." *Alice Munro's Miraculous Art: Critical Essays*, edited by Janice Fiamengo and Gerald Lynch, University of Ottawa Press, 2017, pp. 289-305.

Reimer, Elizabeth. "Desire, 'Narrative Hunger,' and Alterity: Framing Biography as Dialogic Encounter in Carol Shields's *Jane Austen* and Alice Munro's 'Meneseteung.'" *Contemporary Women's Writing*, vol., 9, no. 2, 2015, pp. 200-18, https://doi.org/10.1093/cww/vpu022.

Rich, Adrienne. "Compulsory Heterosexuality and Lesbian Existence." *Signs*, vol. 5, no. 4, 1980, pp. 631-60. *JStor,* www.jstor.org/stable/3173834.

Ricou, Laurence. "Field Notes and Notes in a Field: Forms of the West in Robert Kroetsch and Tom Robbins." *Journal of Canadian Studies*, vol. 17, no. 3, 1982, pp. 117-23.

Robbins, Wendy, et al. "Searching for Our Alma Maters: Women Professors in Canadian Fiction Written by Women." *Journal of Canadian Studies*, vol. 42, no. 2, Spring 2008, pp. 43-72.

Shieh, Wen-Shan. "The Uncanny, Open Secrets, and Katherine Mansfield's Modernist Legacy in Alice Munro's Everyday Gothic." *Tamkang Review: A Quarterly of Literary and Cultural Studies*, vol. 48, no. 1, 2017, pp. 47-69.

"Silica." *Encyclopedia Britannica,* 2 Aug. 2019, https://www.britannica.com.

Simal, Begona. "Memory Matters: Alice Munro's Narrative Handling of Alzheimer's in 'The Bear Came Over the Mountain' and 'In Sight of the Lake.'" *Journal of English and American Studies*, vol. 50, 2014, pp. 61-78.

Simonds, Merilyn. "Free a Challenged Book to the World." *Kingston Whig Standard*, 21 Feb. 2014, https://www.thewhig.com/2014/02/21/free-a-challenged-book-to-the-world.

Simonds, Merilyn. "Where Do You Think You Are? Place in the Short Stories of Alice Munro." *The Cambridge Companion to Alice Munro*, edited by David Staines, Cambridge UP, 2016, pp. 26-43.

Skinner, Andrea Robin. "My Stepfather Sexually Abused Me. My Mother, Alice Munro, Chose to Stay with Him." *Toronto Star*, 7 July 2024. https://www.thestar.com/opinion/contributors/my-stepfather-sexually-abused-me-when-i-was-a-child-my-mother-alice-munro-chose/article_8415ba7c-3ae0-11ef-83f5-2369a808ea37.html.

Smith, Sidonie, and Julia Watson. *Reading Autobiography: a Guide for Interpreting Life Narratives*, 2nd Edition, University of Minnesota Press, 2010.

Söderbäck, Fanny. "Motherhood According to Kristeva: On Time and Matter in Plato and Kristeva." *PhiloSOPHIA*, vol. 1, no. 1, 2011, pp. 65-87.

Stich, Klaus P. "Letting Go with the Mind: Dionysus and Medusa in Alice Munro's 'Meneseteung.'" *Canadian Literature*, vol. 169, 2001, pp. 106-25.

Struthers, J.R. (Tim). "Reality and Ordering: The Growth of a Young Artist in *Lives of Girls and Women." Essays on Canadian Writing*, vol. 3, 1975, pp. 32-46.

Sugars, Cynthia, and Eleanor Ty, editors. *Canadian Literature and Cultural Memory*, Oxford UP, 2014.

Sugars, Cynthia, and Gerry Turcotte. *Unsettled Remains: Canadian Literature and the Postcolonial Gothic.* Wilfrid Laurier UP, 2009.

Sutherland, Katherine G. "Child's Play: Ethical Uncertainty and Narrative Play in the Work of Alice Munro." *Ethics and Affects in the Fiction of Alice Munro*, edited by Amelia DeFalco and Lorraine York, Palgrave Macmillan, 2018, pp. 153-76.

Tausky, Thomas. E. "'What Happened to Marian?': Art and Reality in *Lives of Girls and Women*." *Studies in Canadian Literature*, vol. 11, no. 1, 1986, https://journals.lib.unb.ca/index.php/SCL/article/view/8038.

Thacker, Robert. "'Clear Jelly': Alice Munro's Narrative Dialectics." *Probable Fictions: Alice Munro's Narrative Acts*, edited by Louis K. MacKendrick, ECW Press, 1983, pp. 37-60.

Thacker, Robert. "'The Way the Skin of the Moment Can Break Open': Reading Munro's 'White Dump.'" *Canadian Notes and Queries*, vol. 79, 2010, pp. 24-27.

Thacker, Robert. *Alice Munro: Writing Her Lives, a Biography*. McClelland & Stewart, 2011.

Thacker, Robert. *Reading Alice Munro: 1973-2013*. University of Calgary Press, 2016.

Thacker, Robert. "'This Is Not a Story, Only Life': Wondering with Alice Munro." *Alice Munro's Miraculous Art: Critical Essays*, edited by Janice Fiamengo and Gerald Lynch, University of Ottawa Press, 2017, pp. 3-14.

Thacker, Robert. "'As Truthful as Our Notion of the Past Can Ever Be': William Maxwell, his *Ancestors*, and Alice Munro's *The View from Castle Rock*." *Authorship*, vol. 10, no. 1, 2021, doi: https://doi.org/10.21825/aj.v10i1.20635.

Thomas, Sue. "Reading Female Sexual Desire in Alice Munro's *Lives of Girls and Women*," *Critique*, vol. 36, no. 2, 1995, pp. 107-20.

Treisman, Deborah. "On *Dear Life:* An Interview with Alice Munro." *The New Yorker*, 20 Nov. 2012, https://www.newyorker.com/books/page-turner/on-dear-life-an-interview-with-alice-munro.

Van Schaik, Kasia. "A Life in Transit: Spatial Biographies of Alice Munro's Artist Figures." *English Studies in Canada*, vol. 45, no. 1-2, 2019, pp. 37-59.

Ventura, Héliane. "From Accident to Murder: The Ethics of Responsibility in Alice Munro's 'The Time of Death' and 'Child's Play.'" *Inside of a Shell: Alice Munro's Dance of the Happy Shades*, edited by Vanessa Guignery, Cambridge Scholars Publishing, 2015, pp. 156-68.

Ventura, Héliane. "The Female Bard: Retrieving Greek Myths, Celtic Ballads, Norse Sagas, and Popular Songs." *The Cambridge Companion to Alice Munro*, edited by David Staines, Cambridge UP, 2016, pp. 154-77.

Wall, Kathleen. "Representing the Other Body: Frame Narratives in Margaret Atwood's 'Giving Birth' and Alice Munro's 'Meneseteung.'" *Canadian Literature*, vol. 154, 1997, pp. 74-90.

Ware, Tracy. "'And They May Get It All Wrong After All': Reading Alice Munro's 'Meneseteung.'" *National Plots: Historical Fiction and Changing Ideas of Canada*, edited by Andrea Cabajsky and Brett Josef Grubisic, Wilfrid Laurier UP, 2010, pp. 67-79.

Warwick, Susan. "Alice Munro and the Shame of Murder." *Ethics and Affects in the Fiction of Alice Munro*, edited by Amelia DeFalco and Lorraine York, Palgrave Macmillan, 2018, pp. 127-52.

Wiens, Jason. "Archives Digital and Otherwise: Recent Books on Archiving Canadian Writing." *Journal of Canadian Studies*, vol. 50, no. 3, Fall 2016, pp. 766-77.

Wiens, Jason. "'What Difference': Alice Munro's Fiction in the Space of the Avant-Texte." PAMLA Conference, Los Angeles, California, November 2023, pp. 1-10.

Woolf, Virginia. *To the Lighthouse.* 1927. Broadview Press, 2000.

York, Lorraine. "'The Other Side of Dailiness': The Paradox of Photography in Alice Munro's Fiction." *Studies in Canadian Literature*, vol. 8, no. 1, 1983, https://journals.lib.unb.ca/index.php/SCL/article/view/7989.

Index

abjection, 122-23, 148-49, 178, 201n5

"Accident," 9

Adam and Eve, 133-34

Ahmed, Sara, 113

Alice in Wonderland (Carroll), 175

Alzheimer's (dementia), xiii-xv, xvii, 63

Anne of Green Gables (Montgomery), xxxi, 183, 207n3, 207n4

anti-colonialism, 8-10

Antonova, Anna, xxx

The Atlantic Monthly, 98

Atwood, Margaret, xviii, xx, 29, 30, 170

author-protagonist conflation

    in "Fiction," 137-38

    in "Friend of My Youth," 106

    in *Lives of Girls and Women,* 28, 32

    in "Meneseteung," 112

    in "Simon's Luck," 60

    in *Who Do You Think You Are?,* 35, 66

autobiographical elements

    AM's feeling about using in writing, 109, 125, 157-58

    AM's use of her mother in stories, 106, 174, 184-85

    in *Dear Life,* 155-57

    in "Dear Life," xxxix, 181-90

    and drownings, xiii

    and how its dealt with in novels, 157

    in *Lives of Girls and Women,* 1, 3, 19, 21, 28

    in "Meneseteung," 99, 112

    scholars' view of AM's use of, xvi-xvii

    S. Munro on, xvi

    in "The Beggar Maid," 51, 52

    in "The Eye," xix, xxxix, 172, 174

    and time socialization, 173

    use of Wingham in stories, xxi

    in *The View from Castle Rock,* 128-29, 181

    in "White Dump," 84

autobiography, 173

Awano, Lisa, 203n2

"Baptism," 24-30

Barber, Virginia, xxxv, 35, 55, 69, 199, 205n2

Barry, Elizabeth, 70-71, 75, 76

"The Bear Came Over the Mountain," xiv, xv, 201n2

"The Beggar Maid," xviii, 43, 50-55, 68

The Beggar Maid, 35

Benstock, Shari, 188

Beran, Carol L., xviii, 50
Berndt, Karin, xxv, 5
Besner, Neil, 32
Bigot, Corinne, xxii
Bildungsroman
    and *Lives of Girls and Women*, 1-2, 3, 17
    typical features of, xxxi
    and *Who Do You Think You Are?*, 33, 37
    and "Wild Swans," 46-47
Blin, Lynn, 108
Blodgett, E.D., xii
bodily inscription, 131-33
Book of Kells, 81-82, 94-95
Bowen, John, xxiv
"Boys and Girls," xxi, 10
Brandt, Stefan L., 44
Brendt, Karin, 13
Bronte, Charlotte, xvii, 1, 6
Burges, Joel, 5, 54, 58, 136, 159
Burszta, Jedrzej, 17
Butler, Judith, xxx, 54, 55, 147
Butt, William, 125

Canadian literature, ix-x, xviii, xxxii
capitalism, 5, 24, 53-54, 78, 86, 159. *See also* neoliberalim
"Carried Away," xxxvii
Carrington, Ildikó de Papp, xi-xii, 122, 127, 205n3
Carroll, James, 133, 134
censorship, 196-97
"Changes and Ceremonies," 19, 27
"Characters," 9
"Child's Play," 142-53
    drowning in, xiii
    as ghost story, xxv
    and identities through time, xv, xxvi
    linear time in, xxx

patriarchy in, xxix-xxx
themes of, 129-30
chronological age, 34, 39-41, 43, 54, 67
Cixous, Hélène, xxvii
class prejudice, 162
Coffin, Audrey, 3
Cohen, Leah H., 129
Cohen, Mark, 197
Coleman, Philip, 98
colonization, 9, 93
coming of age, xv, xvii, xxiii, 1-2
Conde, Mary, 83
conflation of characters, 40, 62, 107, 137
corporeality
    and AM's reference to photographs, xxi
    in AM's stories, xv, xxvi, xxxvi
    and body inscribing in "Fiction," 132, 133
    in "Corrie," 164-65
    E. Grosz on, 72-73
    in "Lichen," xxix, xxxvi, 72, 78-80, 82
    in *Lives of Girls and Women*, xxix, 14-16
    in philosophy, 206n2
    in "Privilege," 43
    in *The Progress of Love*, xxvi, 72
    in "White Dump," xxxvi, 94
"Corrie," xxv, xxx, xxxviii-xxxix, 155, 156, 159-72
cursive time, x

Dance of the Happy Shades, xvii, xxii, xxxv, 8, 104
Dear Life
    autobiographical elements of, xvi
    Finale of, 156-57, 158, 172

focus of stories in, 155

as part of this study, xxxviii-xxxix, 156

scholars' views of, 155-56. *See also* "Corrie"; "Dear Life"; "The Eye"

"Dear Life," xxxix, 155, 181-90

deception, 170-71

"Deep Holes," xxii, 8

dementia (Alzheimer's), xiii-xv, xvii, 63

Derrida, Jacques, 79, 164, 204n1

destabilization, 104, 105

Diemert, Brian, 20

disability, 164-65, 166, 195

The Diviners (Laurence), 196

drownings

in AM's stories, xiii, 14

in "Child's Play," xxix, 142, 147-48

in "Dear Life," 182

in "Gravel," xvii

invoked in "Baptism," 27, 29

in "Meneseteung," 122

Duffy, Dennis, 113, 129, 199

Duncan, Isla, xi, xii, 160-61

Dutoit, Thomas, xxiii

Dvorak, Marta, xxi-xxii

Elias, Amy J., 5, 58, 136

environment

danger represented by, 8

as focus of this study, xl

and "Lichen," xv, xx-xxi, 78-80

and "Meneseteung," 120, 123-24

and "White Dump," 90. *See also* feminine bodies-natural environment

ephemerality

in "Heirs of the Living Body," xxii

in "Lichen," xxvi, xxix, 73

of place, 10

in "Privilege," 42

in *The Progress of Love,* 72

epiphany, 179, 186

ethics, 131, 141, 153, 189

"The Eye," xix, xxxix, 155, 172-81

Felski, Rita, xxvii, xxviii, xxx

female agency

in "Corrie," 166, 171

in "Heirs of a Living Body," 16

in *Lives of Girls and Women,* xix, 28, 29-30

in "Meneseteung," 121, 122

female nudes, 71, 76, 79, 87, 92

feminine bodies-natural environment, 70-78, 95

feminism

AM's view of, xviii

in "Boys and Girls," 10

in "Friend of My Youth," 109

in *Lives of Girls and Women,* 2, 13, 14

in *The Progress of Love,* 95-96

in "The Eye," 180

and view of progression, 204n5

in *Who Do You Think You Are?,* 43, 66

in "Wild Swans," 47

and women's time, xxvii

Ferguson, Suzanne, 2

"Fiction," 129-41, 142, 152, 153

"The Flats Road," xxii, xxiii, xxv, 4, 12, 21

forgiveness, 151, 189

Francesconi, Sabrina, 5, 49

Fremlin, Gerald, xxxvii, 21, 36, 47, 67, 194

French, William, 36

Freud, Sigmund, xxix, 10, 202n6, 203n4, 206n2

Index   225

Friend of My Youth, 97, 98. *See also*
"Meneseteung"
"Friend of My Youth," 99-111
  chosen for study here, xxxvi
  compared to "Meneseteung," 112,
    113, 124
  and key themes of *Friend of My
    Youth,* 98
  use of narrator in, 97, 194
Frye, Northrop, xxxii, 202n7

Garner, Lee, 49
Garson, Marjorie, 1, 2, 4, 192
Gault, Cinda, 3, 13
gender
  AM's perceptions of in "Lichen,"
    77
  challenging of roles in "White
    Dump," 92, 93
  in *Lives of Girls and Women,* 10,
    26-27, 31-32
  reversal of roles in "Corrie," 167
  upsetting of categories for in
    "The Beggar Maid," 54-55
ghosts
  in AM's stories, xxv
  in "Dear Life," 187
  in "Fiction," 136, 137
  and imperialism, 62
  in *Lives of Girls and Women,* 7, 11,
    32
Gibson, Douglas, xxxv, 69, 199
Gibson, Graeme, xxiv
gifts, 120, 155, 180, 181, 188-89
Godard, Barbara, xix, 27
Goldman, Marlene, xxv, 32, 41, 46,
  58, 165
Gonzales, Maria L., 1
gossip, 37-39
gothic
  in "Child's Play," xxix

in "Corrie," xxv, xxxix
featured in Canadian writing,
  xxiv-xxvi
in "Fiction," 135, 136
in "Gravel," xxv
G. Turcotte on, 17
in *Lives of Girls and Women,* 10-11,
  14
in "Meneseteung," 117-18
Grace, Sherrill, xxxii, 38
Grant, Patrick, 152, 189
"Gravel," xi, xiii, xvii, xxv
Graves, Robert, 51
Grosz, Elizabeth
  and AM's treatment of time, xxvi
  and bodily inscription, 132
  and corporeality, 72-73
  and Darwin, 79, 89
  and ghosts, 187
  on matter and form, 90

"Hansel and Gretel," 138-39, 140
Harde, Roxanne, 2
Harris, Margaret, 2, 11-12
*Hateship, Friendship, Courtship,
  Loveship, Marriage,* xiv, xxxvi,
  xxxviii, 128, 201n2
Hay, Elizabeth, xvi
Heble, Ajay, 59, 93, 101, 112
"Heirs of the Living Body," xxii,
  xxviii, 14-18, 173
Heller, Deborah, 117, 119, 205n3
Henderson, Heather, xxvi
history
  how scholars see AM approach
    in "Meneseteung," 113-14
  its reliance on miscast memory
    in "Friend of My Youth," 99-
    111
  in *Lives of Girls and Women,* 14-17,
    30-31

as not what it seems in "Dear
Life," 186
rejection of in "The Beggar's
Maid," 52-55
reveals unwanted truths about
Canadian narrative, 57
in "Spelling," 62
unreliability of in "Royal
Beatings," 37-39
unreliability of in "Simon's
Luck," 55-57, 58
use of in *The Progress of Love,* 194
Homer, 66
homosexuality, 44, 146-48, 151
Houle, Karen, 83, 86, 88
houses/homes
of AM, 36, 67
AM compares to stories, 11
in "Child's Play," 150
in "Corrie," xxv, 166, 169
in "Dear Life," 181, 182, 183-84,
185-86
focus on in "Fiction," 130, 135, 136
137, 138, 140
in "Friend of My Youth," 104, 105,
106-07
H. Bhabha on, 202n1
in "Lichen," 73-74, 79, 80, 82
in "Simon's Luck," 58
in "The Flats Road," 5, 12
in "White Dump," 83, 90
Houston, Pam, 114, 115, 122
Howells, Coral Ann., xii, 27, 83, 85,
100
Hoy, Helen, xxxv, 34-35, 55, 61, 193,
198
Huebener, Paul, ix, xxxi, 24, 42, 91,
186
human need for connection, 138, 141
Hutcheon, Linda, xx, 201n1
Hyde, Lewis, 180, 188

hysteria, 123-24

identity
AM's acknowledgement of
female, 78
and AM's view of Alzheimer's
impact on, xiv
arriving at new identity in
"Fiction," 141
awakening of in "The Eye," 178,
179-81
based on ages of characters, 33
in "Child's Play," xxvi, 142, 146-
48, 149, 152-53
in *Dear Life,* xxxix, 187-90
how it changes from past to
present, 153
how it plays out with trauma in
stories, xv
in *Lives of Girls and Women,* 27-28
and queerness in *Who Do You
Think You Are?,* 44
renewal of in "Simon's Luck," 59
imperial time/imperialism
AM fights against in
"Meneseteung," 120
AM pushes back against in
"Simon's Luck," 56
AM's resistance to, 8, 36
in "Child's Play," 144-45
contestation of in "Wild Swans,"
50
in "Dear Life," 186, 187
and ghosts, 62
resisted in *Lives of Girls and
Women,* 32
scholarly view of, 202n2
in "The Beggar Maid," 51
indeterminacy, xviii-xix
Indigenous Peoples, 8-10, 32
innovative literature, 95

Index   227

"In Sight of the Lake," xiv, xvii,
    xxxix-xl, 156, 201n3
intertextuality
    AM sees as gift, 180
    AM's reference to Bronte, 1, 6
    AM's use of, xvii
    in "Friend of My Youth," 104
    in *Lives of Girls and Women,* 11, 12
    in *Too Much Happiness,* 129
    in "White Dump," 94
    in *Who Do You Think You Are?,* 65,
        66, 68
Irigaray, Luce, xxvii

Jamieson, Sara, 33, 39, 40, 42-43, 54
Jane Eyre (Bronte), xvii, 1, 6, 192
Jarrett, Mary, 72, 94, 115
Jernigan, Kim, 113, 120-21
Johnson, Brian, 37
jouissance, xxvii, xxviii, 18, 21, 201n5
Joyce, James, xvii, 1

Kamboureli, Smaro, 25, 27, 30
Kealey, Josephine, 48
Kristeva, Julia
    and abjection, 123, 148-49, 178,
        201n5
    and chora, 124
    on cursive and monumental
        time, x-xi
    and feminism, xxvii
    and monumental time, 192
    and motherhood, xxx-xxxi, 20
    and symbolic dimension of
        language, 18
    and symbolic order, 203n3
    and women's time, xxviii, xxix,
        78
Kroetsch, Robert, xxxii
Künstlerroman, 1, 37

Lacan, Jacques, xiv, xxvii, 146, 173-
    74, 201n5
Laidlaw, Anne C.
    and *Anne of Green Gables,* 207n4
    appearing in AM stories, xv-xvi
    and "Dear Life," 184-85
    death, 19
    and "Friend of My Youth," 98-99,
        106, 204n8
    relationship with AM, xv, xvi, 19,
        174, 184, 189
    and "The Eye," 174
Laidlaw, Bob, 67, 157-58, 184, 203n2,
    204n4
landscape
    as AM's way of exploring time,
        191
    compared to aging women in
        "Lichen," 72-78
    in "Dear Life," 187
    eroding, xv, xxiii, xxvi
    eroticization of, 50
    and feminization of land, 71, 72
    in "Friend of My Youth," 98, 104-
        05
    impermanence of, 10
    in "Meneseteung," 120
    metamorphosis of, 8
    in "White Dump," 84
Laurence, Margaret, xxxii, 196, 197
Lawson, Alan, 17
layering of time, xix, xx
letters
    in "Corrie," 170-71
    in "Dear Life," 189
    in "Friend of My Youth," 109-10
    in *Lives of Girls and Women,* 179
    in "Spelling," 61, 62
    in *The View from Castle Rock,* 128
"Lichen," 72-83
    corporeality in, xxix, xxxvi

228   Index

danger in, 8
ephemerality in, xxvi
eroding landscapes, xxiii
feminism of, xviii
identity in, xv
The New Yorker's attempt to
change, 204n2
photograph in, xx, xxvi, xxix
space and time in, 95
Liddell, Alice, 51
"A Life in Transit," xxiv
liminality, xxiii-xxiv, xxix, 48, 49,
144
linear time
AM shows it's intertwined with
cyclical time, xxx
AM's rejection of, xxviii-xxix,
xxx, xxxii, xxxiii
in "Baptism," 24
challenged in "White Dump," 84
contested in "Meneseteung," 116,
117
contested in *The Progress of Love,*
72
in "Corrie," 159
how AM uses stories to disrupt,
192-93
limitations of in "Simon's Luck,"
56
rejection of in *Lives of Girls and
Women,* 1-2, 19, 28-29
rejection of in *Who Do You Think
You Are?,* 44
resisted in "Fiction," 135
resisted in "The Eye," 176-77
Lives of Girls and Women
banning of, 196-97
change predicted in, 79
coming of age, xvii, 1-2
corporeality of, xxix, 14-16

debate on whether it's short
story or novel, 2-3
and disassociation from
normative time, 12-14, 24, 25,
32
epilogue of, 30-32
feminism in, 43
fight against patriarchal time in,
24-30
greatness of and awards won by,
xxxiv
layering of time in, xix
liminality in, xxiii, xxix
and mother figures, xvi, 18-20
past in the present, 21-23
photography in, xx, 13, 16
and race, 17-18
reverses convention of
bildungsroman, xxxi-xxxii
revision of stories, 19-20
and synedoche, 4
as turning point for AM, xvii-
xviii
used to thwart linear time, 192-
93
view of history in, 14-17, 30-31
Lorre-Johnston, Christine, 8
Löschnigg, Maria, xviii, 85, 110
"The Love of a Good Woman,"
xxxviii, 128
Luft, Joanna, 129

Macfarlane, David, 69-70
Mallinson, Jean, 72
Mansfield, Katherine, xxv
Marrone, Claire, xvi, 155-56
Martin, W.R., xvii, 64
Mary Magdalene, 133-34, 139, 140,
141
Mathews, Lawrence, 36-37
Maugham, Somerset, 170

McCarthy, Dermot, xix, 117, 205n3
McClelland, Jack, 69, 196
McClelland & Stewart, 69
McClintock, Anne, 29, 50
McGill, Robert, xxxiii-xxxiv, 131, 197
McGrath, Charles, 204n2
McWilliams, Ellen, 11
memory
 AM's use of in stories, xii-xv, xvii
 in "Child's Play," 152, 153
 in "Fiction," 130, 136-37
 how it plays in "Friend of My
  Youth," 99-111
 importance of narration to, 63
 study of in "Meneseteung," 112
 in *Too Much Happiness,* 127
 unreliability of for AM, 157
 unreliability of in "Simon's Luck,"
  55-57, 58
 in "White Dump," 84
 in *Who Do You Think You Are?,* 33
Menaker, Daniel, 98, 128, 205n1
"Meneseteung," 111-25
 changed ending to, 116-17
 compared to "Friend of My
  Youth," 124-25
 how closely it relates to "Too
  Much Happiness," 129
 layering time in, xix
 scholars' view of, 112-15, 199
 theme of, 97-98, 99
 as treatment of narrative time,
  xxxvi
menstrual blood, 114, 122
metafiction
 AM's work as, xx, 198
 in "Dear Life," 158
 of "Fiction," 130, 131
 of *Friend of My Youth,* 98
 in "Royal Beatings," 37
 and "Simon's Luck," 60-61

and *Who Do You Think You Are?,*
 34, 35
metonymy
 in "Child's Play," 145, 150
 in "Corrie," 162, 164
 in "Meneseteung," 114-15, 122
 in "Princess Ida," 23
 in "White Dump," 90
Micros, Marianne, 72, 79
"Miles City Montana," xiii, xxi, 70, 72
Miller, Karl, 128
Milton, John, 66
mimicry/simulacra, 65, 204n7
"Mischief," 54
miscommunication, 103, 106, 149,
 205n2
mise en abyme
 and "Dear Life," 185, 188
 explanation of, 201n1
 in "Fiction," 133, 138
 in "Meneseteung," 116, 123
 as rhetorical strategy, xix
 in *Who Do You Think You Are?,* 52
Montgomery, L.M., 207n4
monumental time, x-xi, 120, 192
"Moons of Jupiter," 157
The Moons of Jupiter, xxxv, 69, 70
Morra, Linda, xxxii-xxxiii, 109, 110,
 125, 172-73, 181
Moss, John, 1
mother-daughter relationships,
 xv-xvi, 21, 48, 61-62, 115, 174
motherhood, xvi, xxvii, xxx-xxxi,
 18-21, 90, 115
Mountcastle, Clara, 99
Mulvey, Laura, 75-76
Munro, Alice
 achieves international success,
  36, 199
 banning of her books, 196-97

being beaten by her father, 67, 184, 203n2, 204n4

development as writer, xxiv, 194

effect of daughter's sexual abuse on, xxxvii, xxxviii, 21, 40, 47, 206n3

end of writing career, 157

experimentation with "Spelling," 61

feelings for her father, 157-58

homes of, 36, 67

impact of *Anne of Green Gables* on, 207n4

importance of *Who Do You Think You Are?* to, xxxiv-xxxv

and Jenny's near drowning, xiii

legacy as writer, 191, 200

marriages, xi, xvii, xxxvii, 21, 52, 67, 194

mentors of, 199

non-linearity of her career, 197-98

prolific writing career of, ix, xvii-xviii, xxxix, xl

publishing history, 35-36, 69, 98, 127-28

relationship with her mother, xv, xvi, 19, 174, 184, 189

retirement from writing and death, xxxiii

revising her stories, 55, 169-71, 193

scholars' work on her novels, 198-99

significance of decision not to write novels, 197-98

visits aunt, xiv. *See also* autobiographical elements

Munro, Jenny, xiii

Munro, Jim, xi, xvii, 52

Munro, Sheila, xiii, xiv

Murray, Jennifer, xxvii, 19, 20-21, 49, 174

Nagel, James, 3

narrative framing

and *Friend of My Youth,* 97

in "Friend of My Youth," 101-02, 103, 105-06, 107

of "Meneseteung," 99, 111-12, 113, 115-16, 123

narrative time

for aiding women's view, 52

AM's complication of throughout her stories, x, 8

challenged in "Simon's Luck," 55-56, 58, 60-61

collapses in "Child's Play," 150-51

how AM brought to the fore, 191, 200

and "Lichen," 82

and "Meneseteung," xxxvi

scholars' view of AM's use of, xi-xii, 193

narrative voice, 85, 86, 99, 101, 108, 164

Nath, Debarshi Prasad, xxvii

neoliberalism, 163, 166, 200

New, W.H., xxxii, 85, 104

The New Yorker

and AM's tie to V. Barber, 35-36

and "Corrie," 169-70

and ending of "Meneseteung," 116

importance of to AM's career, 98

and "Lichen," 204n2

and *Progress of Love,* 85

publishing AM's stories, 69, 128, 129

Nietzsche, Friedrich, x

Nischik, Reingard M., 2

No Love Lost, 128

Index   231

normative time
  challenged in "White Dump," 91
  compared to non-clock time in
    Lives of Girls and Women, 4-7
  in "Corrie," 155
  dissociation from in *Lives of Girls*
    and Women, 12-14, 24, 25, 32
Nunez, Mark, 103-04, 111-12, 198

obsolescence, 159-60, 162, 163
off-time, 166
Oliva, Juan I., 1
Omhovère, Claire, 71, 76
Open Secrets, xxxvi, xxxvii
Orange, John, 41
Other, the
  AM's appreciation of, 44
  in "Child's Play," xxx
  as homosexual, 146
  in Lacan's mirror stage, 146
  in "Lichen," 78
  in *Lives of Girls and Women,* 17,
    25, 28
  society's repudiation of, 148
  in "The Eye," 179
ownership, 187

Parr Trail, Catharine, xxv
past in the present
  in "Child's Play," 152
  in "Dear Life," 181
  in "Fiction," 135, 136, 137, 141
  in "Friend of My Youth," 99
  in *Lives of Girls and Women,* 21-23
  in "Royal Beatings," 36-39, 41
  in "Simon's Luck," 56
  in "Spelling," 62, 63
  in "White Dump," 95
  in *Who Do You Think You Are?,* 33,
    66, 67, 68
  in "Wild Swans," 47, 48

patriarchy/patriarchal time
  in "Child's Play," xxix-xxx
  in "Corrie," xxx, 159, 161, 162,
    163-64, 171
  in "Dear Life," 187
  and female nudity, 87
  fight against in *Lives of Girls and*
    Women, 24-30
  looking through lens of in
    "Lichen," 75-78
  and "Meneseteung," 123
  rejected in "The Eye," 177
  in "Simon's Luck," 56
"The Peace of Utrecht," 19, 184
Peck, David, 59
photography
  and aging, 80
  AM's use of in stories, xx-xxi
  in "Lichen," xx, xxvi, xxix, 76-77,
    82-83
  in *Lives of Girls and Women,* xx,
    13, 16
  scholarly attention to in AM's
    work, 201n4
  in "The Beggar Maid," 51-52
place
  AM's talent for writing, 191
  in Canadian literature, xxxii
  and changing through time in
    "Dear Life," 184
  in *Dance of the Happy Shades,* 104
  ephemerality of, 10
  focus on in "Fiction," 139
  impermanence in AM's stories,
    7-11
  unreliability in "Friend of My
    Youth," 104-05
  use of in AM's stories, xxi-xxii
place and time
  bringing together of, xxxii-xxxiv
  in "Child's Play," 144

232   Index

conflation in "Wild Swans," 49-50

in "Dear Life," 182

how AM successfully intertwined, 191-92

in "Meneseteung," 113, 120, 121, 124, 125

in "Simon's Luck," 56, 59

in "The Beggar Maid," 53

in "The Flats Road," xxii

"Places at Home," 67

Porterfield, Anne M.C., xiv

A Portrait of the Artist as a Young Man (Joyce), xxxi, 6, 11, 12

Prentice, Christine, 13

"Princess Ida," 18, 19, 20, 21-22

"Privilege," 41-43, 45, 46

progressive time

AM's resistance to, 8, 116

challenged in *Too Much Happiness,* 127

in "Corrie," 165

in "Heirs to the Living Body," 15

in *The Progress of Love,* 70, 193

questions about in "Child's Play," 143, 144

"The Progress of Love," 70, 72

The Progress of Love

and corporeality, xxvi, 72

experimental nature of, 71-72

ironizing of time in, 193

and "Princess Ida," 20

publishing of, 69-70

as series of disarrangements, 83

stories on middle age of, xxxv-xxxvi. *See also* "Lichen"; "White Dump"

queerness, 43-46

race, 17-18

Radu, Anca-Raluca, 146

Rainville, Lorie-Anne, 8

Rak, Julie, 173

Rao, Eleonora, 2, 47, 49, 53

Raymond, Katrine, 123

Redekop, Magdalene, 80, 115, 165

Reimer, Elizabeth, 112-13

religion, 48, 161-63

renewal

in "Corrie," 160, 165, 168-69, 172

in "Dear Life," 182, 189-90

in "Friend of My Youth," 110

in "Meneseteung," 117, 119, 122, 123

of past in "Fiction," 139, 141

in "Simon's Luck," 59

from stories in *Dear Life,* 155

in "The Eye," 180

in "White Dump," 92

repetition

AM's rejection of, 30, 116, 155

AM's use of, xix, 40

in "Corrie," 163, 164, 172

in "Dear Life," 182

horror of, xxx

in *Lives of Girls and Women,* xxix

in nature, 79, 96

in "Spelling," 62

and women, xxvii-xxviii

retrospective, xi, xii, xxxix, 127, 152, 158

Robbins, Wendy, 203n3

"Royal Beatings," 36-42, 45, 57, 67, 157

Runaway, xxxviii, 156

Sedgwick, Eve K., 45

self-reflexivity

in "Corrie," xxx

in "Dear Life," 183, 184

in "Fiction," 138, 141

Index   233

and "Friend of My Youth," 102
in "Lichen," 82
in *Lives of Girls and Women,* 28
and "Meneseteung," 99
in "Spelling," 61
in "White Dump," 95
in *Who Do You Think You Are?,* 68
semblance, 48
semiotic, x, xiv, 16, 18, 203n3
settler-colonialism, 144
sex, 107-09, 121, 146-48, 167
sexual abuse, xxxvii, xxxviii, 21, 40,
    47-48, 206n3
shame, 41-42, 46, 165, 184, 204n4
Shieh, Wen-Shan, xxv
Simal, Begona, xiv
Simonds, Merilyn, xxii, xxiii, 104
"Simon's Luck," xviii, xxiii-xxiv,
    55-61
Skimings, Eloise A., 99
Skinner, Andrea, xxxvii, 21, 40, 47
Slemon, Stephen, 17
Smith, Sidonie, 157
social time, 160
Söderbäck, Fanny, xxx
*Something I've Been Meaning to Tell
    You,* xxxv, 67
space and time
    connected in "White Dump," 84
    contested in "Meneseteung," 124,
        125
    in *Friend of My Youth,* 97
    in "Lichen," 95
    in "White Dump," 91-93, 95
"Spelling," xiii-xiv, 61-67
split narrative, 193
split self, 129-30, 195
stability, xxii-xxiii
stagnancy, 39, 155, 163, 171, 189, 196
Stich, Klaus, 112, 121
Struthers, J.R. 'Tim,' xvii, 1, 28

Sugars, Cynthia, ix, xxv, xxxii, 17, 62
suspension of disbelief, 180-81
Sutherland, Katherine G., 142
synedoche, 4

Tausky, Thomas, xx, 201n4
teleological time, xxviii
temporal framing, 91, 172
temporal sliding, 127
Thacker, Robert
    and AM's publishing history,
        xxxvi, 98, 128, 205n1
    on AM's use of autobiography,
        xvi, 160
    and AM's use of narrative time,
        xi
    assessement of AM's career, 198-
        99
    and *Dear Life,* 156
    and ending to "Meneseteung,"
        116
    and "Friend of My Youth," 98-99
    and *Lives of Girls and Women,* xx,
        xxxiv, 3, 19, 31-32
    and *The Moons of Jupiter,* xxxv
    and *The Progress of Love,* xxvi,
        xxxv-xxxvi, 69
    and "White Dump," 70, 83-84,
        86, 87-88
    and *Who Do You Think You Are?,*
        xxxiv, xxxv, 36, 67
theatricality, 49, 51, 55, 134-35, 179
Thomas, Sue, 27
time and memory, xiii-xiv, xvii
time discipline, 53
time immemorial, 140-41
time jumping/shiftiness
    in "Child's Play," 143
    in "Corrie," 161
    in epilogue of *Lives of Girls and
        Women,* 30

234   Index

in "Fiction," 130, 135, 136
in "Friend of My Youth," 100, 103, 105
how AM manages to manipulate time, 191
in *The Progress of Love,* 72
in "Simon's Luck," 55
in "White Dump," 83, 85, 93-94
and women's bodies, 115
"Time of Death," xxv
time progress, xxvi, 24, 96, 102
time socialization
  AM rejects, xxxi-xxxii
  of autobiography, 173
  in "Child's Play," 146
  not followed in "The Eye," 176
  and "White Dump," 90
  in *Who Do You Think You Are?,* xxxv, 34, 42-43, 67-68
  in "Wild Swans," 46-48
time trajectory, xxxiii-xxxiv, 173, 176, 178
Too Much Happiness, 127, 129, 195. *See also* "Child's Play"; "Fiction"
"Too Much Happiness," 129
"To Reach Japan," xvi, xxiv, 156
"Train," 156
trains, xxiii-xxiv, 49-50
trauma, xiii, xv, xxxix, 21
Treisman, Deborah, 170
truth and fiction
  ambiguity of in AM's writing, 109, 110-11
  blurring in "Friend of My Youth," 101
  blurring in "Meneseteung," 99
  in "Fiction," 141
  tension between in "Fiction" and "Child's Play," 130-31
  in *The View from Castle Rock,* 128
Turcotte, Gerry, xxv, xxxii, 17, 62

Ty, Eleanor, ix

unreliable narrator, 131
unsaid, the, 38, 61, 67

"Vandals," xxxvii
Van Herk, Aritha, xviii
Van Schaik, Kasia, xxiv
Ventura, Héliane, 94, 150
The View from Castle Rock
  autobiographical elements in, xxi, 181
  compared to "Meneseteung," 113
  and interest in southwestern Ontario, 111
  not part of this study, xxxix, 158
  publishing of, 128-29
violence, xxix-xxx, 36-42, 47, 62, 83, 121. *See also* drownings

"Walker Brothers Cowboy," 8
Wall, Kathleen, 108, 111
Ware, Tracy, 111, 115, 116-17, 122
Watson, Julia, 157
Weaver, Robert, 199
Wee Macgregor, 205n2
"Wenlock Edge," 129
"White Dump," xxiii, xxxvi, 70, 83-96
Who Do You Think You Are?
  importance of to AM's development, xxxiv-xxxv, 67-68
  Indigenous presence in, 9
  past in the present in, 33
  publication history, 34-36, 193
  queerness in, 43-46
  questioning chronological age in, 39-41
  rejection of history in, 52-55

Index   235

rejection of time socialization in, xxxv, 34, 42-43, 46-48, 67-68

and "The Beggar Maid," 50-52

and view of academic women, 203n3. *See also* "Royal Beatings"; "Simon's Luck"; "Spelling"

"Who Do You Think You Are?," 65, 68

Wiens, Jason, 9-10

"Wild Swans," 46-48

women's time

AM embraces in stories, 52

AM's treatment of, xxvii, xxviii, xxxi

AM's view of, x, 78

in "Corrie," 164, 168-69

as factor in banning AM's books, 197

and "Friend of My Youth," 109

J. Kristeva on, xxviii, xxix, 78

in *Lives of Girls and Women,* 16

and "Meneseteung," 123

and rejection of history, 53

and repetition, xxvii-xxviii

in "Spelling," 63-64

"Wood," 129

Woodcock, George, 128

Woolf, Virginia, 81

"Working for a Living," xxxv

York, Lorraine, xx, 201n4